The A to Z of Postmodern Life

Essays on Global Culture in the Noughties

Ziauddin Sardar

First published in Great Britain by Vision, a division of Satin Publications Ltd.

Vision
101 Southwark Street
London SE1 0JH
UK
e-mail: info@visionpaperbacks.co.uk
website: www.visionpaperbacks.co.uk

Publisher: Sheena Dewan
Cover design © 2002 Nickolai Globe
Printed and bound in the UK by Biddles Ltd.

ISBN: 1-904132-03-0

Contents

Acknowledgements

Most lists are lies, but this one is an exception. I must express my thanks to my 'unremittingly brilliant and indispensable' friend Merryl Wyn Davies, writer and anthropologist, for her criticism, suggested rewrites and caustic comments; Gail Boxwell and Jan Mair for their errant e-mails and invaluable assistance; Pat Kane, freelance intellectual, musician and sometime 'E2' editor of *The Herald*, for describing me as 'one of the finest intellects on the planet' and publishing my essays in said organ; Peter Wilby, the indefatigable editor of *New Statesman*, for believing in me and finding regular slots for my essays in 'Britain's premier current affairs magazine'; Cristina Odone, deputy editor of *New Statesman*, for calling me 'darling' and being equally loving with my copy; Angus McKinnon, former arts editor of *New Statesman*, for being such a good friend; and Jason Cowley and Frances Stonor Saunders for being there. All these people have had something to do with one or more essays in this book. But I mustn't forget all those (they know who they are) who have shown me the errors of my (non-Western) ways, corrected my interpretations of Western thought and philosophy, and tried to teach me the true merits of literary canons. May they pull the few remaining hairs from their balding heads, gnash their dentures and wring their decrepit hands.

Introduction

Is it just me? Am I retreating into reactionary mode as my hairline recedes? Or are the times we live in out of joint? Is there something amiss, or have I missed some essential detail that puts things in perspective and makes sense of what's going on in the world? If this is how things are meant to be, is it really what we intended? Did we, the collective, general, we, really set out to produce the state the world is in? Or did we inadvertently unleash the forces that swirl around us by accidentally opening some Pandora's Box?

Not overly prone to doubting my sanity, I believe I am not alone. Most of us are bewildered by what is happening to and in our culture. Where I see paradoxes, legions of my contemporaries are also perplexed. Where I sniff the unmistakable aroma of contradiction, countless other nostrils twitch in unison. We, the confounded, have a case. There is something out there causing our concern and that thing is neither alien nor a case from *The X-Files*. It is everywhere – in the products we consume, the shopping malls we visit, the smells and sounds of our cities and the films and television shows we watch. It produces the contradictions evident in our obsession with lists and celebrity, war and voyeurism, predictions and the Internet. It can be seen in our lack of concern for multiculturalism, our changing perceptions of others – how we see and represent Blacks, Chinese and Japanese – and how we perceive ourselves as 'Europeans' and 'Americans'. It generates our anxieties about sex, rights, children, and our physique. It is a world of absolute liberation and total seduction. We have freed ourselves even from those institutions that gave meaning and depth to our lives – religion, family, community. We relish the seduction and surface illusions of signs and symbols. In our times certainty has ebbed away; now we doubt everything, even science. There are good reasons for all this – except we don't pay much attention to reason nowadays, as we doubt reason too.

But despite perpetual doubt, increasing abundance of consumer goods, better, faster and more accommodating technology, 24-hour entertainment, unbridled freedom, a plethora of choice, we are still far from happy. Mentioning the other side of the equation, the constant increase in absolute poverty in Africa, the perpetual reduction of economic and political freedom and choice in developing countries, the unsavoury aspects of technology – from polluting the world to making the Bomb to producing hopelessly irrelevant gadgets – is not the done thing in polite society. My real problem is whether this new-made world of total disjuncture has been shaped in our image, or has bent us out of shape and made misfits of us all. Why, in a culture with more material abundance, convenience, education and opportunity than any other in history, is there still not enough to go around?

Furthermore, I worry that we – the inhabitants of the 21st century – may be the last group of people actually able to ask such questions, the very last generation whose personal experience provides some perspective on how the world now is. We tend either to live in the past or in the future, but seldom in the present. One half of our culture exists in an invented terrain of myopic nostalgia – for the 1960s, seventies, eighties, and even the nineties. This imagined and frozen past, constantly revisited in television shows like *TV Years* and *I Love the '90s*, is assumed to be happy and innocent. The other half seeks virtue and happiness in some future utopia where technology will solve what humans cannot. Rarely do we pay attention to the present – the point of action within our control where we can transform our futures and transcend our histories.

So, in trying to simultaneously turn backwards and move forwards, we have lost all inkling of ourselves as decisive, judgmental beings whose business is determining where we really ought to go. The last 50 years, a reasonable cricket score, have carried their most favoured children, the citizens of developed affluence, beyond all previous bounds. We have broken all records, all taboos, all boundaries. We are post almost everything that defined and shaped previous centuries, gave modernity its distinctive patterns, promoted and perpetuated inhuman excesses as well as brought out the humanity and imposed it on all humans. We are post-Religion, post-Cold War, post-Ideology, post-Socialism, even post-History. We are all, in some fashion, posties. Our life experience has carried us beyond the mechanistic promise of industrial modernity into a new era.

What defines this new era? An era where the past and the future have collapsed into the present? Where acceleration is everything and everything is confused?

Every morning as I make my stately progress from the comatose content of the bedroom to the breakfast table, I collect the post. Invariably, among the pile there will be a selection of junk mail catalogues. Who put me on these lists? Why do they single me out? In the befuddled consciousness that precedes my second cup of coffee, I distractedly flick the pages of these glossy cornucopias. They have titles like *Innovations*, *Modern Woman* (junk mail is always gender impervious), *House of Bath*, *Modern Originals* and, rather alluring to my generation, *Past Times* and *Ancestral Collections*. Pastiche products, ersatz art, faux culture, and mind-boggling gadgets one never knew one, anyone, ever needed. All are manufactured from the finest products to the highest standards with the most lavish finishes. All are extortionately over-priced, ridiculously useless, resplendently meaningless. Yet they all reek status, lifestyle choices and disposable income to burn. When it is not meaningless *objet d'artifice*, it is holiday brochures or clothing catalogues, such as *Hawkshead* and *River Island*, telling me I am a man about town, about the world, with an image to sustain, a man whose measure is in the look, style and location, the material goods with which I surround myself. After the third cup of coffee I am ready to be at odds with the world, to snarl.

Conservatories, house extensions, makeovers and fantasy rooms pro-liferate on the streets around me. Was it for this, I occasionally ask myself, that my generation marched, leafleted and protested? Mine was the first generation to be alerted to the limits to growth, the 'Silent Spring' on Spaceship Earth, not to mention nuclear winter. We were born with the winds of change whistling in our ears. Yet, the more things change, the more they stay the same. While the absolute numbers of the hungry and homeless continue to grow, global efforts such as the major international concern-ins at Rio and Kyoto hardly seem commensurate with feeding the hungry, sheltering the homeless or saving the planet. We buy natural products and organic food, but the age of big statements, grand gestures to generate genuine change seems long, long past, despite the best efforts of the members of the anti-globalisation movement, God bless them, who are now looked at with even more suspicion after 11 September 2001. Idealism seems to have gone the way of so many other grand certainties – Marxism, Socialism, Religion, Tradition – deconstructed to demonstrate what con tricks they really were. What we have left is the nagging suspicion that perhaps we were better when we really, passion-ately believed and knew something must be done.

Competence seems a major part of the problem. Solutions are 10 a penny, available at every turn. We have the 'know how', it is what to apply it to that causes all the agro these days. When we marched to demand solutions, who knew they would turn out to be such curates' eggs?

We wanted poor little Vietnam freed from the American military-industrial complex at play. Who would have dreamt that free from war they would go in search of the rampant Americanisation of their economy in a desperate attempt to become the next Asian tiger?

We wanted freedom for everyone and everything; now that we surfeit on it, making responsible choices is the uncomfortable corollary: choices about genetically modified foods, embryo research, human cloning.

We wanted all things to be possible – now they are. Why does that make us disconcerted, confronted with intractable conundrums we can no longer render into straightforward analyses? Not even the language has stayed still. In a world of PC, political correctness, one simply cannot call a shovel a spade. With jargon and psycho-babble can anyone say exactly what they mean and hope to be understood?

If these are the tempers of our times then this temperament has a name – postmodernism.

'Postmodernism' is *espiritu del tiempo* – the spirit of the 21st century. It is a product of our realisation that many rationally constructed edifices of the 19th and 20th centuries have turned out to be irrational illusions. A conscious and unconscious protest against the excesses of suffocating modernity, it is the beginning of a new journey, advertised as inclusive and certainly all embracing. From its inception as a critical movement in art and architecture in the seventies, postmodernism has now become a global cultural force underpinned by free market and bourgeois liberalism. Today, postmodernism is everywhere: it has penetrated all spheres of human activity and taken deep roots in daily life. There is postmodern philosophy, history, anthropology, fiction and even religion. The postmodern world is being built by the movie, the television programme, advertisements, design, fashion, pop music, shopping complexes, and the glue that binds it all together: the cyber economy.

So, how do we cope with a world where we have to run faster and faster to stand still? Where we are constantly and perpetually out of breath? I have the greatest sympathy with the pained exasperation so aptly expressed by a friend. A dedicated teacher, much in the mould of the cinematic favourite Mr Chips, he is most at home in his chosen field, history. Yet he finds himself instructing computer-literate, techno-savvy tots, whose pre-pubescent *savoir-faire* shaped by popular culture makes them adults before their time, while pre-programming them for historical amnesia. 'Postmodernism?' he fulminates. 'I haven't caught up with modernism yet!' But there is no hiding place. The 'ism' is loose, we reckon with it or it settles our fate, irrespective of our wishes. Another friend, a suave party circuit animal, is always heard to moan: 'Postmodernism, oh so old hat. We got over that ages ago.' Alas, not so. Its works are with us yet, and everywhere. When an 'ism' ceases to be the buzz-word of smart conversation it begins its real career. It enters the mind chain, fed into and churned out as the coded underpinnings of academic thought. It gets force fed to impressionable undergraduates who enter the world of work programmed with a specific set of attitudes, sensitivities and intellectual instincts. From buzz-word to implicit ordering of how things are done, how choices are presented and ideas elaborated there is a time lag. This time lag is getting shorter and shorter in a culture that venerates youth. If you missed it on the party circuit, watch out. 'Isms' come back to haunt us all, not as polite chat but as the institutionalised consequences of a particular view of the world. To get beyond the 'ism' factor there is no option but to reason with the monster in all the places it has gone to ground – if we can find them.

And that is how I began my one-man campaign for joining up the dots, for seeking the connections. There be dragons in our times too. Like the pathologist in *Silent Witness* or forensic scientists in *CSI: Crime Scene Investigation*, I began taking slices of contemporary life and placing them under scrutiny. Thematic unity, a consistent *modus operandi*, a set of matching spikes like a positive DNA match emerged before my eyes at every turn. I began proclaiming my discoveries in the Saturday editions of Glaswegian daily *The Herald*, and then settled into explaining my find-ings in the pages of the *New Statesman*. Under the appellation 'The NS Essay', I tried to show that the arch destroyer of 'grand narratives', the advance publicity claim of postmodernism, has become a murderous supernarrative of its own. Gradually, as the output of my research accu-mulated, I sequenced the alphabet from which the genome of postmodernism can be read. *The A to Z of Postmodern Life* is the collected end result.

Only by learning to read the message of postmodernism can we form any conclusion about whether this new century is heading off in the right direction or leading us all up some dark, blind alley. We need an alphabet before we can spell out the words: can we go somewhere else please!

Advertising

In postmodern times, advertising has become the eminent domain of our existence. This new lord of the manor has used its superior rights to evict all categories and boundaries within its grasp. The difference between news and advertisement has almost disappeared. The distinction between reality and advertised image has collapsed. Advertising not only informs, educates and entertains, it moulds the very lifestyles we lead. It is everywhere, surrounding us every moment of our conscious life. From the day we are born to the day we die, we hear, read, or see over 70 million advertisements. Advertisement is everything. It is the ether we breathe, the matrix within which we exist.

The conventional understanding of advertising revolves around three questions. The first asks: '*What* does advertising do?' The standard answer is that it distorts and subverts the real, natural needs of human beings and replaces them with 'false desires'. However, the spirit of postmodern times is that desire itself has become an inflationary, upwardly mobile, exponentially expanding, principal justification for existence. In consequence, we don't need advertising to create desires – our insatiable appetite does a more than adequate job of creating artificial needs – advertisement simply brings these fabrications to the fore.

The second question asks: '*How* does advertising work?' The explanation here is that it works by simply or virtually lying. But surely, by now, everyone on the planet knows that advertisements are lies. So why are we still taken in by the deceit? Simply saying that advertisements are lies does not actually reveal much about the way their mythologies are accepted by consumers. We accept many things, such as national myths and religious beliefs, we know to be not literally true. Focusing on the truth or otherwise of advertisements, I think, is actually an impediment to understanding them. As French philosopher, Jean Baudrillard, puts it, advertising is 'beyond true and false'. There is no question of it deceiving us. Like a religion, it is followed whatever its factual or logical content.

So, to the third question: '*Why* do we need advertisements'? The answer, it is usually argued, is to be found in advertising's crucial role in maintaining the free market, capitalist economy. But how does advertising actually sustain capitalism? All religions and ideologies are perpetuated by one vital ingredient: hope. If capitalism is an ideology, then advertising is its language of hope. But the hope is not about needs fulfilled or desires quenched. It is about enjoyment. Enjoyment is the message every advertisement carries as its subtext; it always constitutes the kernel of the promise entailed in the ad. 'Enjoy Coca-Cola'. 'Freshen Up with Seven Up'. In postmodern times, enjoyment is what is really at stake whenever and wherever advertisements are present: car manufacturers now promise you 'advanced enjoyment', as against the 'simple' enjoyment offered by their competitors, to take you wherever you want to go in search of more enjoyment.

Advertising became the bedrock of our existence in the 20th century. It is the metier through which the history of that awful century is best told, an association that is perhaps as dismal a thought as such a century deserves. Of course, the 20th century did not invent advertising; I suspect it has always been with us. Historians claim all those richly backgrounded Renaissance portraits were promotions for their subjects, adverts of their creditworthiness and importance. Ancient monuments and artefacts advertise. Ancient and early modern poetry consists mostly of praise poems to the leader, a kind of nascent party political broadcast. So, advertising has always been there. But it was the 20th century's discovery of distributive abundance and artificial needs without limit that launched advertising on a new trajectory.

The greatest event of the 20th century, outstripping even its horrors – two world wars, mass, mechanised slaughter, the imminence of Armageddon, holocaust and ethnic cleansing – was the invention of the mass market for consumer goods: the apotheosis of the Industrial Revolution. Desiring the accoutrements of a lavish lifestyle is probably a primordial urge, but only in the 20th century did it become a practical proposition for large parts of a whole society. And it was not a hard sell, as advertising from the early part of the century clearly demonstrates. Staid, practical and basically informative, it told the ordinary citizens about goods that were worth having. It was largely text based and lacked strong visual imagery, dwelling instead on informative illustrations of the actual products. The text made large claims for the products, reflecting a sense of wonder at the possibilities of new technology. But advertisements' grand claims for the goods were incidental. What sold was the affordable price tag. The greatest wonder of all was the Model T Ford phenomena: mass-produced products every ordinary person could realistically aspire to own.

The first half of the 20th century stoked up the capacity for production and pent up the desire for enjoyment, with a lot of hardship endured by everyone – stock market crashes, depressions and world wars. Commercial advertising was a poor relation to the real business of fighting for women's rights, economic redistribution and national mobilisation. Product adverts could hardly compare with the visual impact or slogans of political advertising. Think of the suffragette poster depicting a woman in the place of a hapless mouse crushed between the clamped jaws of the voracious, predatory cat. Who does not recall the famous poster of Lord Kitchener pointing a finger at the viewer and proclaiming 'Your Nation Needs You'? And what of the whole genre of Communist posters, idealising the nobility of toil, which became an art form, an unmistakable style in its own right. What product placement slogans could be better than Lloyd George's rallying cry of 'Homes Fit for

Heroes'? The politics and conflict were the great prelude; after came the consumer deluge.

The explosion of consumer culture in the fifties quickly exhausted demand for the provision of basic needs, requiring advertising to find a new vocation. Only when everything is available, everything potentially attainable, does attracting attention for a specific product become an art form, a cultural exercise in stimulating false desire, artificial need. The public confronted itself in the zeitgeist of advertising.

And, advertising became a science – incorporating the conditioned reflex theory of Pavlov and Watson, Freudian notions of motivation, and the whole battery of psycho/social behaviourism – a legitimate object of study and experiment, with a repertoire of sophisticated technique. Consumerism lost touch with practicality, but advertising could not because it was the vehicle that kept economic growth on track. It was 'the hidden persuader' of Vance Packard's bestseller of the late fifties. The purpose of advertising became the creation of desire without discrimination, a yearning for something without discernment.

The great development in advertising during this period was entertainment. In the fifties and sixties, when television became the main vehicle for advertising, we learnt to enjoy it. The bits between the programmes became as memorable and are as fondly remembered as the programmes themselves. People of my age can hum as many advertising jingles, mumble as many catchphrases, as lines from chart-topping songs. Advertisements are as nostalgic and evocative as the songs themselves. They were soap operas (from Katie and the Oxo family to the black horse sagas of Lloyds Bank), the one-liners of stand-up comedy ('naughty but nice' cream cake ads), and situation comedies ('for mash get smash' instant potatoes ads).

But the simple delights of 'Murray Mints' ('too good to hurry mints') and Esso Blue ('boom boom boom') or going to work on an egg are as Stonehenge to the Twin Towers of Kuala Lumpur, the building that has temporarily succeeded to the title of tallest in the world. Simple enjoyment, whether of ads or the economics of material abundance, was not enough. So, in the eighties we moved to conspicuous indulgence; advertising became the symbolic style zone par excellence. It sold images of potential lifestyles we could indulge in. For example, Levi jeans were not just a commodity – they were advertised as symbols of freedom, originality and independence. To buy the product was to buy the idea of yourself; the product encapsulated your values.

In a world ruled by style and image it is ideas that sell. Advertising, the art form that cut its teeth on political messages early in the century, had acquired the scientific acumen to sell the idea and styles of conspicuous consumption. Think how subtle and subliminal it became in all those cigarette advertisements with never a cigarette or a brand name in sight – an expanse of gold instantly evoked Benson and Hedges, while a shimmering grey background cut by a swathe of purple silk immediately brought to mind Silk Cut.

This was sophisticated advertising for a sophisticated audience. As savvy consumers of the 'medium is the message' worldview, we were alert to all the inferences of cultural and commercial reference. Actually, we were being prepared for the wheel to complete the circle: advertising returned to the political domain and thereby expressed the future we would all inhabit. The eighties ushered in the dominance of the political ad and its professional practitioners, the confirmation that politics now had to survive within the logic and eminent domain of advertising. Politics became a commodity; political parties and their leaders items to be marketed as products. The culmination could only be the long-running Benetton campaign, with its bold photographs of AIDS victims, newborn babies and death row inmates, where product recognition made political points.

In the nineties, advertising was transformed wholesale into the business of reality replacement. We entered the era of living our dreams in material terms, led forward by advertising as dream enhancement. Remember those Guinness ads where Rutger Hauer morphed through Impressionist paintings? Or the visual effects wizardry of the British Rail commercials where even the chess pieces settled back with a sigh to enjoy the ride? But once you have gone beyond reality what is there?

There is becoming the dream, incarnating the imagined. We, the people, are becoming the incarnation of advertisements. In the 21st century, the sovereign rights, the eminent domain, of advertising are a quantum leap beyond shaping an enjoyable reality. In the noughties, advertising need no longer sell things. What it must do is merchandise not only our continued existence but also our being. Instead of ingesting advertising, we become its mouthpiece: it is not just the slogan on our T-shirt, but the very essence of our soul.

So, our children watch television programmes that are nothing but genre advertising – cartoons exist to stimulate merchandising, from My Little Pony to Pokémon. Obtaining the products becomes a cultural expression of the horrors of the social formation that begot them. Pokémon wars in the playground and Tamagotchi angst in the class-room, existence defined only by artificial, unreal, but desperate desire. When we use the Internet we are bombarded by tailor-made advertise-ments that know exactly how we behave. Teenagers are constantly glued to youth channels that transmit nothing but advertising; pensioners sit motionless in front of shopping channels that put the crude propaganda of Stalin's regime to shame. We come out of the movies with a subliminal longing for a pizza and a coke. Advertising shapes all our relationships, hopes and aspirations, the very notions of conformity and dissent. Adver-tising has not just assimilated the present, it has also made deep inroads into the past – thanks to computer wizardry, historic figures return from their grave to sing the virtues of the latest mobile phone, long-dead actors get a new lease of life driving the fastest car, drinking beer or eating after dinner mints. The future is nothing but a dream lived out in an advertising nirvana.

We comfort our soul with wry self-knowledge – as in the advertise-ments for the Egg credit card where all the actors honestly admit to participating in a fantastic pastiche of unreal, idealised life. It does not alter the fact that we, the people, are now advertising's greatest artefacts, its ultimate artifice. Advertising is now all about our state of being and existence; its goal is to manipulate and shape our becoming. And should you have any doubts, just pay attention to the series of ads for spicy noodles. In one, a brute of a bloke comes home from the pub desiring a late night snack. Once upon a time that would have been a sufficient story line and pitch for an advertisement. Now the products offer something much more. An instant spicy noodle snack, the lowest form of food one can eat, actually liberates the existence of its consumer, empowering him to don ladies' underwear and indulge his desire to be Madonna. After only a moment's pause for doubt his two sidekicks grasp the significance and unabashedly join in.

This historic progression is not what we should call progress. But it is clear from all the available evidence that the kingdom of advertising is now firmly within us. We, the consumers, are the stuff of which admen dream; they exist to hold up a mirror wherein we can glimpse the misery of our own existential angst.

Americana

America is very good at providing public entertainment on a world stage. In the last decade alone, we have been treated to a whole series of global spectacles: from the thrilling O. J. Simpson chase and trial, to the sexual mysteries and intrigues of Monica Lewinsky's involvement with President Bill Clinton, to the complicated physics of putting a cross on a ballot paper during the 2000 presidential elections. But the arcane perplexities of American social and political life, which often bring the country's bumbling ineptitude to the fore, should not distract us from the fact that America is now an imperial power unlike any other in history. Its military, economic and technological pre-eminence is unprecedented in its planetary reach. No corner of the globe is unaffected by the outpourings of its mass culture – and its political decisions. Everything America does has global consequences and affects us all, and what happens to America, as in the case of the events of 11 September 2001, has consequences for everyone on the planet. In these postmodern times, our very survival depends on what America does and does not do. This is why it is necessary for us all to know how America sees itself and just what makes it tick.

America is not merely the lone superpower, it is a hyperpower and a virtual imperium. Unlike previous imperial powers the US does not have a physical empire. It rules most effectively by proxy while remaining sufficient unto itself. It has vital national interests everywhere but is seldom touched by eventualities anywhere; it is involved everywhere but is ultimately unanswerable, unaccountable and unconcerned about consequences to anyone except United States citizens. Osama bin Laden, for example, had been around for a long time; but only after the US itself was attacked was action against him actually taken.

The ability of America to replenish itself from those over whom it exercises power – virtually all the developing countries of the South and much of Europe – easily outstrips the Roman and British Empires. Like a black hole, it sucks in most of the energy of the planet. America consumes over half of all the goods and services of the world; its population, constituting a mere 3 per cent of the world's total, produces 25 per cent of global pollution. The three richest Americans have assets that exceed the combined gross domestic product of the 48 least developed countries. And Americans' expenditure on cosmetics – $8 billion – is $2 billion more than the annual total needed to provide basic education worldwide. America is the dominant pathogen of the globe. It can destroy, even without trying, the very abode of our terrestrial journey: it has the world's largest accumulation of nuclear weapons (but refuses to sign the Comprehensive Nuclear Test Ban Treaty); it has 30,000 tons of chemical weapons; and it has the world's largest stockpiles of smallpox, anthrax and other biological weapons (but still continues to experiment with new weaponised pathogens). Its colossal military is two and half times larger than the militaries of the next largest potential adversaries combined (Russia, China, Iran, North Korea, Iraq, Libya, Syria, Sudan and Cuba). The hyper nature of Pax Americana is a burden on everyone, it levies real effects on the life of everyone on the planet. But unlike any other imperial power in history a virtual imperium cannot be arraigned.

The cornerstone of Pax Americana is the ideology of Americana, a distillation from the generality of ordinary American life, history, experiences and ideas. As a global ideology, Americana is a successor to Westernisation. The purpose of Westernisation, the dominant theme of the second half of the 20th century, was to transform the world into the image of the West. But whereas Westernisation was like a bacteria that could be fought with the antibodies of tradition, Americana is like a virus that has no cure. It attacks the immune system not just of America itself but all the rest of us as well.

The ideology of Americana has three simple and completely simplistic tenets. The first is the notion that America is the world, so the world had better shape up and be more like America. This dumb certitude manifests itself in everything that America does. America's approach to corporations, markets, drugs, patents and accounting, its notion of freedom, democracy and justice, all must become the world's standard. It is a country comfortable with holding World Championships and 'World Series' when only Americans participate, as in its impenetrable form of football and baseball. Every American takes it as a self-evident truth that the American way of life is the best ever devised in the history of humanity; that America, in Lincoln's famous phrase, is 'the last best hope for mankind'.

But America is also the world on another level. As the Statue of Liberty proclaims so eloquently: 'Send me your poor and huddled masses yearning to be free.' It is the nation created as a refuge for all the world; a nation made up of immigrants. By 1890, after a rising crescendo of immigration, America had become home to huge numbers of Europeans who often spoke languages other than English or who were illiterate farmers. What immigrants know is that wherever their parents or grandparents came from was nasty, brutish and tyrannical – that's why they made their way to America. So the rest of the world by definition is inherently flawed, unable to compare with America, and is, in a fundamental way, not worth knowing.

Americana's self-image of refuge and remaking through hope and freedom did not operate in quite the same way for liberated slaves, conquered Mexicans and the remnants of slaughtered Indian nations. Such people antedate the settlers, or arrived with the first of them – African slaves first arrived in Virginia in 1608. Their eventual inclusion within 'We the People', and tortuous route to the mainly unrealisable

American Dream, neither detracts from nor dents Americana's ideological certainty.

While America is the home of a multifaceted people, it is hardly a multicultural nation. The development of the ideology of Americana has been long in the making and it began with the process of making Americans out of numerous and diverse nationalities. Central to this process was the fabrication of cinematic history. Cinema became mass popular entertainment at the crucial demographic moment. The new immigrants were educated in ideological history by the cinema. The Americans that were manufactured by this educative process were not multiculturalists but proto-believers in the homogenising ideology of Americana. The founding notion of American civil society – '*e pluribus unum*', from many, one – says it all. The one that has emerged from the many is a homogenised unit based on blind conformity.

The simplistic, homogenised mind shaped by Americana and nurtured in the cinema is incapable of grasping the humanity of outsiders. This is why America treats the rest of the world with utter contempt. Every global institution, from the World Bank and IMF to the World Trade Organisation and Multilateral Agreement on Investment must be subservient to America's demands and work to make the world safe for US corporations. Globalisation, often portrayed as a neutral phenomenon, is actually the expansion of a homogenising mass consumer culture, an extension of Americana, to the whole world. Every global treaty, from the Rio agreement on biodiversity to the Kyoto accords on carbon dioxide emissions, carries the imprint of the total insularity and narrow-mindedness of Americans. The Great American Way of Life must be preserved, whatever the cost to the rest of us and the planet itself.

The second canon of Americana reduces all histories, of all the peoples in the world, to American History. As the home of popular culture, America has become the world's storyteller. We have long been familiar with the 'necessity' of historic personalities being portrayed by American actors. But in recent times the movies have taken a quantum leap. The stories that America tells itself and the rest of the world locate and relocate all narratives within America. This is not just the law of the box office; it is genuine and deep ideological correctness. To be worth telling, and therefore worth knowing, stories must be rooted in American experience. Thus, on film, the action in even a classic English story, such as Frances Hodgson Burnett's *A Little Princess*, has to be relocated to New York – despite all the bizarre illogic and anomalies this produces – before it can be represented as universal (ie American) experience. So it is hardly surprising that in films like *U-571* we discover it was American forces and not the British who actually captured the Enigma code machine, the vital ingredient that played an important part in thwarting Hitler.

But to be the world, Americana must disseminate disinformation with an even hand. It not only distorts everyone else's history, it dismantles its own. In *The Patriot*, for example, the genocide of the native Americans and the enslavement of the African–Americans is written off and battles rearranged to British disadvantage. Look carefully at contemporary cinema and you will discover that these are not isolated examples but the product of a deliberate exercise in the manipulation of history. Feeding all pasts into the great narrative of America is a powerful way of legitimising the worldview of Americana.

The function of films like *The Patriot* is to regurgitate the third basic precept of Americana: the total innocence and righteousness of America. As American novelist and critic Gore Vidal has pointed out, America suffers from the 'twin desire' to 'dominate and to be seen as entirely innocent at the same time'. This is the central core of the mythic history that solidified the Union and it declaims something essential about the character of white Americans. They are innocent, simple people struggling to make a good life by taming the wild frontier – whatever or wherever that frontier may be. Simple innocence, the theme of innumerable Hollywood westerns as well as the literary oeuvre of Henry James, is the basis for the devout belief of Americans in their essential goodness. The self-righteousness and insistence upon innocence began at the very inception of America.

America was the first settler colony. It was established against and through the denial of America's original inhabitants, the Native Americans. The first sustained settlement from which America derives was Jamestown in Virginia, recently mythologised by Disney in its animated anti-classic *Pocahontas*. These settlers explicitly wrote of themselves as Biblical Israelites claiming a Promised Land, building 'the city on the hill', the beacon to the world. They saw themselves not as occupiers and colonisers but as virtuous communities fighting against all odds. Or as American historian Richard Slotkin neatly expressed it in the title of his book, the ideology of innocence is the accepted version of *Regeneration Through Violence*. The hero, a John Wayne or Shane who uses violence, is not the innocence venerated in the ideology of Americana. Rather, genocidal violence and ecological destruction, doing 'what a man's gotta do', are performed on behalf of innocence, to protect the poor, honest and humble settlers who are the inheritors of what is legitimated and appropriated by violence. Like Shane, when the nasty work is done, the lone hero figure rides off into the sunset, leaving the tamed and safe land to be administered by the simple, homespun, righteous ethic of the settlers.

Innocence, the assurance of rightness no matter what, is the bedrock of American foreign policy. Just as the destruction and appalling treatment of the original inhabitants, along with slavery and segregation, are subsumed in the ethos of innocence, so the unparalleled suffering that American imperial might has inflicted on the unfortunate of the earth has been absorbed in the presumption of its planetary moral superiority. For example, there is hardly a Latin American state that has not, in the name of democracy and freedom, been subjected to horrific violence and barbarism. From Argentina, El Salvador and Nicaragua to Chile, Honduras, Panama, Guatemala, Haiti and Grenada, the history of US intervention is drenched in blood. Not to mention what the Americans did in Vietnam.

The three precepts of Americana – America is the world, the only relevant history is American History and presumptions of innocence and self-righteousness – subtly reinforce each other and work to short circuit and confound any possibility of reasoned questioning. The entry fee of engagement in America is eulogy, the basic rhetorical form of all public discourse in American life. It is best expressed in the gee-whiz declamation: 'Only in America'. It is axiomatic that no one outside America properly understands America. Yet despite all the assurance of their self-absorption, Americans are hyper-sensitive to criticism. All criticism is jealousy and failure to understand its special perfection and particular mission. Questioning is proof of a desire to undermine the entire edifice, a traitorous act or hostile assault, the ultimate un-American activity.

When all debate must operate within the narrow parameters of the received ideology of Americana, its reduction to the level of the functional and historically illiterate becomes a virtue. Thus Americans take pride in the fact that they know very little about the rest of the world. Politicians vie with each other to cast themselves as innocent frontier folk or simple people from farms 'back home'. Industrialists look at you with sheer amazement if you suggest that their motives are far from innocent. Bureaucrats wallow in the presumed simplicity of their world-view. Depth and complexity are definite liabilities in American society. The ideology demands simple innocence, and the simple is to be taken literally.

So we have the ideology of Americana as the guarantor of a nation that is an ever-more perfect union, a land of innocence, justice and liberty, where opportunities are open to all and all can pursue the great American dream of happiness through material abundance. But, like all ideologies, Americana is a total inversion of the truth.

Consider the great American democracy we are being asked to accept as the ideal model for the world. It is a democracy where the winner need not be the one who gets the most votes. Since only half the population ever casts its vote in any election, the actual electoral victory belongs to those who cannot be bothered to participate in the democratic process. In the freest country on the planet, democratic political campaigns are a ghastly joke. Powerful lobbies, like the gunslingers, have bought everyone who is anyone in politics. You need around $20 million to get yourself in the Congress or the Senate; and it requires $3 billion to put a man in the White House. In the end, the man who gets the most votes, as we saw from the 2000 election for the President, doesn't actually win. The voting process itself involves, as the Florida fiasco demonstrated, an esoteric and complex typology of holes punched, and not punched, in a voting card: chads, hanging chads, pregnant chads...The ideal candidate is a cipher, or a brain-dead actor, or at least someone who can be a Master of Ceremonies at the Oscars. The handlers write the script, build the drama, concoct the spin, and then run the White House. The attack ads reduce political opponents to disciples of Satan. Public debate is all drama and revelations of past misconduct.

Much the same can be said of other American institutions. American justice is as open to everyone as the Ritz, and unthinkingly devoted to the death penalty. Most of the time the American media transmits lies. The social and cultural styles and arguments operate at the level of *Beavis and Butthead*.

Despite its homogeneity, the Union is anything but united. America is deeply divided on the lines of race, religion, ethnicity and gender. To display its innocence and righteousness, one group must constantly be at loggerheads with another. The result, as Pete Hamill wrote in a famous essay in *Esquire*, is a society in permanent, teeming, nerve-fraying conflict: blacks against whites; straights against gays, gays against priests, priests against abortionists; blacks against Jews; Orthodox Jews against reformers; Jews against Arabs, Arabs against Jews; sun people against ice people; citizens against immigrants; Latinos against Koreans; people who work against those who don't; urban folk against suburban and rural dwellers; bad guys against everyone, cops against bad guys, lawyers against cops. Republicans now denounce Democrats as inherently different kinds of people, out of touch with the values, not just the electoral votes, of the heartland. Everyone is fighting to lay undisputed title to the core values of Americana, the American Dream, and to insist that only they are its true inheritors, interpreters or arbiters.

The more tightly Americans cling to the sustaining myths of their Union the more self-absorbed, inward-looking and isolationist they become. Perhaps, after 11 September, this will change. But, so far, the only answer to American problems involves wrapping themselves ever more firmly in the folds of their flag. This is the predicament we all face. As Americana is more narrowly cast at home, it is broadened and broadcast as the inevitable and only possible global dispensation. An alienated, insular and fragmented America is a cause for concern for us all.

Blacks

Black may be hip and cool but it is still the most exploited colour on the planet.

Black actors may have conquered Hollywood, but they still don't get to kiss the white heroines. Black music is all the rage right across the globe, but it still hasn't earned much respect for the black dude in the ghetto.

'Black culture' has come to be equated with Afro-American black culture. We can take it as read that what transpires in American ghettoes migrates to the black community in Britain, with the West Indian islands as the halfway house between the two. So what happens to blacks in America rapidly becomes important for blacks elsewhere. And blacks everywhere, particularly the youth, are explicitly walking, wearing and speaking their blackness. Black popular culture, drawn from a mythic African past, is the hottest ticket in town. We are all walking and talking, dressing and grooming, dancing and grooving like 'real brothers'.

But while we have eagerly bought, appropriated and stolen their identity, we haven't paid much attention to the plight of the brothers themselves. Or their much-exploited sisters. We constantly listen to their music, but we don't really hear it.

Black music has invigorated European sensibilities for decades. It actively subverted the dullness industrialisation foisted on Western popular culture. The blues, jazz, soul, reggae and the like have been an inspiration for forging creative white ways of being. The black presence in British cities has been central to oppositional sentiment for white kids. Mods, skinheads, teddy boys and their respective permutations of 'cool' would have been unthinkable without a black British presence. Northern Soul was the forerunner of raves, with 'all nighters', speed and break dancing a regular weekend way of life during the seventies in northern England.

But all this did not change conventional white perceptions of black people. But then, how could it? The drumbeat and rhythm of African music was always part of the definition of primitiveness, the black condition, and proof of its fitness to be stolen, bought and appropriated. They brought the slaves on deck to dance in their chains as they transported them from Africa to the Americas. The drumbeats and singing in the slave quarters were endlessly reported by writers and travellers, and loomed large in the minds of slave owners as a marker of difference and a source of potential menace.

Music and dance were potent associations. Their potency was magical, where magic was the savage power, pre-logical, beyond the comprehension of civilised reason. African music and dance were wild, libidinous, abandoned, operating outside the restraints that defined rational and civilised life. The insistent appeal and hypnotic attraction of such music and dance, despite their clear associations, was a source of fear, a fear of the fragility of self-control and dominance. Fear structured the relations between the master and slave wherever they were brought into mutual relations: in Africa, in the Americas, in the colony, on the plantation, in the town or the city.

African music troubled the Western mind, just as enforced servility troubled the conscience and stimulated the search for intellectual justification. The chattel slavery of Africans by Europeans was a 'peculiar institution'. It was the partner project of Western domination, along with the eradication of the native peoples of the Americas, those less useful to the purposes of white settlement. The newness of the New World permitted and justified the irreversible servitude of one and the eradication of the other. Who could be slaves and who could not was a matter of debate, public and open discourse that preoccupied Spain and informed the approach of all European powers that followed that nation into the business of the domination of new lands. The 'peculiar institution' that emerged to answer this predicament is not merely what we call racism but the entire philosophical structure of Western reason, implicit in the definition of the Western perception of self. It dances to the beat of Other music in counterpoint, it is the song of supremacy, the rhythm of progress. The harmonics of Western civilisation were fashioned to make evident why things could be stolen and why what was stolen could never be returned, neither for its own good nor that of the takers.

Ownership, whether by theft, appropriation or purchase, is a central precept of the Western worldview. It is the most basic plank of the concept of personal liberty, the fundamental principle of a property-owning democracy. It was as central to the arguments of the English Revolution, which established the basis for parliamentary democracy and the modern career of the Mother of Parliaments as it was for the Founding Fathers of the American Republic. Property made men Man, the rational, real person. Property gave Man a natural right and natural interest in the operation of true liberty, enshrined in and self-governed by laws. The native American had no concept of property, and so legally could be dispossessed of all property. The slave was the natural reverse principle, the true antithesis, a person who could be owned, the person who was property. So owner and owned were neatly bound together. This enduring relationship was encoded in simple black and white. Racism and colour prejudice came after, not before, the 'peculiar institution' of property relations. By conscious act, according to law, within the meaning of law and reason, blacks became a means of production, a function of white ownership, a source of profitability defined by their servitude to their masters.

Being stolen, bought and appropriated was where the relationship began and how it continues to operate. It is perpetuated by the very fact that black cultural production has always been mediated, controlled, distributed and presented by white institutions, a few black-run record companies notwithstanding. The music business is a continuation of the peculiar institutional arrangements that order black existence in white society.

In the history of black music we can read the entire history of Afro-American struggle against racism in the United States. From the great slave songs (with their oral histories), the torch songs, gospel, soul, jazz and funk to contemporary rap, all have been cultural markers of self-determination, empowerment and respect. This is why music is the cornerstone of black identity.

While the profit potential of black music was always recognised, the music industry was not too keen to rock the racist applecart. The problem for the industry was how to market black music without upsetting the white supremacist unconscious of the listener at large. Thus during the thirties and forties, blues and jazz appeared only at the back of recording catalogues under the heading of 'race music', always accompanied with a cartoon of a carefree 'minstrel'. To further ensure that the widely feared power of 'nigger music', particularly its effects on the morals of white youth, was kept in check, critics were employed to write sleeve notes that both celebrated and emasculated black music. Pre-1960s sleeve notes attempted to render the brilliance of black creativity as natural, that it occurred despite 'being black'. Consider the sleeve note for Bo Didley's 'In the Spotlight': 'Lend an ear to his beat... notice the pure primitive rhythm that can only be an inherent quality, and not a studied style. The man works straight from his soul.' This led to a romantic racism in which black culture, particularly jazz, was cast as a vital and natural source of spontaneous, pre-civilised, anti-technological values – the music of primitive, uncontaminated and untutored feeling. Such views not only racialised jazz, they also naturalised the ghetto; the agonies lived therein became a product of the natural order of the world. Thus, while white folks danced and jived to jazz, they seldom paid attention to the message of the songs.

There was also the real fear of the black community itself: subversive political songs, if given wide currency and air time, would fuel the anger of white supremacists. There was always the dread of lynch mobs so eloquently expressed in Billie Holliday's 'Strange Fruit'. In a famous 1946 recording, folklorist Alan Lomax invited southern blues men Big Bill Broonzy, Memphis Slim and Sonny Boy Williamson to perform together in New York. Lomax recorded the men candidly chatting over drinks but as Big Bill Broonzy was to say, 'If these records came out on us, they'd take it out on our folks down home, they'd burn them out and Lord knows what else'. It was only in the late 1980s that it was considered sufficiently safe to release these recordings.

In the face of such obnoxious racism, the 'Uncle Tom' principle and the 'Black Mammie' syndrome were strategies for survival. Playing up to white perceptions was a form of subversion. In his *Invisible Man*, Ralph Ellison captures the essence of the strategy. In the early part of the novel, a dying black grandfather exhorts his family: 'I want you to overcome 'em with yeses, undermine 'em with grins, agree 'em to death and destruction, let 'em swooler you till they vomit or burst wide open.'

For the music industry, the ideal solution was to find and promote white artists who were able, at least to a degree, to capture the energies of black music. Enter Paul Whiteman, Benny Goodman, Dave Brubeck, Elvis Presley and Eric Clapton. These artists went on to achieve much greater success than the black artists whose work they imitate and build upon; but true innovation in popular music was still confined to blacks. Indeed, most significant changes in depth and style are directly attributable to the black community.

The entire history of black music production in the West involves a love/hate relationship between white audiences and black culture, the continuation of the enduring love/hate relationship with which property-owning democracy began. But the emergence of hip hop and rap marks a radical departure from history. Here, for the first time, the white audience encounters a clear 'fuck you' for all the disrespect heaped on black creativity. Rap expresses black identity and self-representation with a compelling (and for some disturbing) 'in your face' immediacy and urgency, while cleverly rooting the whole enterprise in the rich tradition of African–American oral vernacular practice. Explicit about its symbolic (and for some, literal) call to arms in defence of the nation, hip hop's most articulate and most forceful practitioners continue to seize upon and speak about the(ir) realities of being black in 21st century America. Through rap, 'nigger' has been reclaimed as a means of negating its derogatory connotations. It has also spawned a whole movement of whiggers (white niggers) who emulate their black counterparts as 'cool' masculine heroes.

Despite this, white critics have tended to dismiss rap as a postmodern ploy. In particular, gangsta rap has come in for a severe castigation. But to see rap solely as 'sexist', 'violent' and 'racist' is to miss the point. Or, it is to substitute the victimisation and denigration of the victim for genuine understanding. To condemn black 'racism', whether in the political rhetoric of Malcolm X or gangsta rap, perpetuates the problem, which remains how to, or more accurately how not to, include blacks as full, empowered and equal members in the property-owning democracy.

The nihilism expressed by many rap artists tends to be reflective of rather than a glorification of violence. Through Ice Cube, Chuck D and T-Bone thousands of white kids in the United States and the rest of the world have been exposed to a ghetto community as it really is. But the liberal conscience has serious problems dealing with the real oppressions of ghetto life. Perhaps what is truly obscene is the commodification of the ghetto experience. You get to buy, sell and appropriate the experience without living it! This is what we see in white imitators of extreme varieties of gangsta rap, such as Eminem or the white DJ Tim Westwood, who sounds more authentically 'black' than blacks.

Spike Lee has argued that gangsta rap music videos are the postmodern equivalent of the blackface minstrel shows. Both work by packaging entertainment within established racist images. That's why both have been so successful with white audiences. Minstrel shows are a white invention, and one with a very long history. The first record of a blackface minstrel is from 1822 when English actor Charles Matthews did a one-man show called 'A Trip to America', basing his material on the dialect, songs and dances of blacks he observed there. In Britain the tradition of blackface was not new. Medieval mummers and Morris men appeared in blackface, Morris being a corruption of 'Moorish'. The pageants of the mummers included the enactment of role reversal, the inversion of established relationships, the principle of misrule. Such ritualised performances bolstered the established order by defusing and giving a release to the fears and tensions inherent in that order.

In America the tradition of minstrel shows began around 1828 with Thomas Dartmoth Rice, who created the character of Jim Crow and wrote the song of that name. He was the first in a long succession of white performers who popularised this essential American entertainment that encoded the stereotypes of black people through vicious and malevolent parody. The minstrel shows permitted white audiences to love Negro music and dance, find 'darkies' charming as they were neutered through humour and burlesque and romanticise the subservience of the black, just as the image of the noble savage did the Native American. Role reversal was a safe way to appropriate black music. In their classic form, minstrel shows consisted of a whole troupe of blackface performers providing an entire vaudeville entertainment, including topical political satire on the great issue of the day: slavery.

As popular entertainment, minstrel shows outlived slavery and the American Civil War. Jim Crow became the name for the means to subvert black freedom, a case of determined legal role reversal. The Jim Crow laws enshrined the principle of 'separate but equal' to undermine the entire structure of the 1875 Civil Rights Act and the basis of post-Civil War Reconstruction through practices that kept blacks unequal and excluded. In southern states blacks were denied the franchise by the grandfather principle, literacy test and that old staple of the property-owning democracy: a poll tax.

The first talking movie, *The Jazz Singer*, starred the most famous blackface performer of all time, Al Jolson. When radio became the basis of home entertainment the highest rated show was 'Amos 'n' Andy', characters based on the two stock figures of the minstrel shows: Zip Coon (Andy) and Jim Crow (Amos). The show was such an institution it moved to television. The conventions of minstrel shows and blackface defined the permissible ways blacks could enter the entertainment industry. Along with sport, entertainment become the accepted achievement zone for blacks because both reinforced accepted stereotypes. The stereotypes of the minstrel show depended on the white convention that blacks had rhythm and were innately comical. Sport was about 'brute' strength and speed. Blacks were fine physical specimens, bred for the purpose – think of the classic scene in Alex Haley's *Roots*. The family ancestry of Haley is recorded in the plantation's horse breeding book.

In *Bamboozled*, Spike Lee presents a savage satire on the minstrel shows that is truly double-edged. It concerns the Harvard-educated black television writer, Pierre Delacroix (played by Damon Wayans, whose TV series *In Living Colour* Lee allegedly loathed for its representation of blacks). Pressured by his boss to write a cutting-edge series, Delacroix finds his inspiration in Amos 'n' Andy. He devises *Mantan: The New Millennium Minstrel Show*, starring 'two real coons' (Mantan and Sleep 'N' Eat) and set in a watermelon patch. It is a show so racist he expects to be fired – but the show is a huge success, so much so that it angers the gangsta rappers Mau Mau, whose members include Mos Def and Canibus. They plot to take revenge.

On this premise Lee is able to reflect the history of stereotypes through which blacks have been encapsulated by white society. But he is also able to reflect on the role of black entertainers in the era after the Civil Rights movement, arguing that popular black entertainers of today are nothing more than players in racist minstrel shows, for all the megabucks and headline billing they receive. The film takes its title from a Malcolm X quote: that blacks in America have been 'bamboozled' and 'hoodwinked'. The medium of entertainment does not overturn the conditions of black America – by enriching the black artist white America co-opts them within safely established media ghettos and employs them in roles and party pieces that permit the old stereotypes to be refashioned and re-commodified for new circumstances. In this negotiation, power remains where it always has been and blacks are still being bought, sold and appropriated by white power.

Rap and hip hop are the latest functioning of the black mode of production, now reinforcing globalisation, the recycling of the old system of dominance in the age of cyberspace and the borderless world. Black music is the lost leader entrapping the youth of the world in Western consumerism.

There is a deeply tragic resonance in the role played by black music and black generated self-images in the service of Western consumerism. For what the music proves is that the old territorial imperatives are stronger than ever. There seem to be even greater racial, sexual and class-based suspicions and assaults on the black community in America now than in the past. Race remains a central issue of the American political system, an issue that is not debated or analysed. It is merely recorded in statistics about death and destruction, poverty and powerlessness. The statistics continue to indicate that in many respects large numbers of black Americans, particularly the poor, experience the very worst that society has to offer. And fear endures: blacks make up the largest section of the enormous prison population of the USA (still in chains?), a free society that jails a greater percentage of its population and disproportionately its black population than any other nation on earth. Assaults not only come from outside the black community – antagonisms and conflicts between blacks are as intense as ever (the same of course is true of Yardie fights in Britain). Drug culture has become synonymous with ghetto culture, black culture. If the introduction of drugs to the ghetto was, as is often argued, a cynical strategic ploy to divert and contain black people it would seem to be working. It would also make ghetto drug culture another strand in the minstrel show cycle.

Spike Lee argues that today's black artists are different from their predecessors, the first generation who made their names playing the neutered roles of Uncle Toms, Jim Crows and mammies. The first black to join American Actor's Equity was Bert Williams, a black man who made a career wearing blackface in minstrel shows. In the early movies actors like Steppin' Fetchitt, Jack Benny's butler Rochester, and Hattie MacDaniel, the quintessential big black Mammie, were breaking ground by taking the only roles open to them. As Hattie MacDaniel famously said, 'Better to play a maid than be a maid.' And to their appointed roles these actors brought a dignity, a depth in their acting that rose above the menial and bit part nature of their roles. When MacDaniel 'herm hermed' it was a stereotype, but the way she did it made it into a sad reflection on the way white folks were.

Embracing negative stereotypes as a means to empowerment is the weapon of the weak, the choice of those denied freedom to choose. Postmodernism has repackaged this choice, continued its shelf life and turned it into a reversal of role reversal. Gangsta rap is the perfect idiom of self-parody, self-ridicule, the metier of postmodernism – appropriated, commodified, marketed to ensure the old status quo just keeps on rolling along.

Postmodernism makes property all we are, it is a general global enslavement to consumerism, the purchase of who we are. In postmodern times all choices are market choices, and what we buy and appropriate as an identity is defined by what the market will bear. It is a thorny problem for everyone, but especially for black identity, whose history is most intimately tied to the problem of relations of property ownership and market value. Resolution for black identity exists beyond the terms of reference of the postmodern dispensation – that was the message of two of the greatest personalities of black America in the 20th century: Paul Robeson and Malcolm X.

Robeson was a genuine Renaissance man, a law graduate from Rutgers University where he was also a football star. He also happened to have one of the great singing voices of the 20th century. As well as being a fine actor, he was a committed political activist. He used black music as a weapon, a sharpened instrument to make the case for black empowerment. He sang 'Ol' Man River' as a lament on the unwillingness of society to change. His film roles bore all the malign intent of an industry that wanted nothing to do with change. Whether in the US or in Britain — *Sanders of the River* was a classic film about colonialism that Robeson undertook in hopes of reconnecting with his African roots — he was confined to bringing enormous dignity to re-playing the stereotypes. But beyond performance, Robeson's life was a radical war on property, ownership and the continuing use of blacks as a means of production for white profit.

Robeson made only one film in blackface, a film about coal miners in South Wales. It was an exploration of industrial blackface as an issue that transcended colour. He was at home among the radical left-wing Socialism/syndicalism/Communism of the South Wales Miners Federation. It is no doubt a memorial to Robeson that 'Negro spirituals' became a standard ingredient in the repertoire of Welsh male voice choirs. It was his left-wing politics, and making connections beyond the colour line to the nature of property relations, that finished Robeson. Denied the right to perform in the US, he once held a concert singing to an American audience while standing on a stage in Canada — the concert straddled the border. McCarthyism hounded him to his grave.

Malcolm X also made the connection between ownership and control. When he told the black community 'you've been hoodwinked, you've been had, you've been took, you've been led astray, led amok, you've been bamboozled', he was arguing for black ownership under black control. Instead, the postmodern economy has simply projected the classic stereotypes of blacks as entertainers on to an unsuspecting globe. We all wear blackfaces now — in other words, like blacks, we have all been hoodwinked!

Celebrity

What, I used to wonder, do we gain from looking at a panda? The question emerged every time I took my kids to the zoo. We used to go to see the main attraction, Chin Chin, the mega-celebrity panda. I realised that all our visits followed an unvarying pattern. A suitable amount of 'oohs' and 'aahs' were quickly followed by a plaintive admission: 'Pandas don't do much, do they Dad? Let's go see them feed the penguins.'

Gazing at animals in a zoo is unmistakably akin to our passion for human celebrities. Substitute Michael Jackson for Chin Chin and Anne Robinson for a performing penguin and you will see what I mean. Like animals, human celebrities belong to a different genus: *homo celebritus*. This genus exists in an entirely different habitat to *homo sapiens* – an exotic world of inexplicable behaviour far beyond the realm of the ordinary. But here their similarity diverges. While we look down on animals, we look up to *homo celebritus*. We may yet 'evolve' to acquire the bodies of supermodels, the magnetism of film stars, the voice of a pop icon, the imagined sternness of a Robinson. Animals remind us of what we have been. Celebrities present us with images of what, one way or another, by hook or by crook, we may become.

This evolutionary urge – to acquire celebrity status – is the fundamental ethic on which everything in our world now depends. Celebrity is the main currency of our economy, the prime value in our news and the main impetus in our charitable works. It is the predominant means of the giving and receiving of ideas, information and entertainment. Nothing moves in our universe without the imprint of celebrity. This means that the ethos of the zoo has now become the New World Order.

There are as many different kinds of celebrity as there are animals in the zoo. There are the mega-celebrities, the A-list, like the platypus or the kiwi whose improbability cannot be imagined by an ordinary mind – the Michael Jacksons, Arnold Schwarzeneggers and Madonnas of the Western world. There are celebrities who have become celebrities by predatory behaviour among their own kind, like sharks. There are celebrities who have suicidal tendencies like the proverbial lemmings. There are those who like to shock like the jellyfish, those with foul mouths like the parrot, and those vermin-like celebrities who are famous for no reason at all.

But all varieties of celebrities have one thing in common. They like to be looked at. In zoos one looks at the animals and they, in their vaguely mad way, look at you. Nothing actually happens but we leave the zoo thinking that something valuable has indeed transpired; we have gained 'something'. The supposed mutual gain is, however, a work of imagination. One must after all imagine what the 'natural' life of the animal is like. Does the zoo's parody of its habitat contain any hint of the real thing? Is the animal as miserable in the real world as it is in the zoo?

Something similar happens when we look at celebrities in the celebrity equivalent of wildlife magazines: *Hello!*, *OK!*, *Now* and *People* as well as *Vogue*, *Tatler* and *Harpers & Queen*. We are presented with lifestyles every bit as artificial as that of any caged beast. We try to imagine, with some effort at metaphysical abstraction, what the life of people in the pictures is really like. Are they really as happy as they appear? What does it mean to have so much fame and wealth? What are they really like underneath the plastic personas?

But these questions are not a product of enquiry. Rather, they are an outcome of an ecology of desire and envy in a landscape of fantasy. Celebrity lifestyles are a collective fantasy, a daydream in which most of us have an investment. Just as we go to zoos to acknowledge that all the animals we have heard about actually exist, we seek out celebrities to recognise that other possibilities beyond our mundane lives are truly possible. Through celebrities we reaffirm our selves, our deepest desires and our fondest hopes.

This is why not everyone can be a celebrity. No one, for example, aspires to be ugly, so we just don't have ugly celebrities (a few agony aunt types notwithstanding). We don't want to ask too many difficult questions about ourselves, so philosophers and enquiring minds need not apply. Ditto teachers, doctors and other caring professions. Only members of select professions can acquire the mantle of celebrity. Prime amongst these is the acting fraternity – that is, people who are good at pretending to be other people. Actors are followed by pop singers, models, television presenters and sporting types.

However, just being a good actor or singer is not enough to become a celebrity. Celebrity is not based on meritocracy. It is manufactured. The manufacture of celebrities, if one may switch metaphors, reminds me of icebergs. It looks like a force of nature, when in fact an entire industry dedicated to creating the possibility of celebrity exists hidden from view, and works tirelessly to support the visible part. ITV's *Popstars*, a show designed specifically to manufacture celebrities, cynically exploited as well as exposed this process. This manufacturing process was started in the heyday of Hollywood studios. The studios fostered and nurtured a celebrity system in which stars were projected as almost ethereal gods and goddesses. So now stardom and celebrity go hand in hand. Even minor actors with parts in long-running soap operas are guaranteed celebrity status. Some television programmes make instant celebrities not only of their presenters but also their subject matter – witness Davina McCall and Channel 4's dating game *Streetmate*.

Once acquired, celebrity requires serious effort to be sustained. The vicarious engine of celebrity feeds voraciously on three basic elements: attention, excess, gossip.

Attention is the lifeblood of celebrity. It is a two-way process. The celebrities seek constant attention and the public endlessly observes celebrities and dreams of joining their ranks. In a mass society there is just not enough attention to go around, so celebrities are everyone's sublimation of the need to be needed. Attention provokes strange results. A true mega-celeb exists in as real a cage as any zoo animal and some come to hate perpetual and lavish attention. The permanent gaze can be fatal, as we have seen in the case of Princess Diana, Michael Hutchence and Gianni Versace.

What of the observers? Attention, ubiquity and endless reports breed the illusion of knowing. The celebrity becomes a possession of those who attend and observe and thereby feel proprietorial rights over the celebrity they in large measure sustain. But the public also owns the celebrities in another sense. Most people are familiar with Marshall McLuhan's famous dictum: 'The medium is the message'. What many forget is that he went on to point out that 'the content of any medium is always another medium'. Thus, in a media-drenched society, celebrity is both message and medium. And the virtual medium, the persona of the celebrity, is public property. So pity the poor celeb who wishes to cut loose from the strict etiquette of celebrity lifestyle and lead a 'private life'. The Garboesque 'I want to be alone' could only exist in a more innocent and less celebrity-oriented era. It is literally the last hurrah for the likes of Anna Ford, Michael Douglas, Catherine Zeta-Jones and Naomi Campbell, who have sued various tabloids and magazines for breach of privacy.

Excess is the essence of celebrity. It is not hard to be excessive when celebrity reaps unconscionable sums of money. When celebrities were creatures of the studio moguls there was a sensible bargain. Celebs could live as they liked, indulge in as much excess of any variety as they liked, so long as they maintained the cosiest and most moral of public personas. In those days celebs were fictions performed by real people. The temper of the times has changed. Now celebs perform their excesses for public consumption; the very notion of moderation, balance and decorum spells death to celebrity. Hence, the Liz Hurley dress, Elton John's flowers, and the astronomically disproportionate use of alcohol and drugs by all and any self-respecting celebrity. The public lives vicariously through these excesses, and they become not unfortunate incidents but positive delights relished by all and sundry.

One function of excess is to generate gossip – the last essential element of celebrity. Now, there is nothing really new about gossip, it has always been with us. It was, for example, so dominant in 18th-century England that the period has come to be known as 'The Age of Scandal'. But gossip has changed a lot since then. Conventionally, gossip was much more than simply talking about the sordid lives and atrocious behaviour of other people. It was an agency of social control, a definition of standards, decency and moral ideals. The Age of Scandal gossiped and thereby defined the polite notion of propriety that became Victorian morals. Women have always been in the forefront of gossip, but then women have always been the keepers of society's moral conscience. Celebrities were observed and talked about to be judged, and judgements on them could be harsh indeed. Gossip policed the ideals society valued, which did not mean standards were never defied, just that there were standards and flouting them had consequences.

Now gossip is simply malicious talk. Value judgements are no longer in vogue and we have no language to describe what we think is good, proper or worthwhile. The function of gossip is to fuel our insatiable hunger for sordid details, morbid deeds and trivial pursuits. We must know everything that happens in the daily lives of celebrities. Indeed, nothing that happens to celebrities is real unless it is the subject of gossip and everyone is talking about it. It is part of being a celebrity to perpetually generate gossip, to create never-ending fictions of pain and self-pity, to produce invective about all those with whom you come in contact. This is why British television personality Esther Rantzen feels compelled, in her autobiography, to share her bitter and vengeful feelings about her husband's first wife.

Celebrity, as the word implies, involves celebration. But what exactly is being celebrated? Conventionally, celebrity celebrated weirdness, excess, outrageous behaviour – the basic ingredients of gossip. But in media-obsessed postmodern times celebrity has become a celebration of something much more sinister: the unadulterated pleasure of cynical power. Celebrity bestows a power on individuals that is almost unique in history. It is based on three newly acquired abilities.

First, celebrity now has the ability to transcend boundaries. Mega-celebrities, such as Tom Cruise and Britney Spears, are global phenomena and reap macro financial rewards. Indeed, some Hollywood celebrities are worth more than most small countries. In an average year, Tom Cruise earns around £70 million. When celebrity is the driving force of the global economy, such high-earning individuals have real power. When Cruise and Nicole Kidman decided to end their marriage, we saw the true manifestation of this power. They earned more column inches and airtime around the globe than many a good-sized country warrants in a decade or two.

But it is not just geographical boundaries that celebrity now transcends. Even on a mundane and local level, the economic appeal of celebrity means that celebrities now do everything and anything. Serious journalism has been replaced with celebrity columnists regaling us with amusing anecdotes about their choice lives, and giving their opinions on everything from childrearing to rocket science. So a strictly C-list babe like Mariella Frostrup (sometime DJ and TV presenter and daughter of sometime Bond Girl Honor Blackman) can present a flagship news analysis programme like *Panorama*. Leonardo DiCaprio interviews President Clinton on primetime ABC, and *Monty Python*'s Michael Palin is the heir apparent to inveterate travellers like Philby and Thesiger. The power that once belonged to 'the expert' now belongs to celebrity: witness how the once unglamorous professions of archaeology, history, psychology et al are now claimed by 'television personalities'. Minor celebs act as agony aunts, consumer advisers, decorators, cookery experts and gardeners. There is no area of life that celebrity has not invaded.

Second, celebrity has the uncanny ability to persuade the public to suspend belief in reality. We are finding it increasing difficult, in this age of mediated relations, to distinguish between images and reality. More and more people believe that the characters they see on screen or stage are somehow embodied in and personified by the celebrities who breathe life into them. In particular, the belief that soap stars are playing themselves, or that their characters are in fact real people, is widespread. Remember the real campaign to free *Coronation Street*'s Deirdre Rachid? Even Downing Street joined in on this one, tongue in cheek perhaps.

Hence the overwhelming use of celebrities in advertisements. Research has shown that if a celebrity says a product is good, most people would believe it to be true. The familiar presence of a trustworthy celebrity marketing crisps or beer is a sure winner: footballer Gary Lineker is now as synonymous with Walkers Crisps as Rutger Hauer was with Guinness. The super-silly advertisement for Surf washing powder featuring the stars of TV sitcom *Birds of a Feather* produced runaway sales. When Miracle-Gro fertiliser was brought together with sports pre-senter Des Lynam sales increased several-fold. Celebrities, it seems, can sell us any variety of manure.

This is why celebrity endorsement has become a universal principle. If you want to get any idea, project, initiative, campaign or cause started then find a celebrity. No cause is a cause without a star. So we find that David Schwimmer supports a rape treatment centre, Anthony Edwards backs autism research and Susan Sarandon is a tireless campaigner for abolishing the death penalty. Geri Halliwell is a UN Goodwill Ambas-sador for God's sake. For celebrities these causes are as essential as agents and breast implants. The badge of altruism provides some justification for a shameless existence.

Third, celebrity now has the ability to shape identity. In postmodern culture, identity is consciously constructed from an eclectic archive anchored by celebrity. It is not just that the young increasingly model themselves on celebrities. There is nothing really new in celebrities acting as role models. What is new is that celebrity is now the only yard-stick for aspiration. Celebrity culture has replaced all those older human sources of inspiration – oral history, epic poems, legendary myths. Even the old kinship ties that once nurtured and sustained Western society have now been swapped for imaginary relationships with celebrities. So celebrity now occupies us day and night, drives our dreams, inspires our obeisance and reverence. In short, celebrities perform all those roles that were once carried out by religion, ideology and history. It is now the spring from which we derive many of our multiple identities.

The culmination of contemporary celebrity is a new kind of virtual zoo, far removed from the zoo where my children regularly visited Chin Chin. At the end of each visit, we would agree that zoos provided a last chance to preserve endangered species. They were the best places for pandas until we acquired the wisdom and means to enable pandas to flourish once more as pandas should, in sustainable mountain forests far from prying eyes. Old-style celebrity, the kind fuelled by gossip as moral agency, shared this panda factor. It kept endangered values secure from the excesses of which humans are so capable.

In the celebrity-infested virtual zoo both observers and observed are behind bars. Both are products of a caged imagination where aspiration and actuality prowl in narrow confines leading inevitably to madness. Celebrities and their lifestyles are like the tigers that pace dementedly back and forth, back and forth, and consume proffered red meat only to continue their journey back and forth, back and forth. The observers, those besotted with celebrity, chase an empty parody that inevitably drains their own lives of any meaning. We ogle to diminish ourselves. What is there to celebrate in that?

Chinese

Sammo Hung is not a conventional hero. He is short, fat and chronologically over the hill. But as the leading man of the hit action/comedy show *Martial Law*, he is in a class of his own. He can turn any ordinary object – dustbin, toothbrush, a pair of shoes – into a lethal weapon. He can back-flip, high-kick and land a karate chop with supernatural ease.

The plot has our hero move from Shanghai to Los Angeles to join forces with the LAPD. But the fictional move has real-life counterparts. A host of actors and directors have shifted from Hong Kong to Hollywood, taking the style and aesthetics of Hong Kong action cinema with them. The transfer also represents a shift in the conventional representation of the Chinese in American cinema.

Conventionally, the Chinese have been portrayed in the West as untrustworthy, stupid, greedy, superstitious, lustful towards white women, irrationally attached to rather conservative notions of honour and family loyalty, and prone to narcotic addictions. In sharp contrast, the Chinese hero of *Martial Law* is wise, humorous and wholly trustworthy. His integrity and values become a commentary on American culture. He emerges as deeply humane, complex and a rather well-rounded person.

Representation is a function of power. The arrival of a genuine Chinese Hollywood hero on our television screens signals the arrival of China in global politics as a superpower. It is also an acknowledgement that Chinese consumers, both inside China and outside in the Pacific

Rim and all over the world, now constitute almost half of the global market. Clearly, they are unlikely to take someone like the evil Fu Manchu to heart. Sammo, on the other hand, is recognisably one of 'us'.

But within Western culture itself, the Chinese are also becoming 'us' rather than 'them'. Increasingly, they are seen less as objects of fear and subjects of loathing, and more as an integral part of Western civilisation. A running gag in *Martial Law* plays ostensibly on American penetration of China only to emphasise how China itself has been internalised by America. Chinese products are everywhere and Chinese food is in fact better than in China. Buddhism is the chosen philosophy of all fashion-conscious individuals. Kids are addicted to video games like *Street Fighter II* in which players assume the personality of racially marked characters such as Kung Fu master, Chun Li. Chinese martial arts are now a standard feature of Hollywood action films. American and European business no longer fears Confucianism. Indeed, Sun Tzu's *The Art of War* is essential reading for all self-respecting corporate leaders.

The increasing acceptance of the Chinese as an essential part of Western culture has involved overwriting a long string of negative stereotypes. Western representations of China go back to the 16th century and depend on the imagery of the Mongol hordes. The stock embodiment of Chinese cruelty and malign intent is Fu Manchu, whose name means 'The Yellow Peril'. The stereotype of the evil Chinese criminal was created by Sax Rohmer in a 1913 novel called *The Mystery of Dr Fu Manchu*. 'Imagine a person', writes Rohmer, 'tall, lean and feline, high shouldered, with a brow like Shakespeare and a face like Satan, a close-shaven skull, and long, magnetic eyes of the true cat-green. Invest him with all the cruel cunning of an entire Eastern race, accumulated in one giant intellect, with all the resources of science past and present, with all the resources, if you will, of a wealthy government – which, however, already has denied all knowledge of his existence. Imagine that awful being, and you have a mental picture of Dr Fu Manchu, the yellow peril incarnate in one man...'. Its popularity led to a baker's dozen of sequels and a plethora of short stories. During the twenties, the novels were transferred to the screen in a series of British two-reelers; when the talkies arrived in the thirties, Paramount and MGM took over from the British, and Republic Pictures produced a serial, *Drums of Fu Manchu*, to enthral matinee audiences on Saturdays. In the sixties, Fu Manchu returned to British screens in a series of Hammer films, with the cunning Oriental portrayed by Christopher Lee. Thus Fu Manchu films gave to the depiction of the evil Chinese an enduring and international form. By convention from Conan Doyle to Sax Rohmer, Chinatown became a den of iniquity and lurking menace.

The American representation of the Chinese also draws on two seminal works – the 1919 D.W. Griffith film *Broken Blossoms* and Pearl S. Buck's novel, and its 1937 film version, *The Good Earth*. Griffith's film, based on the short story *The Chink and the Child* by Thomas Burke, is a cautionary tale about miscegenation. Its protagonist, Cheng Huan, settles in London with the intention of becoming a Buddhist missionary. Instead, he becomes a recluse and an opium addict. He offers refuge to a young girl violently abused by her drunken father. In scenes of subtle codes, he dresses her in Chinese finery from the curio shop where he works, until she is fit to be a concubine. When the drunken father discovers her whereabouts he breaks in, drags her out and beats her to death, before being shot by Cheng, who then kills himself. *Broken Blossoms* was seen as a sympathetic portrayal of the Chinese. But the intended sympathy only reconfirms the very prejudice it seeks to expose.

The Good Earth, as film and book, piles stereotype on stereotype of Orientalist imagery. The story is the life cycle of the peasant farmer Wang Lung and the former indentured domestic slave he marries, O Lan. The peasants are universalised to some extent, but there is a remoteness about them that is impenetrable. Even more noticeable in the book than the film are the coldness and personal distance shown as innate to the characters. The pride at having a first-born son does not translate into fatherly affection – the children are forgotten appendages once born. The heroic, noble wife is cast aside for a concubine; Wang Lung is betrayed by his nephew; his sons scheme against him in his old age. There is a strong accent on bestiality. China has no redeeming features and is portrayed as timeless, without any sense of history.

Buck was a missionary, born into a missionary family, and lived and worked in China, where *The Good Earth* was written. Hollywood has had a strong relationship with missionary China. It won an Oscar for Gregory Peck as the dedicated Catholic priest who made no impact on the otherness of China in *Keys of the Kingdom* (1944). There were more Oscars for *Inn of the Sixth Happiness* (1958), where Ingrid Bergman played the missionary Gladys Aylward. In all these films, China is cruel, despotic, wrapped in tradition, chaotic, a corrupt 'ruin on the edge of the world' and perennially resistant to change and the West.

To these stock representations, Bret Harte and Mark Twain added the image of the buffoonish Chinaman who speaks only pidgin English. Their creation, Hop Sing, has been recycled through numerous films and television shows. In the long-running TV western series *Bonanza*, Hop Sing is also the name of the comic cook who serves the Cartwright family. Many episodes of *Bonanza* were devoted to improving representations of blacks and Native Americans. But Hop Sing always remained Hop Sing.

The principal Chinese characters in films are usually played by Caucasian actors who give us, appropriately enough, a representation of a representation. Not even Charlie Chan, the inscrutable Oriental detective, was played by a Chinese actor – his most famous screen persona was provided by Walter Oland. He was also played in a number of films by John Carradine, whose son David Carradine has made a career out of recycling Orientalist imagery in the television series *Kung Fu* and *Kung Fu: The Legend Continues*.

As *Martial Law* testifies, the legend does not actually continue. The Chinese are now increasingly representing themselves. In Hollywood they can be found both behind and in front of the camera. This shift is a product of two related developments.

The first is the emergence of a number of Chinese filmmakers, such as Ang Lee and Wayne Wang, who have made it big in Hollywood. In Ang

Lee's first three films (*Pushing Hands*, *The Wedding Banquet*, *Eat Drink Man Woman*), for example, the characters are always complex figures coming to terms with tradition. There is always a wise, dignified father figure, embodying traditional values, who brings out the strengths and weaknesses of modernity and tradition. In his Oscar-winning *Crouching Tiger, Hidden Dragon*, Ang Lee makes hardly any allowances for Western viewers, suggesting a confidence both in his own representation and in his audience. Similarly, Wang portrays the Chinese (*Eat a Bowl of Tea*, *The Joy Luck Club*, *Chinese Box*) as complex characters with intact humanity.

The second is the transfer of Hong Kong action cinema to Hollywood. John Woo led the way by directing action vehicles for the likes of John Travolta (*Broken Arrow*) and Jean Claude Van Damme (*Hard Target*). Then, after the 1997 Hong Kong handover, the floodgates opened, with the mass exodus of the island's film makers. So now high-octane stars, like Chow Yun Fat, Jackie Chan and Jet Li, are fast becoming the staple fare of Hollywood. They still speak pidgin English, but who cares if you can entertain like Jackie Chan, shoot and fight like Chow Yun Fat or land a fatal kick in mid air like Jet Li?

Indeed, it is not just Hong Kong actors and directors that have been integrated – the very grammar and style of Hong Kong film making, with its 'poetry of violence', has been totally assimilated by Hollywood. We can see this not just in films like *Rush Hour* and *Lethal Weapon 4*, where most of the action stunts are performed by Chinese actors, but in a host of films with no apparent connection to the Chinese. This is because American film makers now routinely turn to Hong Kong to train their actors in the physical and mental skills of martial arts film making. For example, the legendary Chinese fight choreographer, Yuen Wo Ping, trained the actors and choreographed all the action sequences in *The Matrix*. The poses that Keanu Reeves adopts throughout these sequence are patterned on the style of Jet Li, whose *Black Mask* was Yuen Wo Ping's last film in Hong Kong.

The Matrix also provides us with an example of how deeply, despite its occasional portrayal as the Great Enemy, China has penetrated the

American subconscious. Tank, the character that defines humanity in the film, is clearly Chinese – played by Marcus Chong, an actor of mixed African and Chinese ancestry. As well as embodying the hope for a future of humanity born and not harvested by machines, Tank is also crucial to resistance. He operates the computers that allow the rebels to fight the machines of 'the Matrix'. In a subconscious slip, the two characters, Tank and Neo (played by Keanu Reeves) who save humanity in the final frames of *The Matrix*, turn out to be Chinese. As most film aficionados know, Keanu Reeves has an English mother and a Chinese-Hawaiian father.

So, it seems, the American psyche is being transformed from within. Clearly, there is more than one way to colonise the world!

Dissent

Once upon a time I used to be known as an *enfant terrible*. I suppose with the onset of ageing one becomes merely *terrible*. But what was really terrible was the growing awareness that quiescent ageing is becoming a general condition. The whole world, it seemed, was going gently into that good night along with me. But, just as neo-liberals in the US and Britain paused for a breath after proclaiming the absolute triumph of capitalism and the end of history, the spirit of the sixties reappeared. Starting in Seattle in 1998, the anti-globalisation demonstrations rekindled rage at the dying of the light and changed the temper of postmodern times. Dissent is not only back on the agenda; it is going to shape the politics of the decades ahead.

The ramshackle and ragged groups of greens, anarchists, socialists, radicals and non-governmental types who go from city to city besieging global institutions, such as the World Trade Organisation, International Monetary Fund and G8, are very special. What makes them special is the fact that they are motivated almost exclusively by anger at the injustices of the world and passion to do something about them. The combination of selfless anger and pragmatic passion is rare at any time, but it is particularly so in postmodern times, whose distinguishing characteristics are complacency and self-interest.

And there is much to be angry and passionate about.

The disparities of our world are grosser now than ever before in history. Never, since the day the original *homo sapiens* first stood on two legs, have so few consumed and controlled so much. The richest 20 per cent of the world's people, that's us and our like, now consume 86 per cent of all goods and services, 45 per cent of all the meat and fish, 58 per cent of all the energy, 84 per cent of all the paper and 87 per cent of all the vehicles. The poorest 20 per cent consume just 1.3 per cent of everything. Indeed, the three richest people in the world have assets that exceed the combined gross domestic product of the 48 least developed countries. The world's 225 richest individuals, of whom 60 are American, own the same amount of wealth as the poorest half of the world's population.

But the situation is far worse than the bare facts. The acquisitive tendency of the great accumulators now rivals the appetite of a black hole. Every aspect of human life, including life itself, has been commodified – and is merchandised exclusively and specifically for the benefit of the rich. Genes, blood, indigenous plants and medicines – you name it, and some multinational holds a patent on it. 'Structural adjustment', which the World Bank and IMF have imposed on over 100 developing countries, is simply a euphemism for privatisation, a process that translates into effectively handing Third World resources to the First World. The economies of the 'Eastern bloc' countries have been worked over, bought up, mortgaged and sold out in almost exactly the same way as those of the Third World. So, since the end of the Cold War, life expectancy in Russia has decreased by 10 years. Absolute poverty continues to increase throughout Africa. While people in the West spend more and more on cosmetics and dog food, more and more people in the non-West are sleeping hungry.

Thank goodness, then, for the 'anarchists' and other 'anti-capitalists' laying siege to global institutions. These people have realised that injustice is not just built into the system; it is the system. Dissent and direct action have become prerequisites, not only for a just world but for survival itself. The very fact that the demonstrators have been demonised – described in disparaging terms, dismissed as Luddites and baton-charged by the police of several nations – suggests that they are on to something real. But how can we ensure that the new spirit of dissent does not end in a whimper, rather than a big bang that fashions a new global order?

Positive dissent at the dawn of the 21st century must begin with four important realisations. First, we ought to remember that yesterday's dissent is often today's establishment and, unless resisted, becomes tomorrow's terror. The great revolutions of the 20th century – from the Bolsheviks in Russia to the Cultural Revolution in China and the 'Islamic Revolution' in Iran – all started as dissenting movements and ended up as even greater authoritarian regimes. The dissenters of the sixties – the hippies, the flower children, the protesters against the Vietnam war – became the corporate managers and free market champions of the eighties and nineties. Who are the anti-globalisation protesters dissenting against? They are dissenting against people like Bill Clinton and Tony Blair who led the counter-revolution of the sixties and seventies – the very people who are demonising the dissenters of the noughties.

Look at it this way: a great number of those who now swell the ranks of the middle class, middle mind, middle of the roaders in the West have achieved their affluent status thanks entirely to the dissenting agenda of 20th century. Just think where we would be without Socialism, the Labour movement, the movement for welfare provision, the suffragettes and numerous movements for Third World independence. The pioneers of these movements were not too unlike the contemporary scruffy ragtag groups of anti-globalisation protesters. The single most important fact is the changes initiated by these movements stopped short, well before arriving at the station of hope for all. Why? Simply because once dissent achieves apparent breakthrough, it produces its own dynamics.

Dissent breaks through to establish a new rhetoric, to make the contemplation of change acceptable, to form a new agenda. And that's when things start to go wrong. Dissenters then have to shoulder the burden of managerial responsibility and potential electability. The outcome is the need to display 'a safe pair of hands', to become acceptable to the establishment order, in terms of the established order. What is transformed is not the world as it has been but dissent itself. Instead of engineering real change dissent makes a career out of tinkering with the window dressing. Dissent is intimated by success, however limited and imperfect. It is manipulated by the gains – freedom manipulates us, security manipulates us, abundance manipulates us, so sustaining and retaining what we have becomes the prime directive. We then succumb to the most ruthless totalitarianism of all – the tyranny of complacency.

Second, we need to appreciate that dissent can actually end up enhancing the very power it is trying to undermine. The ostensibly dissenting practices in Western industrial democracies, as French radical philosopher Michel Foucault has argued, themselves constitute the apparatus of power. In this best of all possible 'free' worlds, dissent is allowed to thrive only when it ultimately enhances the structures of power it appears to defy. Power, to use Foucault's words, masks a substantial part of itself in a number of ways. It creates binary opposites to enhance its legitimacy – just as America has manufactured threatening 'rogue states' hell-bent on its destruction to justify the development of a 'Star Wars' weapons system. It domesticates dissent by co-opting it. A host of dissenting disciplines that emerged in the seventies, such as ecology, feminism and cultural studies, have now been co-opted in the mainstream of academia; their radical edge has been totally blunted. Indeed, non-dissenting dissent has almost been turned into a speculative art in an academic world that is increasingly taking on overtones of corporate management. Power commodifies dissent by making it into a sexy, fashionable and desirable accessory. Witness how the rebellious black youth of America have been turned into a global commodity, their dissent now expressed in terms of designer labels. Most new fads in music and fashion, from mods and rockers to punk to Generation X and the New Beats, start off as dissenting practices before being turned into stylised commodities. You can even go on a package holiday to express your dissent!

Third, we must realise that we do not have any real and original means of expressing dissent. The very language of dissent has itself been colonised. So, the dissenters face a tough problem: how do you signify your dissent from those very political processes, economic forces and epistemological structures that have made dissent an essential part of the dominant power structure and turned it into a fashionable commodity?

The dissenters, as my friend the Indian intellectual and cultural critic, Ashis Nandy, has pointed out, are supposed to be the counterplayers to the game of Western imperialism and domination. Yet, they work *within* the dominant model of imperialism and *with* the dominant consciousness. So, far from articulating and presenting an alternative – the true essence of dissent – they actually promote the dominant model of thought. Thus dissent can lead to further colonisation; indeed, in some cases, colonisation is an essential part of dissent.

We saw this most clearly in the famous Tiananmen Square protests in China. By choosing the Statue of Liberty as their symbol of dissent, the protesters unconsciously signalled their desire to replace one kind of oppression with another. A rebellion against the oppressions of state control based on the command economy ended up by demanding a symbolic as well as actual colonisation both by the American way of life and corporate capital.

Therefore, rebellions that use the common language and concepts of dissent undermine themselves even before they get going. This is particularly so when dissent is associated with violence. Indeed, both in theory and practice, we have made something of a fetish of violent dissent. The Korean poet and novelist, Kim Chi Ha, one of the best-known exponents of the politics of dissent, expresses the sentiment by declaring: 'I loathe the violence of repression and welcome the violence of resistance. I reject dehumanising violence and accept the violence that restores human dignity. It could justly be called the violence of love.'

Academia is similarly in love with violence. Scholars with defiant reputations to protect and promote, like Edward Said, Homi Bhabha and Henry Louis Gates Jr, have made a bizarre fetish of Frantz Fanon, the West Indian French revolutionary, writer and author of *The Wretched of the Earth*. For Fanon, violence has a central, indeed cleansing, role to play in dissent and the future of the Third World. The violence of the oppressor, he argued, is often internalised by the oppressed; it thus becomes necessary for the oppressor to be confronted in violence not just to liberate oneself from his oppression but also to mark an agonising break with a part of one's self. However, if Fanon had more confidence in his culture (this is a problematic assertion as Fanon had no notion of what *his* culture was) he would have realised that his vision ties the victims ever more deeply to the culture of oppression. To articulate dissent with the tools of the oppressor is to actually collude with the oppressor and internalise his (nowadays, frequently also her) essential values. Once violence is given cultural and intrinsic legitimacy, it transforms the battle between two visions and worldviews into a struggle for power and resources between two groups with identical values. Thus the dissenters who begin from the position of being sinned against end up sinning themselves.

Fourth, we need to question why the leadership of major dissenting movements is always located in the West. Domination is only complete when dissent can be foreseen and managed. Predictability – what dissenters will do – is essential to contain and domesticate dissent. Non-Western radicals are notoriously unpredictable and frequently uncontainable. It thus makes sense to those in power to ensure that the eye of the dissenting storm is securely anchored in Europe or North America. It also requires manufacturing and imposing humdrum Western leadership on dissenting movements, comprised of people whose vision of alternative possibilities is limited by the repertoire and experience of the West itself.

Similarly, by subtle but well-organised means, the dominant knowledge industry ensures that the capitals of dissent, along with the capitals of global political economy, are located in the stylish universities, think-tanks and other intellectual centres of the First World. Western academics and thinkers define what constitutes genuine and sober dissent, how dissent is best expressed, and establish the criteria by which it is studied and institutionalised through the university system. So, students and activists from developing countries have to come to the West to study ways and means of dissent; as well as to obtain the finance to give them the freedom necessary to dissent. At least three generations of non-Western campaigners and scholars have learnt the meaning of 'true' dissent and the technology of 'authentic' radicalism from Western academic gurus. Yet, in all the concern for the oppressed of the Third World shown in Western institutions and non-governmental organisations, respect for the Third World's own understanding of its own plight has remained conspicuously absent. While dissent is often initiated in the name of the Third World, the real intellectuals, thinkers and people of the Third World, as well as their ideas, thought and opinions, are seldom allowed to come to the fore.

How does the new spirit of dissent, the emerging anti-capitalist radicalism, fare in the light of these four crucial aspects of dissent in our time? In some respects, the new movement is showing clear signs of domestication. Violent confrontations in the streets of Seattle, Prague, Gothenburg and Genoa have already compromised its moral stance. The leadership is located not just in the West but also in the hands of genuinely constructed vacuous individuals. Consider Naomi Klein. Does suggesting that multinationals ignore people's concern at their peril, or that brands like Nike are screwing the Third World, or that people are beginning to resent the colonisation of their lives, amount to saying something new and original? Why has *No Logo* become a manifesto of the anti-globalisation movement when what it has to say has been said countless times, and more profoundly, before? The fact is that what Klein has to say is not all that relevant. The important thing is that she looks right and can play the part of a dissenter who can be commodified. Ditto Noreena Hertz, her British counterpart. Even the title of Hertz's book, *The Silent Takeover*, is a conscious attempt to recapture the glory of the sixties with echoes of Rachel Carson's *Silent Spring*. Unfortunately, the analysis, as has rightly been pointed out, is at the level of Mills & Boon.

The trail to dissenting fame is itself a form of domestication. Both Klein and Hertz have followed a well-established path. It begins with books containing the obvious promoted as something blindingly new and far-reaching. This is followed by television documentaries (Channel 4 in Britain, PBS in America) and columns in left-wing newspapers – all of which provide ample demonstration that the System appreciates dissent and serves as an illustration of its democratic spirit. After a critical mass is reached, the new dissenting leader is seen and projected by the media as 'natural'. When someone declares the new dissenting movement to be 'the new rock 'n' roll' – in this case George Monbiot, who, according to the *Financial Times* is 'the UK's most prominent direct activist' – you know the rot has set in. Once the leading lights of the movement begin to appear in the pages of *Dazed and Confused* and other style magazines, commodification is complete and the battle is truly lost.

To have a modicum of meaning, dissent has to be much more than a prerogative exercised by those who think they are God's chosen own. The first thing that dissenters have to fight is the very perversion of dissent. Dissent is not a vocation or an identity label or a chic style or an endless source of stories for dried-up style journalists. Ultimately, the survival of the anti-globalisation movement depends on its ability to defy the given models of defiance.

That means the anti-globalisation movement has to look to the non-West both for leadership and inspiration. It needs to constantly re-examine the limits of dissent and the uncanny ability of dissenters to be co-opted, domesticated, colonised and thereby transformed into the establishment. It needs to articulate alternative visions of the future and translate them into practical and pragmatic policies. And it needs to shun traditional hierarchies.

This means something much more challenging than simply remaining unstructured, unorganised and anarchic. Rage for the sake of rage cannot be a substitute for determined commitment to wholesale change. It would be more than enough if the swelling ranks of protesters for once pledged themselves to changing the West rather than saving the rest of the world. For the last betrayal of dissent is the failure to tackle the root cause of the global problem on its home ground.

Europe

Europe is suffering from schizophrenia. The signs of this chronic and disabling mental disease are everywhere.

The common image of schizophrenia as 'split personality' can be seen in all those anti-European Europeans who do not want to be a part of a European Community. The 'disordered thinking', a basic sign of the psychosis, is evident in the emphasis given to the fabricated past and manufactured 'Greek roots' of Europe. All European thought is traced directly to the Greeks, while the history of Europe begins with ancient Rome and then bypasses several centuries of void, the Dark Ages, when nothing happened and no one else existed. From this fabled origin springs the delusion that European thought is the yardstick by which all human thought is to be measured, a delusion that further reinforces the diagnosis. Finally, hallucinations, another characteristic symptom of schizophrenia, are now a common occurrence in Europe: seeing and feeling frightening things in 'immigrant communities' that are simply not there. Indeed, these hallucinations have led to a renaissance of the extreme right across the continent.

The symptoms emerge the moment we try to locate Europe itself. Where is Europe? Where are the outer limits of its borders? How much of 'Eastern Europe', for example, is actually 'East' and can never really be part of Europe per se? Do we really think that Slovakians, Romanians and Albanians – with their totally un-European ways – are European? Is

Turkey in Europe or out of it? And what about Russia? All this, quite naturally, leads to the problem of defining a European; a problem made intractable by the presence of large minorities of Muslims, Arabs, Asians, blacks and other 'Third World' types within Western Europe.

But the malaise really sets in once we move to civilisational, historic and conceptual notions of Europe. As a civilisation, Europe is, of course, everywhere: European civilisation is not located in a geographical space but in these days of globalisation it envelops the world with its desires, images, politics and consumer and cultural products. As a worldview, European thought is the dominant outlook of the globe – the world exists in the image of Europe. Given that other parts of the world, for example North America and Australia as well as the Westernised ruling elites of developing countries, are now more European than Europe, Europe itself becomes rather insignificant in European terms. It is hardly surprising then that Europeans are feeling a bit disorientated and disordered.

'The present', as the Hungarian Marxist critic Gyorgy Lukacs once observed, 'is a problem of history'. To understand European schizophrenia, we need to appreciate how much of its real history Europe has simply suppressed, denied and overwritten. The simple fact is that Europe, contemporary Europe, is inconceivable without Islam. It is not just that Europe shaped its identity in relation to Islam, but Islam also humanised Europe and taught it all those things that make up a civilisation. To deny its true lineage, and reject its real biological father, Europe has gone to incredible lengths both to internalise an elaborately manufactured history and impose it on the rest of the world. This engineered history has three main components: the invention of the Greeks as the origins of Europe and the cradle of all civilisations; the construction of Rome as the foundation on which Europe as an historic entity is based; and rendering all the Islamic history that shaped Europe invisible.

When Europe looks for a sense of self it turns to Greece, the imagined birthplace of Europe as an intellectual project. So what better place to start than the myth of Europa, supposedly the maiden who gave her name to the continent. This is standard Greek myth but the devil, as usual, is in the detail. How do continents acquire names? The question was posed by Herodotus, in *The Histories*. The supposed father of history points out that convention links the myth of Europa to the naming of the continent, even though the actual geographic extent of Europe is unclear. Furthermore, he notes that Europa never even came to Greece and was actually Asiatic. So even for the Greeks their identity as European was problematic, and with good reason.

At the time when the name 'Europe' came to be associated with a continent the Greeks thought only in terms of cities and coalitions of cities as the real extent of their world. Except, of course, when they thought of Asia. All that was essentially un-Greek existed in Asia, home of vast empires and despotic rule by effeminate decadents who knew nothing of the manly independence of Greek life. Asia was old in history and civilisation, while the Greeks themselves were struggling to develop a sense of what we term 'history' and had only vague mythic notions of their own origins.

There is another thread in the tense duality between Greece and Asia. It is the actual subtext of the myth of Europa. The maiden was lured from her home by a white bull. The bull was Zeus himself, the king of gods in bovine disguise. He carried Europa over the sea to the island of Crete where she bore him three sons, including Minos. According to myth, this Asiatic maiden was a princess, daughter of Agenor, king of Phoenicia, the ancient trading state on the Asian shore of the Mediterranean. Her brother, Cadmus, did not take kindly to this abduction and set off to search for Europa. He ended by marrying Harmonia, introducing the knowledge of writing, civilising the rustic Greeks and founding the Greek city of Thebes.

If Europa expresses a sense of European identity in distinction to Asia, her mythic story also represents the indebtedness of Europe to Asia – the detail that comprises the essence of what must be forgotten. Greek myths, as scholars acknowledge, can be read as sagas of appropriation. They are part of the intellectual debt Greece owes to the civilisations of

Asia. Mythos was the medium through which disassociation was fabricated, the commonality out of which difference is made. Far from being an independent invention on the soil of Europe, ancient Greece is a derivative of the civilisations of Asia. Learning passed west, via the Crete of the Minoans. Europa, after her ravishing by Zeus, married a prince of Crete; her son Minos gave his name to the Minoan civilisation of Crete. Greek cities, far from being unequivocally European, were established both on the European peninsula we call Greece and on the Anatolian peninsula, present-day Turkey. The life of Greek cities was deeply intertwined with the life of Asia, not least through trade, the mechanism by which Greece became upwardly mobile and financed its pretensions. The one European fashion decidedly derived from Greece is the wilful determination to see all others as barbarians, especially Asians. Classical Greek drama encodes the Persians, the nemesis of Athens, as barbarian in terms that have clung to the soil of Asia ever since.

Rome supplanted Greece and excelled in engineering. Everything else was left to the devious Greek slaves who did all the teaching, thinking and a great deal of the writing for the Roman elite, leaving them free for their real interests: world domination. As civilisations go you cannot get more venal, bloodthirsty and brutish than Rome. Not that this is our usual perspective on the Romans. Despite everything we know about the perversions, oppressions, tyrannies and excesses of that awful people we still see Roman civilisation as the architect of Europe. The BBC has eulogised this vision of history in the title of its programme *What the Romans Did For Us*. What they did was colonise, exterminate with relish, expropriate and subjugate. Rome is the original home of the colonising mission. Generations of Europeans were schooled from the Roman manuals in how best to dominate other peoples for the benefit of a ruling elite. It is the content of Caesar's *Gallic Wars*, an account of his military campaigns to dominate Celtic France.

But the fact is that the actual origin of Europe as peoples and nations is neither Greek nor Roman. The Greeks, source of all conceptual categories, dubbed Celtic civilisation, the real Britain, the original France, the catch-all name for all Europeans – barbarian. The Celts provided Greece and Rome with an alternative model of savages – the original savages came down from the trees of the north to sack Rome in 390 BC and Delphi in 279 BC. Rome not only forged historic Europe by ruthless subjugation, it gave the people of Europe an indelible inferiority complex, just like the one the Greeks suffered from in relation to Asia. For the Europeans subjugated by Rome the only way to disassociate themselves from their barbarian origin was to internalise colonisation, to re-imagine Europe in the Roman mould and overlook everything else, their true ancestry, as unfortunate. The process has been going on for more than 2,000 years. Consistently, Europe has narrowed and made ever more exclusive and exclusionary its mythologised version of its selected origins.

Europe as an historic entity is doubly barbarian. After AD 410, when barbarian hordes overran Rome, new peoples emerge on the stage of history: Goths, Visigoths, Franks, Vandals. It is the activities of these hordes that carved out the emergent nations of what would be Europe, our Europe. Yet, like the new independent nations of the post-colonial Third World, the newly emergent nations of independent Europe longed for the departed order. The fall of the Roman Empire began the European quest for the recovery of Rome.

The Roman Empire did not, as European propaganda has it, end. It moved East, leaving Rome to the barbarians, and settled in Constantinople. In European eyes it went intensely Asian, in the form of Byzantium. Hence, the history of Byzantium is never part of any schoolchild's study of European history.

Rome rises again as the centre of European concern as the seat of Latin Christianity. The Roman Church became the repository of learning and established the concept of European orthodoxy based on its doctrines, canon law and the recovery of Roman law. The Europe we know today was shaped during a period sandwiched between two seminal events in European history. The first is the Battle of Tours of AD 732, when the people chroniclers refer to as 'Europeans', under the leadership of Charles Martel, defeated the Muslim army, turning back the tide out of Asia. On Christmas Day AD 800 Charles Martel's grandson, Charlemagne, King of the Franks, is crowned Holy Roman Emperor in St Peter's in Rome. Once again the sense of European identity is fictively refashioned in Rome, shaped in distinction to a civilisation out of Asia. The second event occurs in 1453 with the fall of Constantinople to the ubiquitous Turks, the 'present danger of the world'.

It is during the 700 years that separate the Battle of Tours and the fall of Constantinople that Islam actually transforms Europe. The conventional history, defining this period as 'the Dark Ages', sees the long gestation of embattled Europe forged by the antipathy that sustained the Crusades. Unwittingly the enemy prompts the rekindling of the flame of civilisation when, phoenix-like, classicism arises from the fall of Constantinople. The warlike intervention by the Turks permits a flood of Greek manuscripts to come West. This inspires the Renaissance obsession with all things classical, permits Europe to recover its Greek roots, invent modernity, discover the rest of the world and recover the destiny of world domination implicit in its Roman ancestry. It is, of course, the kind of disordered thinking deeply indicative of psychosis.

The manufactured history does get one thing right. The barbarian hordes who overthrew Rome did a thorough job of vandalism. The Roman Church became custodian of all the learning rescued from the wreckage. Knowledge was housed in the monasteries where the fashion was to keep books in chains, as can still be seen at Hereford Cathedral in England. The largest monastic library, it had little more than 500 books, mostly on theology, precious few of which were works of the classical scholars of antiquity.

In contrast to Europe, the cities of the Muslim world had free public libraries and the public purse financed the search for the works of classical scholars, which were translated into Arabic, the common language of a world civilisation. The greatest libraries of Muslim cities, such as Baghdad or Cordoba, contained some 250,000 books. There was a vibrant publication industry, with new books being added to the stock at a rate that compares favourably with today's publishers' lists. There was a well-established network of universities, the public financing of what we would call research, and the practice of private industry supporting technological research and development, which produced a string of innovations.

Quite simply, Europe became an eager student of Islamic learning and Islam conducted itself as a good teacher. And the teaching began at the beginning: Islam taught Europe how to reason, what the difference between civilisation and barbarism is, and what the basic features of a civil society are. It trained Europe in scholastic and philosophic method, and donated the model of its institutional forum of learning: the university. Europe acquired wholesale the organisation, structure and the very terminology of the Muslim educational system. Islam not only taught Europe the experimental method and showed it the importance of empirical research, but it also very considerately worked out most of the mathematics necessary for Copernicus to launch 'his' revolution! It showed Europe the distinction between medicine and magic, drilled it in making surgical instruments and told it how to establish and run hospitals. And then, to top it all, Islam gave Europe liberal humanism.

But while Europe was freely appropriating Islamic learning it was simultaneously constructing a shroud to mask the true origins of its knowledge. The centres of dissemination of black propaganda were the monasteries. What drove the churchmen to despair was the passion for Arabic and Arabic poetry amongst the most able students. In the new-fangled universities modelled on the Muslim originals, the fervour was for Arabic books and the fashion was for Arabic clothes. The likes of Roger Bacon and Albert Magnus used to wander around European universities dressed in Arabic clothes quoting ibn Rushd (Averroes). One such churchman, Alvaro of Cordova, deplored the situation with the words: 'My fellow-Christians delight in the poems and romances of the Arabs; they study the works of Muslim theologians and philosophers not to refute them but to acquire a correct and elegant Arabic style. Where today can a layman be found who reads Latin commentaries on Holy Scripture?'

The dissociation with Islam began during the 12th-century renaissance, the first direct result of Islam's tuition, the period of Peter Abelard and St Thomas Aquinas. One of the main instruments of this fabrication was *chanson de geste*, the medieval romances of questing knights and courtly love that are the foundations of modern European literature. All of this troubadour culture, pioneered in Aquitaine, owes its inspiration to Arabic poetry. The mythic dissociation became a more formalised exercise during the 15th and 16th century and has continued right up to our times. And major figures of European thought have taken part in this civilisational endeavour – from St Thomas Aquinas, to Newton in the late 17th century, to Kelvin in the late 19th century – all have been involved in creating and disseminating the revisionist history of the origins of modern European civilisation and the creation of the Aryan model, which introduced the idea that Greek culture was predominantly European.

From the perspective of Islam, there is a double irony here. It is not just that Islam introduced classical Greek civilisation to Europe, but also without Islam Europe would not have been able to manufacture its Greek roots. Few of the great names of the European Middle Ages could actually read Greek, so what they in fact read was not Aristotle in the original but the Latin translations of ibn Sina's commentaries on Aristotle. Ditto Plato and Neoplatonists. The translation of Arabic texts, which began in the early 12th century, was a major intellectual activity in Europe until the middle of the 15th century. It is hardly surprising that the post-Columbus Renaissance started in the independent city states of Italy, cities whose long history of trading contact with Muslim lands provided familiarity with their sophistication and ready access to Arabic texts.

As long as Europe insists that Greek democracy is the origin of all its conceptual superiority it will remain delusional. Greece and Rome were slave societies, owned and operated by and in the interests of narrow elites with a highly developed sense of their own exclusivity. The Founding Fathers of American democracy made a fetish of littering their debates with reference to ancient Greece. Their articulation of modern individual rights for a narrow white elite is riddled with appeals not only to a mythic Greece, but to Greek writers few of them had actually read. When Thomas Jefferson actually got around to reading Plato he was appalled at the anti-democratic diatribe he encountered. For Europe, for the West, thinking clearly about the realities of Greece and Rome is the intellectual equivalent of the emotional trauma of seeing something nasty in the woodshed – quite enough to disorder the wits of any rational, sane person.

People suffering from schizophrenia are almost always treated with drugs generically known as anti-psychotics. The only plausible solution to the psychotic behaviour of Europe is for it to embrace its Islamic history and origins. Without Islam Europe is incomplete. Without Europe Islam cannot transcend its historic suppression and abandonment. Knowing its true identity, becoming whole, means confronting the nasties Europe has kept confined in the woodshed. Coming to terms with the fact that Europe and Islam were partner projects is the only means of opening a path to a global future grounded in genuine plurality. However hard it may be to renounce the habits of many lifetimes, it is the only way to regional and global health.

Fat

There is nothing better than wholesome, voluptuous fat. Like the fat around the midriffs of all those busty heroines of Indian films who nourished my imagination during adolescence. Or the fat scintillating with desire in so many Orientalist paintings – vide, for example, 'Odalisque' by Eugene Delacroix – that perverted the Western imagination and become the stereotype of all Oriental women. Or the overtly sensual fat that adorned British actress Kate Winslet, ample star of *Titanic*, or the model Sophie Dahl in the famously banned 'Opium' advertisement.

Sophie Dahl, with her chubby ankles, plump wrists and charitable layers of fat, is, for me, an ideal woman. I suspect this is true in most Indian and Middle Eastern cultures. Our heroines, such as the late Umm Khulsum, the last word in Arabic pop, or the Bollywood superstar of the nineties, Madhuri Dixit, have, almost always, tended to be generously wrapped in fat. We have little time for the emaciated stick insects that grace the catwalk. Indeed, sickly, skinny women like Calista Flockhart of *Ally McBeal* are our definition of both poverty and ugliness. In much Eastern thought, thin and skeletal is an aberration, representing both famine of the mind and famine of the body. Fat portrays health, wealth and wisdom. Omar Khayyam would have approved of the liberally proportioned woman in the Marks and Spencer advertisement, running naked up a hill, shouting 'I am normal!'

But fat women are not considered 'normal' in contemporary Western society. No one wants to be fat, yet everyone seems to believe they are. Fat has become an all-encompassing issue, not least an image war fought out in the mainstream of our popular culture. Even my beloved fat icons have thrown in the towel. Sophie Dahl shed pounds to look more like other models. And Winslet, who raised a highly publicised clarion call against the monstrous regimen of dieting, has succumbed to slimming. Admitting the real prospect of never again being cast in a Hollywood film, Winslet vowed never to eat lunch rather than never eat lunch in that town again.

Dieting has become an epidemic. At any one time, two in five women in Britain are on a diet. One in 10, according to some estimates, end up dying in a desperate attempt to lose fat. Hardly surprising, when you consider that some popular diets advocate starvation rations of 1,000 calories a day. In the world's poorest countries, such as India, women on average consume more than 1,400 calories a day. So, fat may or may not be a 'feminist issue', the mantra of Susie Orbach, but it is certainly a big business issue. Even by conservative estimates, the fat business has an annual income of around $38 billion.

And now that science has discovered a 'fat virus', it will expand drastically. It seems that fat people are fat because they are infected with a virus. The virus in question is adenovirus-36, one of the 50 human adenoviruses, which cause such things as colds, red eyes and diarrhoea. A number of studies on chickens and mice have shown that the infected creatures end up with twice as much fat as the uninfected ones. Other studies have shown that obese humans are often infected with a chicken adenovirus called SMAM-1, which is known to cause obesity in chickens. QED: *quod erat demonstrandum*.

So the scene is set for a cure-all for obesity and fatness. Throughout the nineties, medicine went through a trend of discovering bacterial and viral links to all sorts of diseases. It began with the bacteria *helicobactor pylori*, which was identified as the cause of stomach ulcers. Then Borna virus, an animal adenovirus, was implicated in depression in humans.

There is even the suspicion that heart diseases may have viral causes. Antibiotic pills are already available for treating stomach cancers; anti-depression pills aimed at the Borna virus will be available soon. No surprise, then, that a pill for fatness and obesity is just around the corner. This is science touting for a good business opportunity. We have covered this ground several times before. Last time, in the mid-nineties, leptin, a hormone that made fat mice slim, was touted as the ultimate solution for fat people. The wonder drug turned out to be less than wonderful in clinical trials. But even if a successful pill could be developed, would it actually cure obesity and fatness? Would it necessarily be a good thing?

The problem with such cures is that they transform a state of being into a disease and hence a matter for pharmacological and medical intervention. Even obesity, which should not be confused with delectable fat, in general strictly limited to industrialised countries, and the US in particular, is a state of being. It is a product of overconsumption. The Worldwatch Institute in Washington has estimated that there are 1.1 billion obese people in the West, almost as many as are plagued by hunger in the Third World. In the US alone, one in three adults is classified as obese, the result of a lifestyle based on an insatiable appetite for junk food. These people don't need pills; they need to get a life. Their only cure is a radical change in consumption patterns and way of life.

Has the definition of obesity blurred the distinction or totally eradicated the normality of the pleasantly plump, the generously proportioned and the well-endowed, making them all suitable cases for treatment? Think of 'going pear shaped', a popular epithet for gone wrong – yet pear shaped is the average allotment of womankind, well larded around their child-bearing hips. We see this in the Venus of Willendorf, a carved figure of a woman made by palaeolithic hands some 26,000 years ago, and discovered in the 1860s. Not only is this early image of the female form well-endowed, fat in a big way, the modelling emphasises the fertile zones of her genitalia. These palaeolithic figures have been found all across Europe and western Russia. Originally nicknamed *la poire* (the pear), they soon acquired the more ideologically charged name of *venus impudens*, immodest venuses.

Western representations of the female nude, in which various distributions of sexual fat emphasise women's lush fertility, echo the proportions of the Venus of Willendorf. From the 15th to the 17th centuries, big ripe bellies were fashionably erotic and can be seen in the paintings of Rubens as well as the school of Orientalist painters. The early 19th century favoured plump faces and shoulders, progressing towards the end of the century to generously dimpled buttocks and thighs. The only deviation from this was the representation of infantilised women favoured by the Pre-Raphaelites. The Pre-Raphaelites took their inspiration from the sleek, flowing lines conventional in the medieval art they venerated. In medieval times the purpose of art was to emphasise ethereal, spiritual themes, rather than the humanist, corporeal, or indeed corpulent, earthly facts of life. Fashion, and fat, often marches to the tune of philosophy.

It was only with the advent of the 20th century that, as Ann Hollander has noted, 'the look of sickness, the look of poverty, and the look of nervous exhaustion' became the aesthetic for the female form. It is no coincidence that such an aesthetic coincides with the legal emancipation of women in the West. Britain and the US granted women the vote at the same time, in the aftermath of World War I, and ushered in the age of the flapper. The 'Thoroughly Modern Millies' of the twenties used androgynous, flat-chested, uncluttered silhouettes and rising hemlines to declare their fitness to take their place and compete in the market place of a male-dominated world. Femininity and androgyny became linked in a new philosophical complex.

The ideological battle between femaleness and androgyny has raged for the last two decades. The victor, as we all know, has been the gross, emaciated ideal of femininity projected everywhere by popular culture, she of the toned, honed, hard body with not an iota of fat. Where, as recently as the seventies, it was difficult to distinguish between the weight of an average woman and that of a fashion model, now the weight of a supermodel is less than half of most women. As women become more politically and economically articulate, the notions of beauty become more and more ascetic and perverse and for the majority of women positively detrimental. In the bad old days, it was the kitchen that imprisoned women; in postmodern times, the female body itself has become a prison.

So, I say it is time we stood up to the cultural and historical forces that have turned fatness into a disease. For the love of all fat women, all over the world, I am making a Declaration of Fatdependence based on three principles.

First, fat is good and healthy. To appreciate this fully, look at the endemic conditions of anorexia and bulimia in Western nations. Both are mainly gender specific: 90–95 per cent of sufferers are women. Britain's 3.5 million anorexics, increasing at the rate of 6,000 per year, are walking encyclopaedias of disease. Anorexics are likely to suffer from hypothermia, oedema, hypertension, infertility and death. Medical effects of bulimia include dehydration, electrolyte imbalance, epileptic seizure, abnormal heart rhythm and death. Combine the two and you get tooth erosion, hiatal hernia, abraded oesophagus, kidney failure, osteoporosis and death. Not surprisingly, around half of anorexics seldom recover (in contrast, two-thirds of famine victims in Africa recover fully). Equally unsurprisingly, fat people tend to live longer.

Second, fat is sexy. In fact, that is precisely the function fat performs in women. On average, girls have 10–15 per cent more fat than boys. Increased fat ratio in adolescent girls equals sexual maturity and fertility. The male–female disparity then varies with age but is lifelong. Not only do women have a thicker layer of fat under the skin than men but it is concentrated in breasts, buttocks and legs. All this fat needs to be preserved to enhance sensuality and sexuality. One in five women who do rigorous exercise to shape their bodies, such as aerobics, end up with menstrual irregularities and diminished fertility. Fat tissues store sex hormones, so low fat reserves are linked to weak oestrogens as well as inactive ovaries.

Third, fat is desire. Numerous studies have shown that plumper women desire sex more often than thin women, and sexual interests dissipate with dietary deprivation.

Unnatural thinness leads to relinquishing of sexuality; and pleasure in sex is rare for anorexics and bulimics because of body hatred. So *Ally McBeal*'s sexual escapades are fictional in more ways than one. A hungry, malnourished animal has little interest in pleasures of the flesh. And an emaciated insect is a turn-off to other insects. The Ally McBeal syndrome is not so much a fantasy about sexual fulfilment as an unending, impossible quest for mutually contradictory ends.

I want my Declaration of Fatdependence to be seen as a rallying cry to save life, liberty and the pursuit of female happiness. I seek to empower natural female physiology and place fat women where they belong: at the zenith of beauty and galloping good health. So rally round the statuesque, liberate a universal state of being.

Future

Suppose you were frozen in time for the next thousand years. Like Fry, the pizza delivery boy from the animation show *Futurama*, you woke up on New Year's Day, circa 3000. What would you see? Would you find yourself in a world of robots, one-eyed babes and space travel *à la Futurama*? Or a world of warp drives, aliens and distant galaxies, still dominated by white Americans and their European sidekicks – much like the galaxies of *Star Trek*? Or, would it be a world so different that we cannot even perceive it? How indeed would the world of 3000 be different from the world of today?

Exploring the long-term future requires more than extrapolating the current trends. It demands serious thought on positively big questions. Where are we really going? What threats may prevent us from getting there? What lies at the end of our technological rainbow? What do we really know? Will we finally discover who and what 'we' really are? Let us do a thought experiment and focus on the unthought possibilities of the future. Let us assume that after the next thousand years, we will encounter the binary opposite of what we currently expect. So, the long-term future is not going to be about more knowledge but ignorance, not life but death, not Western civilisation but non-Western civilisations, not aliens *à la Star Trek* out in space but aliens from right here on earth. How could we justify these presumptions?

The increase in our ignorance is connected with a future paradox directly attributable to the nature of science. We normally credit progress in scientific knowledge with reduction in ignorance. But ignorance is not something that is only associated with dogma and superstition; it is also an integral part of knowledge. Every advance in knowledge actually increases complexity and uncertainty and hence effective ignorance.

For example, when we thought that the atom consisted of nothing more than a nucleus of protons and neutrons with electrons circulating around them, our ignorance was limited to knowing about three particles. As our picture of the atom became more complex, we discovered that there were numerous other particles about which we knew very little. Now, in a world of 300 elementary particles, and counting, we realise how much more we need to know. Bring in string theory and a universe of 16 dimensions, and what we think we know is dwarfed by what we know we do not know. So, paradoxically, far from being diminished, ignorance actually increases with advances in specific kinds of knowledge.

As we learn more and more about our world and the universe over the next thousand years, we will discover there is more and more that we do not know. Major advances in knowledge will enlighten us to the existence and perhaps the shape of the chasm. This is the biggest and most essential change from the attitudes that have dominated the last thousand years. In an ideal future world this understanding should make us more humble and more prudent.

Technology, too, is paradox ridden. Up to now, we have accepted the idea we would always control and shape technology. However, we have reached a point where technology is turning back on us. Technology is beginning to control us and is reshaping us in the same way it has reshaped the world around us. So the more we try to seek liberation through technology, the more we become the subject of technology. Given the present trajectories, it is a safe bet that well before the dawn of the fourth millennium technology will have totally redefined what it means to be human.

We can see that this is about to happen in genetics. So far, genetic engineering has been limited to the treatment of certain diseases. But we know that with the mapping of the human genome, parents will have knowledge of the genetic makeup of their children. Advances in virtual artificial intelligence technology will enable them to view, as if in a movie, the life patterns of their children, the trajectory of their diseases and their health. Within this century, 'designer babies', physical and intelligence enhancement and genetic therapies will become routine.

Technologies tend to advance as collectives. Developments in one area lead to or coincide with developments in other areas. Thus the complexity of the human genome, which may make manipulating it problematic, could be overcome by developments in computers that would enable us to manage such complexity. In particular, developments in nano-technologies, which operate at the level of individual atoms and molecules, could give us the tools we need to reshape ourselves. It is not difficult to imagine that, in a not-so-distant future, self-replicating nano-robots, which mechanically push atoms and molecules together, will be used for creating new genetic materials. A new synthesis of genetics and computing would be achieved, and the manufacture of human body parts would become common.

All this means that we will live longer and healthier lives. Estimates for life expectancy in the year 3000 are around 125 to 160 years. However, as technology will take care of most things, people will have much too much leisure in their long, perfectly healthy and boring lives. They will be buying experiences, mostly artificial, instead of things. Population numbers will be tightly controlled. The environment will be protected with draconian laws. All this becomes a necessity when you have an overwhelmingly geriatric population on the very limits of earth's carrying capacity.

So, the only control people will have over their own bodies will be suicide. It will also be, in a world of ever-increasing artificial experiences, the only real thing. We may also discover that it is preferable to die relatively young then live extremely long lives quite devoid of significance.

Suicide could provide our lives with ultimate meaning. Plus, there will be lots of encouragement for voluntary euthanasia – to keep populations in balance. The balanced population of the future will be predominantly non-white. The fourth millennium New York of *Futurama* is very much an enclave of Western civilisation. This is a fundamental error. There will be no Western civilisation a thousand years from hence. One reason for this is that civilisations, as macro historians all the way from ibn Khaldun to Paul Kennedy have been telling us, rise and fall in cycles of around five to six hundred years. The expansion of Europe can be dated to the start of Portugal's exploration of Africa in 1413. Almost precisely half a millennium later, the Great War began. So Western civilisation is now reaching its 'sell by' date.

But there are also strong demographic reasons. If we could shrink today's world population into a village of precisely 100 people, with all the existing human ratios remaining the same, we would discover that only 16 people were Western Europeans and Americans. But these 16 folks would be rather old, compared to 57 Asians who would be rudely youthful. Current estimates suggest that we will have a sustainable population of 30 billion by the year 3000. By then, our shrunken village would only have 3 faces that are recognisably white. So, most of the faces you will see on New Year's Day 3000 will be Chinese and Indian, followed by Hispanic and African – even in New York!

Thus, many of the shapers and makers of the next millennium will be non-Western, a point amusingly demonstrated by Michael Hart, the author of *The 100: A Ranking of the Most Influential Persons in History*. Under the pseudonym of Arturo Kukeni, Hart offers us *A View From the Year 3000: A Ranking of the 100 Most Influential Persons of All Time*. Out go the likes of Pasteur, Newton and Einstein. In come such delicious fictional creations as Chang Po-Yao, who develops a technique for growing new brain tissue *in vitro* and uploading all memory and personality into computers; Rkumini Gopal, who devises a set of safe, quick, and completely reversible techniques for sex-change operations; and Kim Won Lee, who is responsible for the engineering of the planet

Mars into an exhilarating human environment. The innovations may be fictional, but the names do have a rather prophetic ring to them. (So you might as well learn how to pronounce such names sooner rather than later.)

And so to my final prediction. At the start of the third millennium we seemed to be obsessed with aliens. No doubt, in the coming centuries, our uncontrolled desire to contact other sorts of intelligence will lead to an exponential increase in space travel. But space exploration will not be a world of intergalactic travel and countless encounters with aliens imagined by *Star Trek* and its clones. It would only be possible if the laws of physics had no bearing on the fourth millennium. Unfortunately, 'the final frontier' is an awfully big place and the speed of light is a dead end. Had Mr Spock got his calculations right, he would have told Captain Kirk that, even at a warp velocity of several times the speed of light, it would take a thousand-year journey to reach Romulus III!

Which means we will be confined largely to our lonely solar system. We will discover that space simply echoes our own inner emptiness. Instead, we will meet aliens here on earth; and they will be aliens of our own creation. Genetically modified individuals will be distinctly different from all those who, for religious, ethical or other reasons, refuse to take part in the genetics revolution – the 'natural' humans. Over centuries, GM individuals could evolve into a new species. They may turn out to be cold and malevolent or enlightened and wise. Either way, in evolutionary history we may be remembered less for ourselves and more for the species we may end up creating.

So, when you wake from your thousand-year slumber, you may discover that you are not human at all. You may be a computer, an amalgam of person and machine, or even a new species of GM human. In many respects, *Futurama* has got it right. The long-term future will be more (artificially) diverse. As we increasingly intervene in evolution, we will create all varieties of new life forms, ranging from chimeras, cyborgs and robots to possibly even biologically created 'slaves'. You may wake up to a noisy demonstration about the rights of robots!

Of course, it need not be like this at all. The long-term future is neither determined nor inevitable nor indeed a flight of fancy with no connection to the present. It is and will always be a function of our choices. The unthought elements of the present can become a nightmare future or the means to unmake that horrid future before it gets started. Thinking and acting upon our unthoughts could even deliver a dignified world with the humility to place meaning before gratification. In which case, the world of January 3000 might be well worth waking up to.

Globalisation

I discovered the meaning of globalisation in Singapore. Indeed, the moment one arrives at the city-state's Changi Airport, one can see globalisation running riot in an impersonal consumerist cornucopia of designer labels. Changi Airport is also dedicated to being the world's premier transport hub. From here you can go anywhere, ushered along by the ubiquitous 'Singapore Girl', as the much-advertised stewardesses of the national airline are known. Whenever I arrive in the building, I leave as rapidly as possible, hoping for a talkative ride into Singapore city centre, courtesy of a local taxi driver.

And that is how the full scale of the culture crisis overwhelmed me. I was spared the usual inquisition that introduces conversation – where are you from, how's the economy there, how long are you staying, what do you think of Singapore. Enough to say I was down from Kuala Lumpur for the weekend to invoke a deluge of angst. 'Ah, no need sorry for my Singlish, lah. You boleh Singlish, ah? Very bad, ah. Prime Minister say Singlish cannot, ah. So now what, ayoh?' A few rapid-fire enquiries on my part and the full enormity hit me, as surely as if I'd been in Delhi the fateful day the British took over. Phua Chu Kang was to take English lessons! The End.

Let me elaborate. *Phua Chu Kang* is the highest-rated show on Singapore television. It is a locally produced sitcom about a lovable, rascally private building contractor, the said Phua Chu Kang. In the rich mix that is Singapore, Phua Chu Kang is played by local superstar Gurmit Singh, a born-again Christian Sikh who is married to a Chinese. His greatest comedy creation is a know-all operator who knows nothing and botches everything. The comedy emerges from the delicious observation of everyday, indigenous life expressed in the full tropical profusion of the native dialect. Phua Chu Kang, like most Singaporeans, speaks only Singlish. Singlish is the exotic *lingua franca* nurtured from English by way of Chinese, Malay and various Indian subcontinental accretions. It is as rich, encrusted and lush a dialect as the road bridges across the highway from Changi Airport. These concrete structures are completely enveloped by green vines intermingled with brightly flowering bougainvillaea. They look like natural phenomena, outgrowths of the earth.

Singlish is authentic local repossession. It is an indigenous cultural form that has dug its roots deep into the fabric of imperialism, the force that created the artificial nation state of Singapore and its ethnic mix. But, Singapore now has globalised visions of future riches. The most successful of the Asian tiger economies, it is the Switzerland of the region. It is an attainment-oriented, high-achieving, paternalist autocracy. Singapore's leading politicians always strike me as men at home with Singlish. But that is not the kind of place their Singapore is destined to be. To globalise one must Americanise and Singapore is Americanising with a vengeance.

Prior to my arrival, the government had denounced Phua Chu Kang for polluting the airways with his native patois. Singlish was diverting the youth of the nation from their mission to succeed. It was no random outburst. Nothing in Singapore is random. In precise terms the attack on Phua Chu Kang defined the meaning of globalisation. Globalisation is cultural homicide writ large, and television is the mirror wherein the future is displayed.

Success means inculcating globalised manners, mores and values, as seen on TV. Consequently, internalising global identity means eradicating what comes naturally. Singapore culture must be ersatz, like all the renovated shops and houses around the downtown marina. These elegant buildings, in colonial fusion style, have been lovingly renovated to service global yuppiedom. They house French, Spanish, Mexican, Mediterranean, any nationality except Asian, franchise restaurants. Here tourists and upwardly mobile local entrepreneurs indulge in fine wining and dining to the strains of the latest pop 'classics'. Local architecture is just a quaint backdrop.

When you globalise everything what you get is Singapore. When you want to know what Singapore is about you watch SBC, the Singapore Broadcasting Corporation, local purveyor of television. Once upon a time SBC was modelled on the BBC, who even seconded staff to train Singaporeans in public service broadcasting. But that is not the kind of animal globalisation is. SBC has become a multi-channelled hydra. Its main outlet provides 24-hour entertainment-driven programming, mainly consisting of imported American series. It also runs its own CNN clone news channel. In Singapore it is easier to find out who is dating whom in Hollywood than anywhere in the world, except perhaps Hollywood.

Being Singapore, the change of direction is deliberate, planned and purposeful. The objective: to be a regional broadcasting hub, a production centre selling regionally, thinking and looking globally, synergistically intermeshing the entire communications revolution experience, IT-savvy, hotwired into mass global popular culture. And that is why Phua Chu Kang must learn to talk proper English, or at least a mid-Pacific variant.

The moral of this tale is rather simple. If the richest, most highly educated, most nationalist country in the developing world will willingly sacrifice its cultural identity, the last, best bastion of its individuality, to globalisation, we can be sure the pandemic has already happened.

Globalisation is now sold as the best chance for economic uplift of the excluded masses of the world's poor. It marches forward by stripping them of all that civilises them in their own tradition, history and cultural expression. Imperialism produced mongrelisation. Given independence and time, mongrelisation could and does generate indigenous creativity and revitalisation, the Phua Chu Kang effect. But to be successful globalised economic empowerment requires something quite different. It needs naked entry into mass popular culture manufactured in America, recycled and parodied by pale imitations everywhere. Indeed, The End – of civilisation as the peoples of the world have known it, lived it and cherished its richness and diversity.

Like a scavenger seeking nourishment, I ingested Singaporean television in the hope of finding a glimmer of a cure, only to get larger doses of disease. I found locally made documentaries on 'disappearing Asia', designed in imitation of and for sale to such outlets as Discovery Channel. They had recruited Lea Silonga, Filipina star of the hit musical *Saigon*, to front disparaging, patronising looks at quaint exotica. The programmes outdid classic Victorian lady travellers. Indeed, the commentary sounded as if it had been written by a Victorian lady traveller, titillated but less than amused at what old Asia once was, and should not be allowed to remain. The victims have become the perpetrators. That is what globalisation means.

Globalisation is about information. The lifeblood of the future economy is instant access, instant comprehension of global information. What this flood of information says is money makes the world go around. To get money requires hooking on to trade, identifying markets. Simply put, it means replicating as swiftly as possible the places where money is centred, derived from, value added to: those G7 giants.

The port of entry into the new global dispensation is the media. Television is both It and IT, the acme of information technology. Television shows the market what is marketable. It disseminates the style, generates and popularises by constant repetition the merchandising opportunities. It makes global popular culture the only reality. Every home has a TV, every home becomes a portal on the superhighway to a globalised, homogenised world full of Singapores. Literally, one teleports direct to the new dispensation. The youth of the world are the sacrificial lambs offered up in this slaughter of cultural identity.

Youth is a diminishing resource everywhere except in the non-West. While the civilisations of China, India and Islam support young populations with average ages of between 20 and 25, the population of Europe and North America is ageing. The average age in the West is fast approaching 50. The baby boom of the post-war years reshaped marketing and advertising to create a youth-oriented consumer culture afraid of ageing. Now, postmodern consumerism takes on a global focus to meet the demographics of the 21st century. The increasing spending power of East and South-east Asian youth is the lodestar of globalised marketing techniques and multinational merchandising concerns. An advertisement for the Hong Kong Bank says it all: 'There are 3 billion people in Asia. Half of them are under 25. Consider it a growing market.'

This 'growing market' is being targeted in a specific way. Through television, advertising, movies and pop music they are force-fed a total lifestyle package. What matters is the look, the affectation, the cool – and each of these abstractions can be translated into a merchandising equivalent available at a nearby shopping mall. What in the West operates as a culture of narcissism finds embodiment in Asia as hero worship. The heroes are the pop stars, the movie stars, the TV stars, the sports stars, who rule the global stage mirrored on your TV screen. The audience is positively brainwashed to talk, act, think and live as their heroes do.

Star power is not Asian. It is Madonna, Britney, Brad and Mel, Ronan and Michael, Manchester United and Agassi. The stars and the worldview marketed with and by them are hyped and hyper ventilated. They are the tools of the global economics of TV.

The Hollywood television factories make their money in the American market. The content of their programmes is driven by the internal dictates of Americana and its predilections. From its beginning American television has been a marketing device, pure and simple. It is organised and operated to serve the tastes and interests of commercial sponsors and advertisers.

What Hollywood makes in the global market place is profit. It sells costly, high production value, glossy programmes for discounted prices to the television networks of the world. If it costs Singapore, or Malaysia, $100,000 to buy an episode of *The X-Files*, they are getting a product that cost $5 million to make. The cost of bought-in programming is internationally regulated – the poorer the country the less they pay. So it is impossible for Third World countries to produce local programmes with such production values. Locally produced programmes look poor in comparison to imports and seldom attract advertising.

While the global economics of TV are compelling, they are not the full story. What is seen on TV takes on an educational meaning; it is the substance of which global success is made. So the children of the elite in newly emerging economies in Asia buy into and act out the lifestyle of the rich and dominant in the West. The studied disaffection of urban youth culture in the West produces the epidemic of *lepak* in Malaysia. *Lepak* are young people who spend their days hanging out in shopping malls, affecting the style of young Westerners and perhaps being bored out of their skulls.

But acquiring the look, the clothes, even the videos and CDs that comprise global popular culture is not a straightforward transmission of purchasing power into the pocket of multinationals. Asia is counterfeit country, home of the genuine imitation 100 per cent fake. The street markets in every city and town are awash with clothes, bags, sunglasses, watches, electrical and electronic goods, music tapes, videos and computer software cloned, pirated and all locally reproduced. For a pittance, young Asians can emulate their heroes while simultaneously stimulating local enterprise. The WTO hates it, Asian governments must promise to exterminate it – but the black economy is proof positive that resistance is not futile.

Globalisation is a disease. But it just may be the kind of virus that requires the patient to get worse before they can recover. However much television pushes the youth of Asia to venerate global icons, super megastars, one fact remains. The biggest audience is always for local shows. Cheap and cheerful Singaporean, or Malaysian, or Indonesian, or Thai programmes may be. *Friends*, *ER* or *Star Trek* they are not. But Hollywood stars don't speak Singlish, or Malay, or Urdu. No matter how young Asian people try to emulate them, such icons do not and cannot look or know or experience what makes young Asians tick. Eventually, we all want to look in a mirror and see ourselves.

Maybe Phua Chu Kang is right after all. His catchphrase, 'best in Singapore', is proved by the ratings war – he is the king of comedy. So beyond the global noise of the information superhighway, perhaps we should be listening for the siren song of local heroes calling us to a new departure. Perhaps local routes in developing countries can lead us back to the place we belong: a self-made world, rich and various.

Hype

Hype kills. Hype devastates societies. Hype strangles politics. Hype annihilates economies. Hype produces wealth for a few undeserving individuals while destroying the livelihoods of the vast majority. If that wasn't enough, hype has made lies, blatant, malicious lies, the foundation of civilisation as we know it.

Civilisation, as we have built it, functions on hype. It is both the chief symbol and the *modus operandi* of global capital. The market operates on hype: stocks and shares skyrocket on exuberant, speculative projections of potential riches, only to fall back to earth when reality sets in. Such was the dot.coms bubble. Technology evolves by perpetual hype: 'must have' technology is every child's inheritance, a mindset that creates the means for market saturation. The spectacular implosion of hi-tech companies, such as Marconi, will have to be the springboard for developing new techno toys – it's the only way this economy knows how to work, and the only hope the now superfluous labour force has of finding another job.

Science, the engine house of technology, now advances with hype: a potential breakthrough is immediately peddled as a vision of unlimited new possibilities for commercially viable applications, no matter how ridiculous or absurd. Headline-grabbing hype is what makes science possible, so it determines what science gets done, irrespective of the real outcomes. Consider the hype surrounding the mapping of the human genome. It was sold as the answer to life, the universe and everything. In the end it told us what thoughtful science had long known and considered likely. For all the hoopla, the hyped potential cures and dividends are nowhere to be seen.

What is hyped is not what we get, but we have become accustomed to the symbiosis. It is the stock-in-trade of the entertainment industry — film, television, theatre — which lives on hype. The more execrable a Hollywood movie, the greater the hype. Think of the fanfaronade surrounding such banal and dumbfounding films as *Star Wars: The Phantom Menace* and *Pearl Harbor*. Barry Norman, the doyen of British film critics, described *Pearl Harbor* as 'a classic example of hype gone mad'. The film is 'rubbish' and everyone involved in it knows it. The purpose of hype, Norman tells us, is 'to make people forget it's rubbish, leave their brains at home, and get to the cinemas early'.

Brains and hype have an inversely proportional relationship. The first thing hype kills is the mind. The word 'hype' is derived from two components: hypodermic — as in syringe, and hyperbole — as in extravagant and obvious exaggeration. The two strands dovetail into each other, producing 'spin', the guardian angel of New Labour and the exclusive domain in which modern politics is done. So hype begins its magic as a drug, and under its influence, the victim comes to believe the exaggerated lie as a viable truth.

That hype acts like an 'injected' drug was first spotted by a group of German intellectuals bundled together as the Frankfurt School. Seeking a revolutionary philosophical variant of Western Marxism, which later came to be known as 'critical theory', the School thought that the media 'injected' values, ideas and information directly into each individual. A largely passive and atomised audience swallowed the hype they were fed uncritically. Nowadays, we tend to look down on such a 'mechanistic' and 'unsophisticated' model of media–audience relationship. But members of the Frankfurt School — which included thinkers of the calibre of Theodor Adorno, Walter Benjamin and Herbert Marcuse — were no fools. They had witnessed the impact of hype at first hand in Nazi Germany – they knew it could transform a rational society into a murderous mob.

Indeed, hype achieves its goal largely by generating a mob mentality. Which brings us to the second thing that hype kills: reality. In fact, hype manufactures an inversion of reality that is used to generate mass hysteria, the condition of being hyped. Under the Third Reich, German racism presented rabid fear, the bogeymen vision of age-old fairy tales, as a genuine natural phenomenon. The medieval blood libel against Judaism (that Jews murdered and drank the blood of Christian children) was recycled, along with films depicting Jews as rats infesting German cities. They wrapped racism and other phobias in fashionable scientific theories. Eugenics was not a Nazi invention, it was a general scientific theory. The human perfectibility eugenic science sought contained all the necessary rationale for the mass annihilation of those members of society deemed imperfect. It stimulated xenophobic resentment by converting the war reparations and peace treaty that ended the First World War into a victimisation of and aggression on the German people. These insidious elements were packaged and sold with the practised skill of modern advertising executives, through all the media where advertising hype thrives: films, radio, newspapers, the gamut of available popular culture. The regularly injected synthesised cocktail was a potent drug that induced pathological hysteria. The pathology may vary but hysteria is the essence of all hype.

A more innocent proof that we are in no way immune to the pathology of hype is *The Blair Witch Project*, one of the first films to fully exploit the Internet's hype capabilities. New technology, same old strategy, same old hype. The film opens with a caption explaining that in 1994 three student film-makers hiked into the woods in Maryland to shoot a documentary about a local legend, the 'Blair Witch', and never came back. A year later, footage from the documentary and the team's video diary was found. What follows, we are told, is an edited version of that footage. The success of the film depended on the incredible lengths the producers went to in creating a real-world legend of Blair Witch. They began with a real town, Burkittsville, the site of the 18th-century township of Blair. An Internet site presented the Blair witch mythology as if it were real, manufacturing plentiful background material, footage and photographs on the 200-year 'history' of the Blair witch. Through colleges and universities across America word spread that the film was based on a true story, stimulating a dedicated mob following for this constructed reality. When the film opened, students and young 'experts' on the legend travelled hundreds of miles and queued for hours – generating a self-feeding frenzy that ensured that the film was a runaway success.

To generate a mob mentality, hype need not be as elaborate and thought out as in the case of *The Blair Witch Project*. It could be as callous and crude as the manufacture of the pop group assembled by the television show *Popstars*: Hear'say. Their debut single, 'Pure and Simple', became the best-selling debut single of all time and their book *Popstars: The Making of Hear'say* followed suit. So, the Frankfurt School were on to something after all. Tap into the psyche of a generation and watch hype work like crack cocaine. Hitler Youth, Hear'say groupies, greedy dot.com investors, high-tech manufacturers and the lunatics who queue up to watch the latest hyped rubbish from Hollywood – all operate with the same pathological pack mentality that is incapable of separating pure illusion from any notion of reality.

If you cannot distinguish between fantasy and reality, or just don't care which is which, you are hardly in a position to distinguish between good and bad. Quality is the third thing that hype kills. On the whole, hype works on the lowest of common denominators. It foregrounds the mediocre and gives common currency to the pestiferous. A casual glance at any bestseller list will confirm this. Trashy (but glossy) food and cookbooks, autobiographies of pop/sport/fashion stars who have hardly lived and embarrassing accounts of (mostly imagined) childhood wrongs rub shoulders with madcap mythology, tacky romance and the latest film tie-in.

It is all at about the same level as the home page of Mahir Cagri. Mahir shot to fame in 1999 proving the rule that hype, including self-hype, is directly proportional to crudeness. When you log on, you are greeted with the words 'WELCOME TO MY HOME PAGE!!!!!!!!!!!!! I KISS YOU'. Underneath, we have pictures of Mahir, supporting a flamboyant moustache below a hefty hooter, in everyday poses: playing table tennis, lying on a beach, lounging in leisurewear. Below that, we have the personal details: 'I like sport, swimming… I like sex'; 'my profession journalist, music and sport teacher, I make psycolojy doctora… I like to take foto-camera (towns, animals, nice nude models and people)' (sic). Now, who would want to give time, attention or indeed hand out money to someone like Mahir? Yet, by rather skilful hype, Mahir turned, or has been turned, into a global phenomenon. When the site was first put up, he was inundated by visitors and callers wanting to (a) correct his English; (b) marry him; (c) write his profile for the *Guardian* and the *Washington Post*; and (d) interview him for television. Soon Mahir was a snowball rolling down K2. CNN was negotiating an expansive interview, advertisers were queuing to take space on his site, critical theory specialists were deconstructing his narrative and presidents were seeking his endorsement. A simple Internet search will now reveal some 25,000 Mahir sites selling Mahir products, promoting Mahir's style, analysing Mahir's impact – there are even parodies of his site. An interesting thought this, as surely Mahir himself is only a parody of the hyperventilated way we parody our own capacity to be duped, deluded and diverted.

In the end, Mahir has to be seen as a work of art. In a hype-infested society, almost anything that is crude and puerile can be justified, and hyped further, by dubbing it art. Much of what goes under the rubric of Brit Art, hyped up in shows like 'Sensation' and 'Apocalypse', would put Mahir to shame. Witness how much pure pornography – in films like *Intimacy* with its real scenes of fellatio – is now hyped as 'art'. The object of all this is to push boundaries – not of art, but of consumerism. What has always been seen as shameful, by means of hype becomes a new chic consumable.

The postmodern audience is able to see through all this. If we are to believe what they teach in media studies courses around Britain and the US, we are all media savvy. The hip young in particular, according to the theorists, are resistant to hype. This is total codswallop. On the whole, the hip young are fools. Give them a meaningless buzz-word and see them lap up hype like ice-cream on a cornet. A couple of years ago it was 'ULTRA' – ultra experiences (as in white-knuckle rides), ultra tooth-paste and ultra bras. Now it's 'EXTREME' – extreme sports (bungee jumping and other lunacies, now a mega cult), extreme travel (such as a celebrity going to the Arctic Circle, the ultimate in television hype), extreme endurance (as in reality shows like *Boot Camp*, *Survivor* and *Castaway*), extreme animals, and no doubt soon to make its appearance, extreme sex (pornography again!). 'MAX' is on its way; 'MEGA' has been there; no doubt 'SEVERE' is looming somewhere on the future horizon. Indeed, the youth of the globalised world have been so infected with hype that simply labelling plain old H2O 'aqua' generates a major new trend in aqua drinking.

Nothing works better on the young than ironic anti-advertising or self-parodying anti-hype. Think of the copy line from *Austin Powers: The Spy Who Shagged Me*: 'If you see one movie this summer, see *Star Wars*.' The clothing brand Diesel made a name for itself by giving ironic, back-handed compliments to other brands for improving the life of consumers. Its own catchphrase is: 'Thanks Diesel, for making us so very beautiful.' If something can be a critical talking point, or better still a source of study in the university, it's guaranteed to be hyped up as anti-hype. Benetton, with their controversial posters of dying AIDS patients, black and white angels and newborn babies, and Wonderbra with their outrageously sexist posters have been very successful at this. Studios now regularly set up Web sites to criticise and abuse their own films to drum up word-of-mouth hype *à la The Blair Witch Project*.

It is hardly surprising that hype-injected youth don't have any time for politics – for the real struggle to change the world. Politics is the fourth victim of hype. When people would rather vote on which members are to be expelled from *Big Brother* than use their right to vote in the general election, we know that politics has entered a terminal stage.

A great deal of the blame for voter apathy has been placed on the New Labour style of spin politics. But New Labour did not invent spin. In Britain, Margaret Thatcher is the real pioneer of hype and the spin approach to politics. It was Thatcher who transformed party political broadcasts from talking heads to Saatchi & Saatchi advertisements for a political brand. The 1979 election campaign, notable for the use of posters with the slogan 'Labour isn't Working' and a photograph of a dole queue, transformed electioneering into advertising campaigns. Thatcher's government was a leader in the skilful use of public information films on the state of the nation. The chilling AIDS campaign advertisements – gravestone sinking into the sea – established the standard for public information commercials. Whether she was fighting an election or an epidemic like AIDS, Thatcher used panic-ridden hype as her standard bearer.

New Labour's achievement is the transformation of hype into a natural, organic phenomenon. Think of Blair delivering, at the death of Diana, the famous 'People's Princess' speech: eyes wet, voice teetering on the edge of controlled emotions, pauses calculated to be half a heartbeat, hands skilfully demonstrating spontaneity. Or the other potent symbol: Blair emerging from his official car in tight, faded blue jeans flashing his cute buns (allegedly Blair's bum has been voted the sexiest in politics), carrying in one hand his battered guitar case and in the other a battered red box. This is spin at its best, invisible rather than transparent, seemingly accidental and spontaneous rather than stage-managed. Much better than kissing babies or donning a hard hat for touring a riot-ridden city.

Finally, hype kills trust, confidence and hope – in other words, it chokes community. We are sufficiently self-aware to know we are being hyped, but completely incapable of seeing how we can extract ourselves from its self-perpetuating cycles. When illusion is reality, the only reality that is marketed, can we traverse the yawning void to get back to solid ground? Castles in the air generate wealth, employment and the service-driven world of post-industrial society. What happens to affluence and its consumerist idyll if we should decide to try reality, organic living, less profligate lifestyles, more responsible ways of living? Surely, in that way lies only utter ruin for everyone? So cynicism is all we have left, and we dignify it as art, the highest accolade of our creative imagination. Today, we are our own art forms; the individual, the body, the mind as an isolate. In its aloneness is the only work of art, the ultimate expression of all that can be expressed. When everything is hype we can trust only ourselves, even if we are only following the hyped predicates along with the rest of the mob. We know we see through it; we cannot be sure anyone else does.

When cynicism rules and trust is merely a relic of distant antiquity, when we can be confident only that we are being sold a bill of goods, community suffocates on mob hysteria. To stand against the tide of the unreal, to demand an end to the manufacture and manipulation, is to threaten everyone else's investment in a self-sustaining delusion. It would be hopeful if we could talk about the need to rescue ourselves from this invidious spiral, but all forums of debate – art, media, politics – are the centres for hypercreation. A world of glitz, glitz, glitz is indeed bleak, bleak, bleak.

Hype, as theatre critic Robert Gore Langdon once noted, is a form of passive smoking. But while Langdon thought it is something we ulti-mately reject, I would argue that it is something we are getting so addicted to that soon it may be impossible to escape. In these post–ideo-logical times, hype has become an unconscious ideology to beat all historic ideologies. And like all extremist ideologies, it acts as a pathogen on society. The dread words of the Patron Saint of Political Spin return as in a haunting nightmare. What if really 'there is no alternative'?

Identity

We are in the midst of a global epidemic of identity crisis. Most of us do not know who or what we really are. Some of us have impossibly romanticised notions of what we should be. We desperately cling on to an imagined 'heritage', subscribe to the preservation of an unchanging 'tradition', and are ready to kill and be killed to save some 'essence' of our idealised identity. Many of us have altogether abandoned the very idea of having a fixed identity: we change our identities with as much ease as we change our jackets. All of us are suffering from a disease that is slowly but surely eating us from the inside.

The symptoms are everywhere. In Northern Ireland, men in balaclavas are not just 'scum', they think of themselves as either Ireland's or Ulster's 'finest' and will unite in violence for the sake of the difference. Britain seems perpetually in limbo, not knowing whether to become more American or more European. For much of the 20th century, American identity, and its foreign policy, was shaped in opposition to a 'Communist bloc'. In a post-cold war world, America has to deal with real and imaginary villains ('Muslim terrorists', rogue states such as bankrupt and starving North Korea, 'the Chinese menace') in an inane attempt to resolve its predicament of self-identity. The collapse of the Soviet Union has produced a plethora of new, artificial, national feuding identities, pitting Azerbaijanis against Armenians, Chechens against Russians, Kazakhstanis of one kind against Kazakhstanis of another. The

Balkans has just gone through one of the most brutal balkanisation of identities in all its history. In the Muslim world, traditionalists and modernists have been engaged in battles over what constitutes true Islamic identity for decades. The very idea of being 'White' has now become so problematic that 'Whiteness' is studied as an academic discipline in its own right.

In short, identity is being contested everywhere. That is why the politics of identity has become one of the dominant themes of postmodern times.

To 'know thyself', as Socrates put it, is both a fundamental human urge and a basic question in philosophy. Having some idea of who or what we are helps us to determine how we ought to live and conduct our daily affairs. A little self-knowledge also provides us with a little coherence in our metaphysical and moral outlooks. But in a rapidly globalising world, it is almost impossible to have even a modicum of self-knowledge. All those things that provided us with a sense of confidence in ourselves – such as nation states with homogeneous populations, well-established local communities, unquestioned allegiance to history and unchanging tradition – have evaporated. The sources of our identity have been rendered meaningless.

Consider, for example, the territory called 'England'. It is not the sole preserve of 'the English' any more: the population now is much more heterogeneous, with 'Englishness' (however it is defined) as only one segment in a multi-ethnic society. Moreover, the history and tradition that are associated with this 'Englishness' – the Empire, House of Lords, fox hunting, the national anthem – are either questionable or meaningless to the vast majority of new English who now live in England. Worse: this Englishness becomes quite insignificant when it is seen in relation to a new European identity which itself is an amalgam of countless other cultural identities. Not surprisingly, 'the English' feel threatened.

While the concrete foundations of identity are cracking away everywhere, the shifting context adds another layer of perplexity. Identity is a label, a toolkit, a compass bearing. It permits us to find not only ourselves but discern similarity and/or difference in everyone else. When the foundations of our identity crack we lose not only the sense of who we are but essential elements of how we connect to all other identities. All labels become confusing, multiple and problematic.

Think of the rather common label 'black'. It has no global connotation; there is no universal black identity. Being black has different meaning and significance in different places. In New York, being black is a mark of difference in contrast to the whites, the Italian, the Irish and the Hispanics, and a symbol of being cool. In Nigeria, it is not important whether you are black or white but whether you are Yoruba rather than Hausa; and the only way you can be cool is to be totally Westernised. In Jeddah, nothing is cool, and what really matters is not whether you are black or brown but whether you are a member of the royal family. In Cape Town, to be black is, almost by definition, to be confused: once excluded, now technically empowered, a dominant group in the rainbow, but still practically marginalised by the history that created and continues to operate practical exclusion. So, from the perspective of identity, context redefines meaning and we end up not talking about the same colour at all.

In addition, the very notions and ideas we use to describe our identities are changing radically. What does it mean, for example, to be a 'mother' in a world where in vitro fertilisation and surrogate motherhood are rapidly becoming common? What happens to conventional ideas of parenthood in the case of the French baby 'constructed' from the egg of a 62-year-old woman and sperm from her brother, and 'incubated' in a surrogate mother? What does it mean to be a 'wife' in a homosexual marriage? Or 'old' when you have rebuilt a 65-year-old body through plastic surgery and look like a young starlet?

Identity has become a perilous notion. It is not, if it ever was, monolithic and static, but multiple and ever changing. And the most fundamental change is this: all those other categories through which we in the West defined and measured ourselves – the 'evil Orientals', the 'fanatic Muslims', the 'inferior races of the colonies', the immigrants, the refugees, the gypsies – are now an integral part of ourselves. It is not just that they are 'here' but their ideas, concepts, lifestyles, food and clothes now play a central part in shaping 'us' and 'our society'. We thus have no yardstick to measure our difference and define ourselves.

Descartes could say with some confidence, 'I think, therefore I am' because his thought had already defined the Other, the darker side of himself, through which he could confirm his own civilised and thoughtful existence. Today, our thought has to be directed towards a more frightening question: how much of the Other is actually located within me? The quest for identity is essentially an attempt to answer this question. And it is the fear of the answer that transforms, in the words of Amin Maalouf, the Lebanese-French novelist, 'a perfectly permissible aspiration' into 'an instrument of war'. This transformation occurs through some basic associations.

The first of these is the conventional association of identity with power and territory. Identity always conferred power, defined the essential character distinctive to its own territory, and familiarised people with the proper means of domesticity, living comfortably within the homeland. America, for example, began as a declaration of identity: a new world emptied of meaningful past and ready for migrants who would build an identity based on the power of a new territory. But the very definition of American identity provided power and privilege for those who were conceived as the insiders. The term 'ethnicity' has its roots in the American provenance where, apart from the European immigrants, all other immigrants are defined as ethnics. The distinction is between hyphenated Americans – Italian, German, Polish, Irish, Russian – and ethnicity. American identity offers the hyphenated Americans the idealised American Dream of inclusion and opportunity. Thus, only hyphenated Americans have ever made it to the White House.

But ethnicity is very different: blacks, Hispanics, Native Americans are ethnics, problematic and different kinds of Americans. Ethnics make excellent domestic servants, a significantly different thing from domesticity. Ethnicity is the politically correct term for race, for a hierarchy within American identity and for the power of definition that is exclusive to white America. Asians too are ethnics. Chinese Americans had their identity neatly stereotyped in the works of Mark Twain and Bret Harte. Japanese Americans were the only people interned as real 'enemies within' during the Second World War, an unthinkable reaction to German, Italian or any other quisling state Americans.

In British identity, power and territory are expressed in hierarchies of race and class. It is a little too glib to argue that British identity had the luxury of seeing race as external, the definition of difference beyond its shores. But the exercise of power that created an empire on which the sun never set, and a notion of class that defined and shaped modernity and was not a stranger anywhere in the world, are essential attributes of what it is to be British. Without it the British could not be simultaneously xenophobic, internationalist and parochial – the sort of people who go on Spanish holidays to eat fish and chips and drink warm bitter ale. British identity is based on an assumption of authority that makes the world a familiar place, a proper theatre in which to continue being British. It also produced its own internationalist perspective: Britain has had its share of 'old India hands', 'Africa men and women' – urbane cosmopolitans who know Johnny Foreigner better than they know themselves.

The problem with identity as power and control over territory is what happens when power wanes. Johnny Foreigner is now within; ethnics are demanding the American Dream. Power has been debunked, denounced and vilified. Does all that identifies the Self go down the plughole with it? How can we be comfortable with accepting the identity of villains? Which leads us to the second association: to exclude the unsavoury foreigners from our identity we have to anchor it in romanticised history and frozen tradition.

Collective identity is based on the selective processes of memory. British identity was (is?) the acknowledgement of a common past. Sharing and having been shaped by this common past is what makes us different from all other identities. The trouble is, history is a deliberate human creation, itself another wilful act of power, artificially constructed to support an artificial identity. Europe engineered a cultural identity based on a common descent from the supposed traditions of ancient Greece and Rome and two thousand years of Christianity. British history books always begin with the arrival of the Romans. So British history begins by submerging, barbarising and differentiating itself from Celtic history. Celt and Welsh are words whose linguistic roots, one Greek, the other Saxon, mean stranger. The history of Britain, as written in the age of devolution, records not a common shared past but continuous contest and conflict within these isles. Whatever Britain is, it is the creation of dominance by kings and barons and upwardly mobile yeomen who practised colonialism at home, and after perfecting the technique, moved abroad.

It was Oliver Cromwell who noted that Britain had its 'Indians' at home, in what he called the 'dark corners of Britain'. He referred, of course, to the residual Celtic corners. It makes perfect sense that Margaret Thatcher, whom I always regarded as Oliver Cromwell in drag, should propose the solution to the Ulster problem as relocating Northern Irish Catholics to the Republic. It was Cromwell's policy – if they will not reform, be educated and submit, then they have no place within the identity, history and society that is Britain. That no one seriously proposes sending the Union Jack-waving Ulstermen back to where they came from, or removing the Union from them, itself suggests a strong allegiance to a constructed history, the history of irreconcilable difference. As Orangemen so often say, marching with fife and drum to intimidate and demonstrate their dominance is their culture. In an age of the politics of identity, culture has its rights. But how far can you defend the rights of a culture whose only reason for being is to retain dominance?

It really is quite dumbfounding how much of Britishness, and by association Englishness, is based on fabricated history. Consider the whole notion of Anglo-Saxon Britain. Winston Churchill and Rudyard Kipling were devotees of Anglo-Saxon history for a reason. John Townend, the disciplined and disgraced ex-Tory MP, invoked Anglo-Saxon identity for precisely the same reasons when he argued that only Anglo-Saxons could be truly English. It enabled them to avoid acknowledging how genuinely European British history has always been. Norman kings hardly ever spent time in Britain, spoke French rather than English, and were most concerned with dominating Europe from their French possessions. Of course, the Saxon bit of the Anglo-Saxon has its own problems. After the Welsh Tudors, and Scots Stuarts, a brief quasi-native interlude, German monarchs were bussed in to reign over Britishness that was to be marked by Englishness alone, and that wanted nothing to do with Europe.

The selectivity of historic memory is part of its inventiveness. History always seeks ancient roots, the better to justify its innovations. Ancient Anglo-Saxon liberties were purposefully invented on a number of occasions to fashion the Mother of Parliaments. This foundational institution was not a true popular democratic institution until 1929, the year of the first election based on universal adult suffrage. The statue of Oliver Cromwell quite properly stands outside Parliament. His insistence that ancient Anglo-Saxon liberties rested on property owning was the novel twist that secured class hierarchy, made the Restoration of the monarchy easy, and enabled manufactured history to continue its work. The pomp and ceremony of the British monarchy was a late-Victorian invention. The Royal Family as the model for the normative family, an ideal for a nation, is a post-Edwardian invention, Victoria's libidinous son Edward hardly being a suitable candidate for model husband and father. And so it goes on.

Thus, the notions of race and class are intrinsic to the self-definition of the English. As despairing Tories clearly demonstrated in the 2001 election campaign, without the idea of race there is little left for English identity to hold on to: only being a disadvantaged minority within Britain, the complete inversion of received history. What works well for youthful addicts of street culture, with their heterogeneity and multiple and hybrid characteristics, does not suit the aspirations of new English identity, and that's why the appeal to the barricades, sending them back, locking them up has to be made.

As recently as 1940, George Orwell could state that 'when you come back to England from any foreign country, you have immediately the sensation of breathing different air'. Identity as difference is less easy to define in a world already awash with globalisation, whose most notable feature is rampant Americanisation. Where is the British sandwich? Surely that defined the difference of being here. But McDonalds, Starbucks, pizza parlours, doner kebab, chicken tikka masala, the rise of ciabatta and the Pret a Manger syndrome have transmuted the familiar air of England into wafts of everyone else's fragrant confections.

These culinary metaphors have become basic to redefining British identity. The new culinary repertoire is not so much a smorgasbord as alternative choices. Do we embrace the global Americanisation of the high street, the merchandised model of individualism, the free market identity of buying into who you want to be in terms of dress, sex and politics? Or are we really as European as ciabatta and our passion for fine wine? Are we more the kind of people who opt for a common European history of struggle for public ownership and secure, quality public services? In facing that choice we have to discover how and in what way the spiced diversity of real curry, as opposed to an invented dish to suit only white tastes, fits into the feast of identities.

So we arrive at the third association: the negotiation of identity between the alternate poles of desire and death. As American scholar Cornel West has suggested, we construct our identities from the building blocks of our basic desires: desire for recognition, quest for visibility, the sense of being acknowledged, a deep desire for association. It is longing to belong. All these desires are expressed by symbols – pomp and ceremony, national monuments and anthems, cricket and football teams, etc. But in a world where symbols are all we are, all we have, holding on to these symbols becomes a matter of life and death. It is for the glorification of these symbols that the bloody tale of national history is written and enacted in nationalists' campaigns everywhere around the world.

Identity not only invokes the desire to be different, it also summons the desire to express similarity. Indeed, there can be no difference without similarity. But similarity is always seen as the opposite pole of difference, as appeals to making everyone the same. It is often posed as 'our' similarity against 'their' difference. Once the doctrine of similarity was the underlying principle of the Communist ethos; now it has become essential to the internationalist–libertarian–individualist doctrine that underpins globalisation. 'Workers of the World Unite' has been replaced by 'Liberal Capitalism is the Only Way'. Such championing of similarity can become war on those who fight to maintain their difference. Similarity in such contests becomes an ethos to die for.

In coming to terms with the contemporary crisis of identity, we need to transcend certain apparent contradictions. To reject the demonisation of difference does not require the abandonment of difference. The desire for similarity is not the same thing as the aspiration for homogeneity. Traditions and customs that do not change cease to be traditions and customs and are transformed into instruments of oppression. Identity has historic anchors but is not fixed to a limited, unchanging set of traditional signs. Identity is not what we buy, or what we choose, or what we impose on others; it is something from which we learn how to live, discover what is worth buying, and appreciate what it is to be different.

What we need is to recover our confidence in identity as the product of various and diverse traditions. We need to recognise that any identity is the means to synthesise similarity through difference and to see difference as a discrete means of expressing basic similarity. We need to move away from the politics of contested identities that heighten artificial differences towards acceptance of the plasticity and possibilities of identities that focus on our common humanity. Living identity, as opposed to the fossilised to die for variety, is always in a constant flux. It is an ever-changing balance, the balance of similarities and differences as a way of locating what it is that makes life worth living and what connects us with the rest of the changing world. The challenge of postmodern time is to transcend difference and thereby enable it to fulfil its real purpose.

Japanese

To see things clearly, it does not always help to look at them directly. To understand the role Japan plays in Americanised global culture, it would be more productive to look at a place other than Japan. The place I had in mind is *Star Trek*, the virtual world of high technology and exploration that reflects Japan's own historic love affair with know-how and virtuality.

The Star Trek (ST) enterprise, with all its films and multiple television shows, is a great barometer of American consciousness. For the past 40 years it has been exposing the latent fears and anxieties as well as the visible hopes and aspirations of the great American people. Whenever the shows begin to sag and the ratings drop, a new villain that taps into the American consciousness is introduced to restore order. When *Voyager*, the third ST progeny, was declared by even its most zealous fans to be dull and ready for an early grave, it was revived with the introduction of the half-Borg character 'Seven of Nine'. Thanks to Seven, Voyager's warp drive was restored, and thanks to the Borg, the lost space-ship returned home on a triumphant note.

Seven, as played by the svelte and curvaceous Jari Ryan, is clearly every man's dream babe. But when we first meet her, she is a different person, a Borg. Draped with wires, fitted with mechanical arms and eyes and complete with Zombie skin, she is all machine, with no individual identity. She is linked to a 'hive mind' that exists as a 'Collective'. This drone collective is the most dangerous foe of the Federation. But what or who are the Borg?

A major element in the success of the ST siblings – *The Next Generation* (TNG), *Deep Space Nine* (DSN), *Voyager* and now *Enterprise* – is the representation of aliens in terms of the deep-seated anxieties of Pax Americana. The xenobiology of ST is littered with marauding aliens constructed like a patchwork quilt from the fabrics of Orientalism. The main foe in TNG is the warrior race of Klingons, who, with their genetic predisposition to treachery and fatalism and their emphasis on honour at the expense of justice, contain more than a shade of the 'Saracens' of the Crusades. Indeed, to ensure that we transform all the Orientalist illusions into contemporary geopolitics, they even fight, in the age of phasers, with scimitars. The Cardassian Empire, engaged in a life and death struggle with Commander Sisko of DSN, contains more than a passing reference to contemporary China. Like the Orientalist representations of the Chinese, the Cardassians love family and tradition, revere their elderly and ancestors, eat anything that moves and have a herd-like instinct. And like today's China, they are determined to seek a dominant position in all matters. The Borg are to *Voyager* what the Klingons and Cardassians are to TNG and DSN. But there is a major difference that makes the Borg rather special.

The central question ST shows address is the very common and collective problem of how we are to imagine 'the undiscovered country' that is the future. This question is explored in an explicit, indeed overstated, framework of double diversity. The shows are not only grounded in multiculturalism but also work within a number of different and highly specialised disciplines. The latest theories, controversies and ideas from anthropology, sociology, linguistics and psychology to physics, astronomy and electronics can all be debated and deconstructed in the episodes of TNG, DSN and *Voyager*. As such, ST is constantly questioning the modernist underpinnings of Western civilisation – the notion of perpetual progress and economic expansion, the Truth of reason and science, the self-assurance of morality, authority and identity – all those categories that we now know, thanks to a herd of postmodern theorists, to be 'in crisis'.

As such, ST aliens, even with all their Orientalist make-up, are never painted in black and white. They are always complex and amenable to change – today's foe may become tomorrow's friends. This framework is further enhanced by the Federation's principles of non-interference, encapsulated in the 'prime directive'. Thus, the ST crews seldom make moral judgements about other cultures and are always open and willing to learn from new aliens they encounter – a direct reference to contemporary dilemmas about the limits of the political and cultural representation of various 'Others' and what it means to be responsible in these postmodern times.

Yet the Borg, who have featured in the most successful ST episodes and films, have escaped this postmodern logic. With the Borg we have the nineties' reworking of the body-snatching, Commie-pod-people aliens of cold war science fiction. A race of totally evil cyber zombies, the Borg cruise in spaceships that look like big black cubes or dense solid spheres, looking to evolve by absorbing new races. What makes them so terrifying is their superior technology and collective will. They have a simple and direct mantra: 'Resistance is futile. You will be assimilated.' As the distillation, in its purest form, of all the Orientalist stereotypes of Japan, the Borg provide us with an early warning signal of an approaching cold war. The Borg are the American fear of Japan writ large.

Japan occupies a special place in the lore of Orientalism. Like the rest of the Orient, it has been seen as an exotic culture, the land of karate and the geisha. It has been admired for its aesthetics (exquisite gardens, curious architecture, strange *kebuki* theatre and funny tea ceremonies) and feared for its 'inhuman' martial traditions (samurai, *bushido*, *ninja*, *kamikaze*). In contrast to evil and treacherous Muslims and cowardly and effeminate Hindus, Orientalism represented the Japanese, as ST now represents the Borg, as emotionless sub-humans, a robot-like people hermetically sealed in their Zen spirituality and communal outlook.

But Japan also differs from much of the Orient in two distinct ways.

First, it was never colonised. So, Japan was able to protect itself from the onslaught of the Orientalist scholars. The histories of all Oriental civilisations have been written by Western scholars in a framework that makes them small tributaries in the great universal river of Western history. But Japanese studies, unlike Islamic, Chinese and Indian studies, have been, and continue to be, very much the preserve of Japanese scholars. So Japan was able to control its own past; and the West was unable to shape a modern, Westernised Japanese identity. This is the key to understanding Western representations of Japan. It is based on the fear that the West has no control over the past, present or the future of Japan. Japan is thus destined to remain irreducibly different from the West and impenetrable to the total embrace of Western humanism.

Second, Japan was able to adopt, appropriate and transform Western technology. Indeed, a technologically advanced Japan has 'Japanised' technology itself. If the future is technological, and technology has been Japanised, then it is reasonable to assume that the future too is Japanese. Or rather, Japan is the future – a future that displaces and transcends the West. This is a deeply frightening thought for the West!

It is also a thought that has produced a new variety of Orientalism. The fears of an irreducibly different Japan, a Western culture about to be overwhelmed by the Japanese Other, a Japan comfortable with high technology, all come together in techno-orientalism. In techno-orientalism, Japan is not only located geographically, but also projected chronologically. It is located in the future of technology. This reinvented Japan – a land of Manga comic strips and film animations, *Godzilla*, video-games, video-phones, techno-porn, PDAs, mobiles, hand-held intelligent computers, smart buildings, sardined bullet trains and overcrowded cities – can be sampled in cyberpunk novels like William Gibson's *Neuromancer* and futuristic movies like *Blade Runner*.

The Borg are the most pernicious representation of techno-orientalism. As symbols of a future Japanese society, they represent the end product of dehumanised technological power, the nightmarish dimension of capitalist progress. But this representation is based as much on animosity as on jealousy. The mutant Japanoids are better suited to survive the future. As *Voyager* makes clear, the Borg adapt very quickly and are totally future proof.

If the Borg are the fear, Seven is the hope. In her Borg incarnation, she is modelled on two icons of contemporary Japan. The first is the kids of the otaku generation, who are 'lost to everyday life' by their immersion in information technologies. Techno-orientalism imagines these young people mutating into machines, a cyber-biological mode of being for the future. The second is a brand of technobody horror imagery (drills entering eyeballs, wires bursting the flesh) that comes straight from Shinya Tsukamoto's cult film, *Tetsuo*. The two icons are combined to produce a single, distinctive image of future Japanoids.

But as Seven is 'humanised' and assimilated into the crew of the Voyager, she begins to lose her horror make-up and transforms into a ravishing beauty. We return from techno-orientalism to the old-fashioned variety. The West has always seen the Oriental woman as a functional instrument. Seven becomes an automated doll, an empty vessel ready to receive all that Western individualistic humanism desires.

It is significant that the Borg first appeared in the aftermath of Shin-taro Ishihara's influential book *The Japan That Can Say No* (1991). Ishihara argues that Japan needs to stand up for itself and shape its own destiny, independent of the West. American commentators immediately attacked Ishihara as a 'Japanese chauvinist' and called for the containment of a Japan with ideas way above its station. The Borg are the first major exercise towards that containment. As *Voyager* demonstrates, there are only two ways to deal with the Borg: destroy them totally or turn them into a replica of the American self. In the final episode of *Voyager*, we see that only by destroying the Borg can Voyager and its crew attain their own salvation. Seven shows the alternative: what the Japanese, drained of their ugly 'Asian values', and overlaid with a Western humanistic framework, could become. A ravishingly beautiful, curvaceous and industrious cog in the grand narrative of Western humanism.

Kids

Dedicated viewers of CNN may have noticed the series of advertisements made for UNICEF, the global guardian of the child, occasionally punctuating news bulletins. The ads depict idealised little children in various predicaments, and end with a statement of children's rights. Children, the ads tell us, possess inherent rights, like the right to survive and flourish, to have a sound environment, to be protected from child labour. All very laudable. The ones that perplexed me somewhat were the rights to privacy, expression and freedom of thought. Perplexing because they called into question exactly how we define the concept of childhood.

The Enlightenment bequeathed us potent notions of childhood and the rights of the individual. These notions have been refined, transmuted and appropriated in various forms by modernity and postmodernism. Today, as UNICEF asserts, we are wedded to the notion that children are individuals and as individuals have all the rights we associate with individual adults. But in their isolated single status we hardly know what to make of these little angels/monsters/moppets. Or to put it another way, as individuals children are society's problems writ miniature.

And society – well, our society in any case – is gripped by a strong sense that something is seriously wrong with children. Today, our children have far more than those of times past, yet they are perpetually unsatisfied. They are more educated and sophisticated, yet less responsible; they have more amusements and entertainment, yet they are frequently bored; they are more looked after yet more seditious and out of control. Child murderers are multiplying. American school kids seem to go on violent rampages with tedious regularity. Teenage boys now rape little girls. What's gone wrong?

Actually there is nothing wrong with children. But everything is wrong with our notion of childhood – which is another way of saying that we need to re-examine ourselves and our society. As a cultural symbol, the child in Western society has carried the burden of contradictory notions – it simultaneously represents innocence and evil. And both these notions stem from Christianity.

The child is a central metaphor of Christianity, working through the imagery of the Christ child of Christmas and underscored by those well-remembered ringing phrases like 'suffer the little children... for such is the kingdom of God' (Mark 10: 14), 'except ye... become as a little child' (Matthew 18: 3), and of course Isaiah's ringing paradisaical vision: 'and a little child shall lead them, when the lion lies down with the lamb' (Isaiah 11: 6). What is conjured up for us is a concept of simple innocence and purity, a purity that is instructive and associated with regeneration, renewal and a heavenly vision of perfectible humanity – 'out of the mouths of very babes and sucklings hast thou ordained strength', as the *Book of Common Prayer* put it.

But at the same time, the idea of original sin ensures that every child is born condemned for the unworthy behaviour of Adam and Eve in paradise. By definition, a child is an inferior, lower level of being. Only after the child had been baptised by adults did it in fact become human and its citizenship had to await confirmation. This Christian theology makes the child an evil, inferior entity, straight from the moment of its arrival. Evil and immorality are inherent in the child; and if it is left alone, if uncared for and unshepherded by adults, the intrinsic evil and immorality will consume the child on its way to adulthood. From this root come all varieties of 'spare the rod and spoil the child' ethics.

William Golding's *The Lord of the Flies*, which most children read at secondary school, plays on this notion of childhood. A critique of flag-waving Boy's Own adventures, Golding's children personify the evil that lies beneath the surface of civilised society. One group of Christian boys embraces an atavistic paganism and the society they create for themselves is based on oppression and subjugation. The strongest are simply evil; the weak, as personified by Piggy, are ugly and incompetent. The strong are intent on murdering the weak. Order returns when an adult arrives and the murderers are revealed as the children that they are. There are strong Christian connotations here – the character of Simon has many similarities with Jesus – and Golding relies partly on the notion of 'original sin' to make clear that the defects of society are in fact defects of nature; it is in our nature to be innately evil and in unsocialised children this evil simply comes to the fore.

So from the outset there is something enigmatic and paradoxical about the child. This duality got great play in colonialism and modernity.

It is useful to spare some thought for the meaning of childhood as it was before modernity. Childhood is not a self-evident period. Children did not just 'grow'd' like Topsy. The points of demarcation between what is a child, a youth and an adolescent have all been made by culture and society and the opportunities they offer. Society has worked on the demographics and economics and philosophised the changes as it went along. The Biblical child was what we would term today a pre-schooler. For most of human history childhood was the years before six or seven, the years of dependence. After childhood, youth was not that different from adulthood, except in being a period of acquiring skill, learning and increasing dexterity in the habits and concerns of the adult world.

Putting away childish things at around six or seven meant labour and economic usefulness. Service became the human lot and that was educational whether it took place in a school or not. Formal education was an opportunity for very few until the end of the 19th century, which is perhaps why and how so much of what we think of as childhood dates back only that far.

The Enlightenment and its political discontents both sentimentalised childhood and mobilised it as a powerful part of its utopian vision. The image is captured in Delacroix's iconic painting of the French Revolution, 'Liberty leading the People', where liberty is personified as a boy and a youth leading the mob. Whether the allegory was inspired by Isaiah or by pagan notions of youthful fertility and regeneration, the place of childhood was at the very heart of social, collective action.

The Romantic apotheosis of the child is provided by the poems of Wordsworth. When the liberty children led society to turned sour, as it did for Wordsworth and the entire Romantic movement, when the French Revolution became totalitarian state terror the child became an even more potent harbinger of something quite different. The child became what Wordsworth termed an 'intimation' of our 'immortality' as spiritual consciousness. The child embodied the clouds of glory adults could only longingly ponder as they looked 'through a glass darkly'. Back to innocence and purity with a huge increase in spiritual competence went the little angels.

The notion of the child as an evil, immature and immoral being was distanced from the Western self-consciousness. It went abroad and became the foundation of European colonialism and imperialism, as well as the idea of modernity. The patriarchal Biblical language of the Father and his children was appropriated to new ends. The noble savage or savage barbarian was recognised and treated according to ideas that are nothing more than the transmutation of European social values into natural laws that explained the rise of civilisation as a developmental process. The Other peoples beyond Europe were simultaneously young, as in new forms and childlike, and old, in the sense of original, living in a state from whence the West had already emerged, and to which at all costs it must not degenerate.

European colonial writers often described non-Western cultures as childlike, needing moral guidance and looking after by the Imperial powers. Thus James Mill, the 19th-century liberal and utilitarian thinker who provided the intellectual justification for the colonisation of India, saw the relationship between colonisers and their subjects in terms of father and son. His own childhood and how he was treated by his father become the main metaphors for the mission of civilising the Indians. Rudyard Kipling, who also had a devastatingly cruel childhood in England, projected his lost childhood on the Indians by describing them as 'half savage, half child'. Cecil Rhodes described the South African blacks much more darkly: 'the native is to be treated as a child and denied franchise. We must adopt the system of despotism… in our relations with the barbarous of South Africa'.

The use of the metaphor of the child legitimised the use of barbaric laws and violence and demanded unconditional obedience to imposed authority. What their fathers and teachers did to the colonial administrators in their childhood, on and off the playing fields of Harrow and Eton, they in turn tried to do to the subject people they ruled. After all, how does a father enforce rules of behaviour among his unruly children? He occasionally boxes their ears or gives them a good thrashing to put some sense in their heads. In Western society itself, this notion of childhood justified the economic, social and psychological exploitation of working-class children. Dickens' England is an apt place to observe this.

While Wordsworth was maundering about these 'six year darlings', using the age-old notion of what is a child, the newly established factories of England were stuffed full of those who had just left this period of innocence. In the first decades of the 19th century, it has been estimated, 80 per cent of the workers in English cotton mills were children. Children were also hard at work down the mines, up the chimneys and wherever they could find a livelihood. These wretched young workers had to await the economic empowerment of childhood as a much longer period of sentimentalised dependence before there was any change in their lot. The new vision of childhood, the Victorian paternalistic variant, got underway thanks to the wealth accumulated by the middle class, wealth created by all those child labourers.

Childhood, as we have come to be confused by it, is a creation of the bourgeois notions of the mid-19th century, a vast Victorian complex. Philippe Aries has described this stage as the impulse of 'helping the children to rise in the world individually and without collective ambition'.

Or you might say that childhood, as we have come to conceive of it, is a riposte to the chilling notion contained in Delacroix's painting. Send them to school, formally teach them, encourage thereby their dependence on adults for their sustenance and well-being, divert them with hobbies and interests and generally make them carefree.

Consumerism aimed at children is not a new discovery. It began in the Victorian era as part of the process of establishing the new nature of childhood. It found expression in a range of associated crafts like toy making (think of those wonderful dolls' houses and lead soldiers), comics (the real *Boy's Own*) and children's literature – the most powerful disseminator of the new ideas of what childhood should be and what was expected of the child. As the concept developed it became the fashion to send them to Scouts and Brownies to learn acceptable social aspirations – but for goodness sake make individuals of them, not bearers of a collective conscience, since children by cultural convention have all too much conscience and consciousness as it is.

Nor is youthful irresponsibility and tension between generations anything new. Nor was gang behaviour first encountered with the Mods and the Rockers. All this had a long, long history. Youthful despair was the Bohemianism of the early 19th century and the Romantic movement. As Alfred de Musset put it: 'Young people found a use for inactive strength in the affectation of despair.'

What was at stake in the Victorian construction of childhood was a concern with a contemporary ring. Should children be forced to hasten the change from childhood to adulthood, or should the idealised period of childish innocence and dependence, the period through which they must be nurtured, instructed and shepherded, be extended? Matthew Arnold was of the opinion it was a sin not to hasten the transition if it were possible. Yet, by effectively creating the model for the English public school during his years at Rugby, he produced the institution that facilitated the prolonging of childhood for the emergent middle classes. Youth could play at being adults, but it was just play, the new concept that filled up this extended period of becoming.

Postmodernism has expanded and made a fetish of consumerism along with youthful irresponsibility and despair. Childhood has been turned into a commodity, chopped into smaller and smaller market niches. It all starts with baby's first this or that and moves on relentlessly in small segments – '1–2 years', '3–5 years', 'pre-school', 'teens' – each step inexorably leading to more and more consumption. And everything that the adults do, children do too. So now we have infant fashion, teenage fashion, children's films, children's supermarkets and low-cost children's holidays where parents come free! Toys are not toys any more, they are concepts intended to be internalised by children. Dolls come with the entire package of adult pornography: big breasts, slender waist and long legs ready for action. Pop music and videos usher the young into a world of hypersexuality, a world where youthful irresponsibility is essential for being 'cool' and despair is a fashion statement.

If childhood is a commodity, it can easily be consumed by adults. Hence the exponential increase in child pornography and child abuse. The romanticised idea of childhood is the lost kingdom of the adult world, so it is only natural to desire and yearn to possess all that the care-worn adult has forsaken. When childhood is invested both with innocence and sinless purity and overlaid with bursting sexuality it positively invites paedophilic obsession. The new construction of childhood was effected by increasing the sense of difference between the child and the adult, leaving youth to be a troubled arena of turmoil.

The process began with Rousseau and naturally Freud had a great deal to do with identifying the complexes acquired in one stage only to be repressed in another. The upshot is that popular culture now makes a cliché out of child abuse. No longer is childhood synonymous with 'trails of glory', where what we cannot exactly recall is knowledge of spirituality; what we now have to wrestle with is suppressed memories of sexual and physical abuse. Child abuse is now the plot of a thousand dramas in literature, theatre and cinema. A huge industry has emerged around the fabrication of recovered memory syndrome. One hardly stands a chance of being interesting unless one can attest to being the product of abuse.

Write a book about how you had sex with your dad and become a celebrity. Child abuse has been made so generalised and so decidedly an idealised cause of the problems of adults that we no longer know how to mobilise repugnance. We are even less sure of whether it is a real, increasingly prevalent problem, or whether the frequency is created by the attention devoted to it.

Conspicuous consumption, we have known for some time, produces deprived and undeveloped personalities. By turning childhood into a commodity, postmodernism not only fosters an 'I want it now' mentality, but transforms childhood – 'the best years of our lives' – into a cultural wasteland. It imposes a precocious individuality on those whom we at the same time have been conditioned to see as dependent by custom, convention and the law. So long as children participate in an innocuous youth culture, the mass global culture of today, they are being the children we want them to be. So long as they dress like adults, don make-up and adopt adult sexual and social sensibilities they demonstrate their individuality. How they will rise through this is pretty much their own individual concern. But when individual children in increasing numbers do what individual adults do we are shocked.

Child murderers and criminals and child parents perplex us to the very foundations of our being. They are a total paradox in the face of the stern strictures we have made about the nature of childhood. They present us with a whole set of irreconcilable impossibilities because of the rights of individuality we have conferred on children who are no longer a responsibility of society or community or the family or any collective, while clearly being of and within all of these groups. The unruly adolescents – so beloved of postmodern marketing – have become both problem children and problem adults simultaneously precisely because we are not sure which category they most resemble. In adolescence whole histories of conflicting ideas meet unresolved. And we have collapsed all historical, colonial and modern notions of childhood in a great mess so now we have no idea of what or who is a child.

But what would the offending young have to say in their defence if, as Blake once demanded, 'the voice of the children were heard in the land'?

Once upon a time the generation gap and youthful rebellion were associated with great causes: liberty from brutal oppression, increasing the masses' rights of participation in the decision-making processes of society, and application of moral principles, such as virtue, justice and altruism in the life of society. The rhetoric of adult politics constantly invokes the child, the future generations for whom and on whose behalf things must be done. But the truth is the West has arrived at a postmodern terminus, the end of history, where all has been decided and the only thing left is to be a consumer. On the philosophical front doubt is all we can cling to, it is virtually impossible to discuss belief, and ethical and moral certainties have been relegated to the time before the Ark landed in Lah-Lah Land. Society, community, family and the transmission of imperatives, norms, things to believe have become bogey men, the preserve of fundamentalists, traditionalists and other unsavoury types. Cynicism rules OK! and determines the relations between youth and age.

The voice of a child that rings in my ears is of a perfectly nice, ardent youngster, whose angst is summed up in the phrase: 'I wish I had a culture, something to believe in.' Western society has empowered the young only to consume – all other rituals and any formal rites of passage have been rigorously stripped away. We have made it politically incorrect to pass on any other attachment to certainty to the child and that mass of youthful individuals we have groomed with knowledge of their rights. The collapse of the Left and the demonising of tradition and religion leave the notion of society in an emasculated limbo. People are free-floating individuals, children and adults, over-endowed with rights and with no accepted language in which to discuss their responsibilities to anyone or anything beyond themselves. Perhaps we are so keen on stressing the rights of the child to do just what any adult can do because we fear children are malleable conformists. It is not children who have a problem with society but the adults of the breed.

We have gone about as far as it is possible to go in leaving children to their own devices. Parenting has become the exercise of permissibility, where it would be radically unchic to tell children what they should, ought or must do. Patriarchy is out; and, should it look anything like imposition, so is matriarchy. This pervasive attitude constrains the institutions constituted by law to be responsible for the welfare of the child and the operation of the family, which cannot be left to itself lest it harm the welfare of the child.

When children emerge unable to distinguish that there are such concepts as right and wrong, good and bad, virtue and villainy, it is because this is the overarching culture of contented dubiety we have taught them. Postmodernism is not a rightful freedom from imposition. It is the imposition of disregard for anything except the individual. And that is what we are force-feeding our children, and fretting and worrying about when we see the results.

To alter the dynamic, to find a better definition of children and childhood that generates better and more balanced people, we have to begin again with the meaning of family and society. We have to recover a balancing concept of something beyond ourselves to which we bear responsibility in the midst of freedom. We have to return to the debates and twists and turns of history not as a closed book after which we have written 'The End', but as a continuing saga that relates us to ideas, concepts and even beliefs that are greater than ourselves.

We are not the first era in history to have to deal with problem children. We are merely the first era that has abandoned idealism about the possibility of human improvement and deserted all references beyond ourselves. If we want our children to be good and wholesome, we have to begin with ourselves.

Lies

'Size matters', says a stylish French woman. The advertisement for the Renault 'New Clio' claims that 4 centimetres can make all the difference. She is apparently referring to wheel tracks. But in the context of the minimalist postmodernism that frames the advertisement, and the way the overtly sophisticated female plays with the measuring tape, we are intentionally led in another direction. This double entendre has all the refinement of a *Carry On* film.

Size matters both down there for men and up there for women. So what do the vast majority of people who do not have the right size do? Well, if they really think that size matters, they fake it. Men go for penis enlargement and women have their breasts 'enhanced'. In Europe and America, where fewer than one in four women breast-feed their children, many are happy to pay huge sums, risk their health, suffer discomfort and pain, just to increase the size of their breasts to the magical 38DD.

No matter how slender and toned the rest of a woman's body may be, a huge pair of pomegranates stuck on the front is considered to be – well, wow! Witness Pamela Anderson, Brigitte Nielsen, Carmen Electra, Melanie Griffith and Britain's favourite television presenter, Melinda Messenger. The only assets, if you forgive the pun, that these women have is their plastic, fake breasts. But it says something about us and our times when silicone breasts are the only requirement for becoming a star or an overnight sensation, and Wonderbras, delivered to American department stores in armoured vehicles, are the subject of serious cultural analysis. Indeed, it seems to me that the world is awash with fake breasts. Every naked or bikini–clad breast that one encounters on television, films, magazines, the tabloids or cyberspace, is almost guaranteed to be plastic.

But something profound has happened here. In the process of becoming obsessed with fake, and frankly grotesquely large, breasts, we have lost sight of and downgraded the natural entity and forgotten its true function. Size has come to determine personality. But 'party tits', as the novelist Jay McInerney calls them, have only one function: to fulfil the fake desires of fake individuals. As Marilyn Yalom argues in her book, *A History of Breasts*, the more society becomes obsessed with breasts, and huge fake breasts, as the object of erotic desire, the further breasts depart from their original nurturing function.

Fake breasts are, of course, a form of lie. Celebrities supporting fake breasts are basically lying about themselves. But there is more: the lie has actually redefined reality. The fake breast is not just bigger, better, sexier and more desirable than the real thing, it has also reshaped social and cultural behaviour. Fake breasts define glamour, therefore most women think this is the only way to be glamorous. Most young men are not just attracted to large, fake breasts, they even think that when a woman lies down, her breasts are supposed to stand straight up, like rockets ready for launch. Real breasts, which come in all shapes and sizes, have therefore been subverted, perverted and declared inferior and undesirable; fake breasts become more real than the real item and more socially and culturally potent.

What is true of breasts is true of the world at large. It is not just that we are lying about the size of our breasts, and in some cases our noses, cheek-bones and other parts of our anatomy – as in the case of Cher – but we are lying about most things. Indeed, our culture has become deeply embedded in lies. Take real life. It is complex, messy and not very entertaining. So to make real life entertaining it has to be embellished with lies; or, like fake breasts, it has to be enlarged and thrust in your face. This is precisely what happens in many television documentaries about 'real' people. Television screens on both sides of the Atlantic are awash with programmes that purport to present a real slice of life – they have titles like *The Real Birth Show*, *Cheaters* and *Single Girls*. But childbirth, ordinary single girls and folks who cheat on each other are – well, forgive the pun – as flat as a flat chest. To make them desirable, dramatic and entertaining, you have to make them larger than life – and present real life as though it is a long-running drama.

What happens when we see ordinary people leading ordinary lives as though they are characters in a play? Lives that seem to consist of nothing but heightened tension, outrageous behaviour, high drama? Ordinary people watching these ordinary people wonder: why are our lives missing the drama, the excitement, the bravado? There is a kind of invisible feedback loop: the enhanced reality sucks in the audience and persuades them to behave in a larger than life way. This is best illustrated in Sky television's 'Uncovered' series: *Ibiza*, *Caribbean* and *Greece Uncovered*. Here the producers persuade young holidaymakers to behave in an outrageous and grotesque fashion. When real holidaymakers visit these places they assume that this is how one really ought to behave. Thus, the enhanced fake reality feeds the real; and the real itself acquires the dimensions of enhanced reality. This is the equivalent of young women looking at Pamela Anderson and rushing out to acquire their own silicone breasts.

The first casualty of a society obsessed with size is the loss of distinction between lies and truth. If the lie, the fake, is more real than the real, why bother with the real and the true? It is not just that truth is boring, it is also much more difficult to confirm and even harder to film. Television documentaries have for a long time played loose and fast with truth. The very grammar of film makes it difficult for the subject matter to be portrayed wholly truthfully: even a simple sequence such as a person opening the door may require half a dozen different shots that have to be edited together. During my childhood, I used to be totally enchanted by

Disney wildlife films, which I always assumed to be true stories. And even today, we watch nature films as though they were unfolding a wild drama in all its stark reality and truth.

But how true to life nature films are is well illustrated by Jacques Cousteau, patron saint of environmentalists. Cousteau devoted his life to revealing the secrets of the oceans and his documentaries introduced a whole generation of young folks, myself included, to the 'undersea world'. But Cousteau's documentaries were total lies – they were deliberately structured to reveal a dramatic narrative. In one episode, an expedition around the Cape of Good Hope, we saw the story of two sea lions captured by the crew of the *Calypso*. The sea lions were given names and trained to walk on the deck like dogs before being returned to the ocean, apparently unscathed. But the story was a lie. There were four, not two, sea lions and the understudies were needed when the first two died. They were kept out of the sea for filming so long that they died of dehydration. In another case, footage of an octopus scrambling out of a perspex tank before hopping overboard was obtained by pouring bleach into the container. Shots of a shark attacking a baby whale were recorded after the *Calypso* had injured the creature with a glancing blow. A sequence of two octopuses fighting was stage-managed by divers who threw them together at the entrance to a narrow cave. Virtually all of Cousteau's films were fakes, including two Oscar-winning documentaries. In reality, the fishes, octopuses and other marine creatures are not living a dramatic story – they are just living. The only way to turn them into a story is to fake it.

Television journalism is not far behind Cousteau. Indeed, we now have a new variety of journalism that either does not bother with truth at all or presents falsehood as truth. At least when *Bridget Jones's Diary* started in the *Independent* it did not pretend to be true. But many such columns do. The most famous of these columns appeared in the pages of the *Boston Globe*. The characters populating award-winning journalist Patricia Smith's columns were purported to be real people. Smith wrote pithy stories about city life and black culture. But almost everything she wrote, it was eventually revealed, was a lie. At *New Republic* magazine, Mike Gallagher wrote gripping features about teenage computer hackers and sex-mad White House interns – they were dramatic largely because they were fabricated. Then there was the famous exposé of Carlton TV's documentary 'The Connection'. The award-winning film claimed to be a risk-laden investigation into the Cali cartel's heroin route from Colombia to the school playgrounds of Britain. The film followed drug carriers from start to finish. But it told a story that was not true with evidence that was false.

One could dismiss these incidents as isolated cases. But the trend towards infotainment, that is, journalism that is also drama and pure spectacle, is now well established. When I worked as a reporter for London Weekend Television during the early eighties, we did something called 'current affairs'. It was hard-hitting journalism that by today's standards was definitely laid-back but always tried to tell the truth. But by the mid-eighties 'current affairs' was dismissed as boring talking heads. I left television because I was not interested in 'heightening' my journalism with 'reconstruction', slow motion and special effects. The boundary between constructing television journalism as drama and entertainment and falsification of facts is a thin one. It is a boundary that is evaporating rapidly. Most contemporary docu-drama, including 'fly on the wall' stuff, is plainly constructed lies.

Of course, constructed lies are not limited to television. Almost every country now has a thriving black market for counterfeit products – watches, videos, perfumes, electronic and other consumer goods. Before the 1998 Asian crisis, an astonishing 20 per cent of the region's economy was based on fake products. After the crisis, it rose to an estimated 30 per cent. The Asian counterfeit product comes in two forms: as dishonest fakes and as 'genuine imitations'.

The dishonest counterfeit product is cynically promoted by some original Western manufacturers themselves. When some multinational companies carve out a new market in a non-Western state, they do not manufacture their usual products themselves. Instead, they subcontract local companies to manufacture their goods and then market them under their brand names. The advantages to the parent companies are obvious: they can avoid all responsibility for exploitative practices such as poor working conditions, wages well below the legal minimum and use of child labour; they can keep the costs to a bare minimum and ensure maximum profit; and they can boast about helping local businesses. But what of the product itself?

While it carries the brand name of the multinational corporation, it is in fact a totally different product, not least because its formulation has been changed and original ingredients have been replaced by inferior ones. Thus, these branded products are lies, simulacra: while they look like the real things, and have been marketed by real Western companies, they are in fact shoddy replicas.

The genuine imitations are local products. They are normally sold for peanuts and are outwardly almost indistinguishable from the real things. It is almost impossible, for example, to tell the difference between a real Gucci watch and a fake without opening them up. Counterfeit CDs not only look the same as the real ones but have exactly the same sound quality, making it practically impossible, even for industry experts, to tell the difference. But it is not just fake watches, cassettes and CDs that are being marketed in Thailand, Taiwan, Hong Kong, South Korea, Malaysia, Indonesia and Singapore. Counterfeit culture produces everything from designer clothes to shoes, leather goods and even antiques. A common sight in the cities of South-east Asia are people totally dressed in fake designer labels, looking every bit as chic as their rich neighbours with the real goods or their Western counterparts on the streets of New York, Paris and Geneva.

This counterfeit culture is very adaptive. Among the most popular fakes are the pirate videos of Hollywood films which are often available even before a film is released in the US. When the videocassettes lost their technological appeal, they were quickly replaced, first with video-CDs and then with DVDs. In both cases the (re)production quality matched the original but the cost to the buyer is less than a tenth.

I am not entirely against this economy of the fake. In some ways it strikes a blow against capitalism and enables the poor of Asia to eke out a living. But it does have a darker underside: when it comes to fake spare parts for cars and counterfeit industrial processes we are on to seriously dangerous ground. It is relatively easy in cities like Bangkok and Kuala Lumpur to have your car fitted with totally fake parts – carrying labels such as BMW and Renault – which have not been rigorously tested and are not altogether safe. An estimated one in four accidents in a city like Kuala Lumpur is caused by fake parts.

With fake history we move on to even more dangerous ground. If all lies are, to use the title of a famous postmodern film, *True Lies*, then what difference does it make whether history is based on historical facts or mythology? No one would argue that history is open to different interpretations. But these different interpretations have to be based on facts and data that can be reasonably and objectively verified. Fake history does away with historical objectivity altogether. And the traffic in fake history moves in both directions: historical facts are mythologised and pure mythology is transformed into factual history.

The best examples of this tendency come from India. Under the Hindu Nationalist government of the Bharatiya Janata Party (BJP), Indian history has become a major contested territory focused on the construction of 'the new Hindu history'. BJP equates this with 'national history'. Here, the mythological characters of Hinduism are painted as real and real history is presented as epic mythology. Consider Ram, the central god of Hinduism. The traditional Ram of Hindu religiosity is a tender and tolerant god, a mythological character that inhabits the memories of traditional Hindus. The new Hindu history turns him into a historical fact: a linear construction totally devoid of the multi-layered complexity and richness of the Ram of mythology. He now becomes an intolerant, violent Ram hell-bent on war against Muslims – despite the fact that even if he existed, he existed several thousand years before Islam. As a real historical figure, he has real historical sites, places and buildings associated with him, which must now be cleansed of the influence of other religions and cultures. This has led nationalist Hindus to demolish the famous Babri mosque in Ayodhya where Ram is supposed to have built a temple. They have also declared over 2,000 Muslim monuments, including the Taj Mahal in Agra and the Jamia Mosque in Delhi, as originally built by Hindu rulers, or built on the site of Hindu temples.

Factual history is turned into mythology by submerging it in politics and ideology and attaching 'epic qualities' to historical events and situations. So, for example, specific historical battles between Muslims and Hindus are transformed into perpetual and eternal struggles. In this way, history is rooted out of its context and becomes timeless. The mythic time schemes leak into historical, realist time, giving much leeway to a politicised 'Us' against a perceived historical enemy, 'Them'. The historical narrative simultaneously becomes narrow – trapped in certain places and events with external villains and internal victims – and circular, returning to the same events, symbols and sentiments over and over again. So history becomes a sacred blend of cultural logic, social organisation, ideological convictions and political programme. Fake history can thus be anything and often becomes everything.

Of course, this is not unique to nationalist Hindus. The Islamic history on which the Taliban constructed their Afghanistan was just as fabricated, mythologised and politicised. Afrocentric history often elevates African myths to the status of historical facts. A great deal of postmodern history suffers from the same cultural logic. Works which selectively cut and paste characters, events and situations from a span of a thousand years run the risk of presenting history as though it was a designer consumer product. Such fake histories often confuse interpretation with the interests of particular groups or fashionable trends.

What is lost is not just history but the very craft of the historian. Historical objectivity disappears and history is reduced to propaganda. Fake history is propaganda masquerading as scholarship. Propaganda, by definition, is a means of social control that relies on techniques that induce individuals and social groups to follow sectional interests and emotional drives. Propaganda is a matter of expediency and not morality so it makes no difference whether the 'facts' it is based on are true or false. The moral force of history is thus undermined and history becomes a mere instrument.

Fake history brings us back to fake reality. Virtual reality, as we all know, is more real, more heightened, more fun. But it also expunges life of real blood and sweat, dirt and grime, pain and suffering. And just as fake history loses its moral imperative, fake reality has no place for morality – only expediency and contingency. It is not just that we are incapable of telling the difference when the fake is better than what it imitates – we can never really discover the difference. Thus all realities become on a par with each other, all truths become relative and all objectivity is reduced to a charade. No wonder most politicians have serious problems remembering whether they slept with someone or not!

So what becomes of real pain and suffering, injustice and oppression out there: is it all lies, mere simulations, or are there real people enduring real hardship and cruelty?

For a world that claims that all reality is socially constructed, which promotes lies as the norm, the pain, suffering and death of other people are particularly unreal. The culture of lies and fakes serves as an insulating space that isolates those who live in a world of countless choices, including the choice to acquire fake breasts and identities, from those whose only choice is to be the unwilling victims of the modern and postmodern world. This is why real pain and suffering, hunger and famine, seldom move people. Six thousand children have died in Iraq every month since sanctions were first imposed in 1990, yet when 6,000 people died in the World Trade Centre attacks a war was started – it was real because it happened in their own country. People are happy to give a few pence to charity, but they do not really want to do anything positive about it – attack its real causes, stand up and defend the poor and the oppressed or speak out and fight against an unjust global economy. Notice how often 'charity' is combined with entertainment – its real function is not to eliminate suffering but to increase the enjoyment of those who wish to ease their guilty conscience. Fake reality, and the extreme anti-realist and irrational doctrine that goes with it, generate complacency and a permanent crisis of moral and political nerve among the middle and upper classes – the very people who are capable of raising their voices against policies and actions undertaken, often in their name, by those in power.

It is not possible for us to morally justify ceaseless oppression of non-Western societies and cultures or of the poor and the marginalised in Western society. So the culture of lies provides us with a new alibi. It postulates that no moral stance is actually possible. Since all moral positions are equally valid or equally absurd, none is possible, and one might as well learn to enjoy the status quo. From the patently sensible assertion that culture cannot be grasped as a true or false representation of reality – as Marxists, for example, have argued for decades – we now have the absurd postmodern theses that all is fake and fake is better than anything real. That real is no longer real, that reality is but an illusion, that there is nothing but a perpetual and endless reconstruction of realities, that truth, history and arguments are nothing more than free-floating language games.

From here, the next step of showing that oppressive and imperialistic policies and actions are nothing but representations of social reality and proving them to be totally unreal is a short one. Pain, suffering, oppression become as fake as Pamela Anderson's breasts.

Yet there are factual and moral truths out there that are as real as the 'smart bombs' that (mistakenly?) landed on civilian dwellings in Baghdad during the Gulf War or the daisycutters that landed in Kabul and other cities of Afghanistan. There are real truths that stand above disagreements between competing viewpoints, that can be argued, that are amenable to historical evidence, and that involve standards of verifiable warrant and accountability. There are real people who are going through real suffering right now.

The most famous line in Orwell's *1984* reads: 'Who controls the past controls the future; who controls the present controls the past.' This formula now is slightly out of date. Today, who controls the fake controls reality and thus controls the past, the present and the future. In our post-modern world, fakes and simulations have grown so large that they entirely cover the things they imitate. Lies not only make you look good, they can also bring you untold riches and power. In the case of celebrity breasts, this is literally true. The culture of true lies, of imitation, of fake bodies, fake reality, fake commodities, fake history, is all about power and control.

Unlike the real, which is unpredictable, unmanageable and therefore uncontrollable, the fake is totally predictable and manageable, thus so much easier to control. And, it seeks to control all those things that we value most in ourselves – our Self, our identity, our bodies, our imagination, all that makes us human. The only size that matters is the size of our humanity. We ought to remember this next time we ogle a fake breast.

Lists

Unbridled generosity has arrived at my local Sainsbury's petrol station. A few weeks ago, they awarded me a medal simply for filling my car with their petrol. The medal is a splendid silver coin: one side is adorned with an optimistic logo and the declaration 'into a new millennium'; the other side contains an impressive portrait of Gandhi encircled with the legend, 'Makers of the Millennium'. I was invited by the attendant to buy a richly illustrated album to store my collection of medals as a unique record of the achievements of the last thousand years.

Sainsbury's list of 21 men and one woman 'whose vision and determination, flair and compassion have shaped the world we live in' is only one of numerous lists out there. To begin with, there is Random House's *Modern Library* list, Waterstone's the bookseller's list of *100 Books That Made the Century* and Sky television's list of 'Movies of the Millennium' (an interesting concept given that motion pictures have been with us for only a century). The National Portrait Gallery offers the 'List of 100 Iconic Images', while radio station Classic FM has the 'Music of the Millennium' list. The television station, Channel 4, combines with the *Observer* newspaper to produce a 'Power List', not to mention lists of best actors, directors, pop music and restaurants. Indeed, you can have lists of anything; and apparently there are people who collect lists of lists. Journalist Hunter Davies has even produced a *Book of British Lists*; as if that wasn't enough, he moved triumphantly to *Hunter Davies' Bigger Book of British Lists*.

The trouble with all these lists is, of course, the universally attested truism that they are perversely inaccurate. The top 10 of anything, in list form, invariably puts the most obvious first choice well down the order in favour of some inane, unworthy or purely modish selection. For example, Waterstone's *100 Books That Made the Century* has Tolkien's *The Lord of the Rings* miles ahead as number one, while Joyce's *Ulysses* struggles for the number four spot. So the list has controversy built in. Indeed, the existence of a list excites one's comparative juices only to appal and confound one's sense of justice and cast doubt on other people's powers of reasoning.

This is why lists are guaranteed to attract attention and generate fuss. Which makes them a good bet as a promotional gimmick. All you need is an anniversary, some timely hook. Hence, each year, during the what-to-give season, books of useless lists, all topically updated, crowd the shelves of bookshops. There was never an anniversary quite like the millennium. The overtones of millenarian foreclosure, the end of everything frisson, positively required summation and summary judgement. So all the organs of the media went totally bonkers and filled every free space, air wave and visual signal with a dumbfounding variety of lists.

All of which suggests that lists are useless things. They are a passing fad, and like the millennium they too will pass away. We should be so lucky! Lists are now a standard feature of our cultural landscape, and will exist as long as we continue to exist.

A number of obvious reasons explain the continuing utility of lists. First, lists have become the intellectual counterpart of shopping. The album that comes with Sainsbury's 'Makers' is designed like a catalogue from 'Past Times'. You read it like a shopping catalogue – but it has the added illusion of communicating knowledge. That which is mentioned on the list is a 'must have' item of connoisseur living, readily available from some vendor if it's a book, or film, or something that can be commodified. In a postmodern era when fragmentation is the norm, lists present scattered bits of information as synthesised knowledge. Not for nothing are the collected parts of the *Independent*'s weekly lists of 50 best clubs, 50 best gardens, 50 best museums and so on *ad nauseam*, dubbed *The Knowledge*. The inference is that knowing the top 10 of anything is equivalent to knowing the thing itself; knowing the top 10 classics is like actually reading them. The list is the route map to familiarity with the essential landmarks of cultural orientation. To know they exist, to be able to drop their names in conversation, is the contemporary alchemist's lodestone of cultural competence.

Second, lists provide assurance of certainty and quality in a world where everything has become relative and all things are supposedly interchangeable. For example, the whole idea of excellence has become a subject of parody and its very existence is questioned. So, lists of canons and classics, best films and actors, greatest scientists of the last century, most memorable celebrities, however much we may dispute them, create an illusion of standards and quality in a world where 'dumbing down' is the norm. They suggest that excellence is still out there, even though popular culture itself is awash with mediocrity.

Third, lists are a very good device for setting an agenda. Consider one of the most amusing juxtapositions in Sainsbury's 'Makers'. Wolfgang Amadeus Mozart is selected as the key personality in the performing arts category. Meanwhile, the category of music belongs to Live Aid, which, if memory serves, was an event, a cause, a brief heady moment rather than a specific musical endeavour or achievement. Moreover, while the list pigeonholes a thousand years into 21 names, it needs two whole categories for sport: Sport 1 and Sport 2. Clearly, this is a nod to pop music and our youth- and sport-obsessed culture. An agenda is at work here, and a list is nothing if not a product of an agenda: cultural, political, populist and intellectual. And one must say racist, since the only representation of African-Americans, or indeed Africans at all, is in the doubly selected field of sporting endeavour: Jesse Owens and Muhammad Ali. And by the way, when it comes to the millennium of anything China just need not apply. Which, like it or not, is perverse when you consider how much this millennium owes to paper, compass and gunpowder!

But there are deeper reasons why lists will have a constant presence in the future. We are going through a phase of rapid change. Three forces in particular are making the world anew: globalisation, democratisation and decolonisation. Each of these forces is transforming the shape of culture, art and literature and the way they are perceived and studied. Globalisation, for example, has enabled a modicum of cultural products to travel from the East to the West. Hence, the sudden popularity in Europe and America of such things as Quawwali, the devotional music of the Sufis, exemplified by the sky-rocketing sales of cassettes and CDs by the late Nurat Fatahullah Khan. Or the discovery that Iran and China produce more original, and truly cinematic, artistic films than Hollywood. The appearance of so many Indian novelists (including the Indian Diaspora) on the Booker Prize list suggests that India, rather than England, is the true home of the contemporary English novel. Not surprisingly, such developments are (consciously and unconsciously) perceived by the West as a threat to its cultural domination. Lists provide a way of reclaiming increasingly dissipating power.

Ultimately, lists, like Sainsbury's 'Makers', Waterstone's *Books That Made the Century* and Sky's 'Movies of the Millennium', are expressions of cultural power. The relationship between lists and power is best demonstrated by the grandest list of all: the Western canon. The Greek word 'canon' means 'reed', and also 'measuring stick'. The canon is supposed to represent the yardstick for measuring civilisation. But a canon is also a cannon – an armament for bombarding other pretenders and their claims to civilisation, such as India, Islam, China, Japan, Africa. This is why so much cultural energy is spent on producing lists of canons and classics.

Lists derive their power partly from their educational value, their use in nurturing the future generation. The debate about Western canons, for example, is a debate about what should be taught at universities. Or: how should we indoctrinate our children with our (Anglo-Saxon) culture.

This is why so much academic blood, particularly in America, has been spilt over lists; and why they are so hotly disputed and discredited by blacks, Asians and other 'post-colonial' people. In his highly praised tome, *The Western Canon: The Books and School of the Ages*, Harold Bloom presents the debate in terms of a holy war. The Canon is always capitalised and perpetually under attack from anti-canonisers: Feminists, Afrocentrists, Marxists, Blacks, Asians, etc.

Bloom is right in seeing the battle over the canon in particular, and the whole notion of lists in general, in religious terms. Classics do not elect themselves; they have to be selected. Lists have to be made by somebody, preferably by highly placed opinion formers. Like saints, classics are canonised. In a world that has lost all notions of the sacred, classics serve a religious and spiritual function. Lists thus acquire a holy connotation; they provide us with something to admire, to look up to, to believe in.

We now read lists as once we read the Bible – just as devotedly and seriously. Sky's 'Movies of the Millennium', for example, will be pored over and endlessly analysed by countless media and film studies students. Sainsbury's 'Makers', clearly aimed at schoolchildren, will be the subject of study in the classroom.

The religious connotations of lists are enhanced by claims to universality. Anything that is at the top of the heap of the best this-or-that must, by definition, be 'timeless', and therefore universal. The National Film Registry of the Library of Congress has a list of 200 classic films (all American, need I add) that have been saved for all time. The British Film Institute has its own list of 360 films, one for each day of the year we are told (they can't count at the BFI), which are supposed to have universal appeal and, as such, must be saved for posterity. Just as all those who are exposed to the truths of a religion must adhere to the faith or be judged as heretics, so we must acknowledge the universal truth inherent in these films or be judged philistines. And, if by chance some calamity strikes us all, we can die happy in the knowledge that civilisation will be salvaged by these timeless and universal cultural products.

As a device for arresting multi-culturalism and other forces of cultural contamination, lists perform their magic in two basic ways. First, they tie the past, as imagined by the West, to a global future. So advances in contemporary philosophic, historic and sociological scholarship, that have exposed the notion that the West is the beginning and end of all civilisation as a grand delusion, are brushed aside. Lists rely on a paradoxical cultural memory that, on the one hand, is firmly rooted in the age of Empire and, on the other, relies extensively on yesterday.

Take – and take it as far away from me as you can – Sainsbury's 'Makers'. You can rest assured that nothing of any importance happened during the millennium until it was almost half over. The earliest name on the list belongs to Leonardo da Vinci, who lived in the 15th century and who makes the list in the category 'Visionaries and Inventors'. This is the nod to name identification, since as a visionary and inventor Leonardo cribbed a great deal from Roger Bacon, of whom popularisers know no one has heard. And anyway, Roger Bacon was a product of an intellectual upsurge, the 12th-century Renaissance, sponsored by Europe's debt to the learning of Muslim civilisation, a connection far too close for comfort. We can of course brush over the fact than none of Leonardo's inventions worked – in scientific terms, as a visionary and inventor he was a jolly good painter – since such concerns are not the interest or province of simple listing. The point, however, is that by starting with Leonardo's doodles the previous five centuries of largely non-Western history are wiped clean. All of the work of the millennium falls on the shoulders of Britain and the US, with the occasional input from Italy, Germany and Holland. Of the 21 categories listed, only six have anything to do with the past, that is a past beyond the 20th century. The life we live now, our current perceptions, are what will take us into the new millennium. For all the supposed backward reflection, we can safely rid ourselves of almost everything that is not of the 20th century. In the category 'Time' we have John Harrison, of whom no one had heard until the publication, in 1995, of Dava Sobel's bestseller, *Longitude*. It is as though we have made no intellectual progress in the last four decades;

the world continues, as it has always done, in the way of the West.

The perception of the nature of time is one of the things that has changed most during the last few decades, and most dramatically over the millennium. In recent 'time' the notion of linear progress stands thoroughly discredited. But it was even more incomprehensible to anyone before the Enlightenment. 'Time' as an entity in which continuous progressive change takes place was only firmly established in the post-Darwinian era, basically the last 100 years. But Sainsbury's 'Makers', like so many lists, offers us a sense of history that is deeply linear and unashamedly Victorian. The last thousand years were created and shaped solely by the West; other cultures were merely passive spectators. A list that begins with 'Time' and ends with 'The Future', which you may not be too pleased to learn belongs to Bill Gates, obviously has concerns other than historic accuracy, fair representation of non-Western cultures, or just plain common sense. It is hardly a work of the mind, but it is certainly a work of power and dominance.

Second, while the world becomes increasingly plural, lists create a delusion of monolithic unity. Demands for pluralism are forcing many institutions, course outlines and reading lists to include a wider range of cultural products, to incorporate material from outside the mainstream of European and American culture. Lists counteract this tendency by suggesting that a homogeneous and overarching culture is endorsed throughout the globe and everyone, no matter what their creed or colour, will enjoy and endorse the selected items.

So who would object to Henry Ford, selected in the Sainsbury's list in the 'Transport' category? He was, after all, the man who enabled us all to have a car in any colour we chose so long as it was black (though I prefer to believe he earned his place on the list by declaring that 'History is bunk'). Or who would dare say anything against Neil Armstrong, everyone's 'Space' hero? But the cynics could ask: did Armstrong, or even Kennedy and NASA, take us to space? Or was it Werner von Braun? Would the space programme of the US or Russia be imaginable without the capture by each side of the leading minds of Hitler's rocket programme? But to concede that humanity's supposed achievements in space owe their inception to the militarist racism of Hitler, and his ability to capture the German scientific class to do his bidding, would be nothing short of serious cultural pollution. It is not the kind of thing we can teach our children. The aim of list-making is not to recognise foundational achievements or inspire historic honesty, but to present instantly recognised names and a sanitised trajectory for understanding how a recreation of the past is involved with how we live now and will make our way into the future. An iconic name makes a list look and sound good and creates the illusion of cultural consensus and unity while allowing the list to advance its real intentions, to work as an instrument of power and dominance.

There is, however, one area where lists have succumbed to historical forces. We can now notice the impact of the democratic 'winds of change' on most lists. Sky's 'Movies of the Millennium', for example, is a product of popular opinion. And what a sorry lot the public turns out to be. The greatest film of all time? *Star Wars.* Arguably a contender, if only because it is the highest money earner of all time – another list. But how on earth did the execrable *Titanic* get to be number 2? The answer is contained in the list itself. Of the 100 films listed only six were made before 1950. So all time turns out to be a very short period in the public memory, a suspicion borne out by the fact that the nostalgia films for the eighties and nineties are already with us. It goes without saying that the people who bother to fill in the questionnaire have seen very few films indeed. Which means that such lists can be easily dismissed.

In contrast, the expert list purports to be a matter of considered, mature and reasoned judgement. 'We have thought long and hard', says the introduction to Sainsbury's 'Makers'. That's why they included Gandhi, one of the two outsiders (the other being Mother Teresa) on the list in the category of 'Great Leaders – Peace'. The Mahatma would have understood perfectly that his name has a wide currency, though I doubt he would have taken it peacefully. The cornerstone of his philosophy was *ahimsa*, or non-violence. His cause was non-violent guerrilla war against all forms of subjugation, which in his mind was associated largely with colonialism. He laid the blame for colonialism solely on the shoulders of Western civilisation. Indeed, he wasn't too happy with putting the terms 'Western' and 'civilisation' next to each other. When a reporter asked him what he thought of Western civilisation, Gandhi replied, 'I think it would be a good idea'. So, it is more than a little ironic that a list that so violently glorifies Western civilisation uses Gandhi as an instrument for legitimacy and wider recognition. It is as though all that the Mahatma stood for, said and wrote excites only silence. His name has recognition value, but his philosophy is irrelevant. In lists you can do what you could not do in history: you can colonise the very idea of Gandhi.

Multiculturalism

Multiculturalism stinks. This is the consensus of both the Left and the Right. Stench is the usual fate of produce left out in the open air for too long. And multiculturalism has been around for decades, it has been looked at, into, poked and prodded more diligently than the most interesting medical curiosity, reported on, bemoaned and ventured beyond. We are still as far as ever from delivering a modicum of multiculturalism, or, indeed, understanding what it ought to mean.

We understand multiculturalism to be the recognition that societies are pluralistic and consist of distinct cultures and different ethnic components. This view of multiculturalism is little more than a truism. Most societies are, and have been in history, multicultural. India, for example, has always consisted of a plethora of cultures and ethnicities. Even Britain was multicultural before multiculturalism was invented: the Welsh, the Irish, the Scots are not just different people, they are also different languages, cultures, histories, a fact now acknowledged by devolution.

A more specific view of multiculturalism describes it as an eclectic mix of races that now live under the same geographical umbrella in Europe and America. It is assumed that at some point this mix of cultures would synthesise, generating hybridised cultural experiences, influenced by various strands and practices from all the different races. In some respects, we have already reached this multicultural nirvana. The food we eat, the clothes we wear, the way we furnish our homes, all show strong influences garnered from immigrant communities. And our art, literature and movies now reflect the many voices and cultures that make up the racial mix of modern Western society. Yet, despite all this 'ethnic' influence, racial harmony is conspicuous by its stark absence.

In Britain, multiculturalism comes chronologically after 'assimilation' and 'integration'. In the fifties and sixties, the politics of assimilation aimed at wiping out the cultural identity of the immigrant communities. In the seventies and the early eighties, integration policies were designed to transform immigrant groups into indistinguishable 'members' of the dominant culture. Multiculturalism appeared after the failure of such hegemonic exercises and focused on 'celebrating difference'. It was actually imported from America where it replaced the 'melting pot' of earlier black and immigrant generations with what David Dinkins, the first African-American Mayor of New York, called a 'gorgeous mosaic'. The emphasis, once again, was on racial and ethnic difference. So accent on difference became a key component of multiculturalism.

Indeed, champions of multiculturalism have turned difference, and ethnicities based on race and difference, into a fetish. The 'vision' of *The Future of Multi-ethnic Britain* (2000), the so-called Parekh Report, for example, is based squarely on difference. 'The fundamental need, both practical and theoretical', the report says, is to 'treat people with due respect for difference'. Over the past decades, both Conservative and Labour governments have been insisting that minorities demonstrate and interminably celebrate their difference. Difference is a hot commodity in our art galleries and museums where it is regularly constructed, fabricated and paraded as a sign of enlightened plurality.

The undue emphasis on difference and ethnicity has not only turned multiculturalism into a commodity, it has made true multiculturalism an impossibility. This is not an accidental result, but a product of initial design. As currently understood, multiculturalism is intrinsically an American construction and incorporates all the assumptions and experiences of American history. To appreciate why multiculturalism has failed so demonstrably, we need to grasp why America does not work as a pluralistic society.

The US is a nation conceived, born, reared and nurtured by immigrant communities. The nation was invented from the essence and as the epitome of all that should be learned from the failures of the Old World. Yet, even constitutionally, it is unable to get from '*I pluribus unum*' to '*in unum pluribus*' – from official motto of 'from many, one' to a sustainable, acceptable reality of 'in one, many'. Why? Because America is the ultimate product of Western colonialism. Whereas colonialism was what European nations did abroad, it is how America came to be on the ground it stole and ethnically cleansed to call home. The ideology of colonialism, with all its assumptions about race, ethnicity and difference, is how Europe looked at the rest of the world; but it is how America looked at itself and forged its self-identity at home.

So, the American notion of multiculturalism is constructed securely behind the walls of colonial structures of power. What it had to say about self-evident truths concerning life, liberty and the pursuit of happiness was the extent of its multiculturalism. The visions of equality before the law and separation of power between church and state were designed specifically to make a multicultural white society possible. These were lessons well learnt from the Old World, where, as Thomas Jefferson so cogently argued, inordinate amounts of blood had been spilled and still failed to make everyone conform and produce uniform orthodoxy. The question avoided rather than overlooked was how the principles of libertarian rights could apply to non-whites – to native peoples seen as savages and blacks owned as property, both, nevertheless, being extant non-persons within the nation state.

The horrors of America's historic failure to include Native Americans and blacks and then the Chinese within its notion of plurality were addressed during the seventies and eighties in two ways. The first option was ethnicity. Ethnic pride was the entitlement the system bestowed on those whites it assimilated but who were not the ideal, the archetypal WASP, white Anglo-Saxon Protestant, such as the Irish, the Polish, the

Russians and the Jews. When the question arose what to do about the excluded ethnicities, the answer was simply to indulge them. So, the hitherto excluded Native Americans and blacks acquired ethnic labels and permission to wear their ethnicity and historic victimhood on their sleeves.

The second option may be called legal individualism. Individualism is the cornerstone of Western liberal thought and the basic premise of American constitutional philosophy. The very idea of equality is based on individualism. So, treating the excluded ethnicities as equal meant giving them equal treatment before the law. What this means for true equality turns out to be, in American history, a double-edged sword. One way southern states subverted the abolition of slavery, for example, was by inventing the 'separate but equal' formula that led to separate black schools, lunch counters, drinking fountains and the like. Similarly, equal individualism for Native Americans meant the drive to convert tribal reservations into individually owned plots of land. It was also the impetus behind the sixties Civil Rights legislation where the law was supposedly 'colour blind', treating each individual citizen equally irrespective of race or ethnicity.

But far from making multiculturalism a reality, mixing equality and ethnicity generates new kinds of problems. Talking up ethnicity leads to fragmentation. And if each individual has an equal and immutable right of attachment to distinct and separate ethnicities with full rights of self-expression, difference becomes an unsolvable, enduring problem. Worse, those who do not regard themselves as members of distinct and separate ethnicities – like the youth – then manufacture new ethnicities to show their distinction. The insatiable desire for difference can never be satisfied – it can only lead to perpetual dissatisfaction, frustration, animosity and riots.

When black Americans travel the ethnicity route they have to begin by creative recovery of a diverse identity out of Africa. They face the problem of identity ripped from them and the discovery of an identity that is equally demeaned and disparaged by white, Western civilisation.

African ethnicity is not one entity, but any African ethnicity, along with any non-European ethnicity, becomes another battleground because of the impossibility of equivalence. The white majority do not see African ethnicity, or various Asian ethnicities, as anything other than completely different and inferior. When American blacks show pride in their ethnicity by teaching black children their ethnic heritage, howls of protest are raised about diluting the inviolable sanctity of the Western Canon as the true embodiment of all that is noble in the human heritage. Afrocentric education, far from providing positive reinforcement for black children, centres them in another vortex of marginalisation. Afrocentric ethnicity is not an option for inclusion but proof of why they have been excluded. And it does nothing to combat the social and economic legacy of their marginalisation within America and its history. This is precisely why the ethnic route does not deliver multiculturalism.

The legal route does not fare much better either. The law signals the intentions of society, but is a rather blunt instrument for actually changing the attitudes of society. So equality may be declared through law, but it cannot be delivered by law. At law, black Americans are more likely to be charged, convicted, incarcerated and executed than any other group. As the legal rolls in the famed Florida recount debacle of the 2000 presidential election proved, blacks are more easily and more likely to be disenfranchised by law. Laws that make everyone equal fail to address enduring disadvantage or redress the issues of communal repression. Perceptions about groups and communities, the weight of history, and the differences of historic experience all affect the reality of what is called equality of opportunity and ensure that the status quo continues to generate inequality. Making the law theoretically colour blind effectively works to keep non-white ethnicities in their place and leaves ample scope for whites to evade the problem of equality by moving to the suburbs, removing themselves from contact with the non-white underclass.

By following the American model, Britain is repeating the failures and experiences of American history. We promote multiculturalism as an ideology of difference in a legal framework that insists that everyone is the same and makes no allowances for difference. Our courts, police and prison system, as in America, are institutionally biased against non-white ethnicities. We even have our own version of the 'long hot summer', the epithet first coined for the 'racial urban unrest' in American cities in the sixties.

All this, however, does not mean that multiculturalism is a bad idea. In fact, it is a profound idea, the very thing we actually, in practical reality, genuinely need. Multiculturalism is a necessary quest not just for any self-respecting society, but for human social evolution as such. Multicul-turalism is failing simply because the version on offer does not and cannot make concessions on the hierarchical superiority of the Western worldview. Multiculturalism has escaped us because it cannot be recon-ciled with liberal individualism, the cornerstone of Western society. Multiculturalism has been so unsuccessful because it is offered as a one-way traffic, something that the white community does for the 'ethnic minorities'. Multiculturalism is coming under attack from all sides, because both the Left and the Right realise that any socially viable version challenges the vindication of their inherent rightness and right-eousness. In the final analysis, multiculturalism fails because what is on offer is not *multi*-cultural at all.

Multiculturalism is essentially about two things. First, it is an issue of power in all its aspects. The fear of many right-wing critics is totally jus-tified: multiculturalism is all about subverting the power of Western civilisation. This was obvious from the moment multiculturalism became a movement in America. That crucial moment occurred in 1987 at Stan-ford University when Reverend Jesse Jackson led a march by about 500 students chanting 'Hey hey, ho ho, Western Culture's got to go'. The stu-dents were referring to a specific course and seeking its replacement with one that stressed the cultural accomplishments of women and ethnic minorities. I wouldn't say that Western culture per se has to go but its power to define what it is to be human, different, rational or ethnic, what is valuable, worthwhile, successful and proper, certainly has to go.

Listen to noted American historian Arthur Schlesinger Jr and you will know what I mean. Europe, writes Schlesinger in *The Disuniting of America: Reflections on a Multicultural Society*, is 'the unique source' of all the 'liberating ideas' of 'individual liberty, political democracy, equality before the law, freedom of worship, human rights, and cultural freedom that constitute our most precious legacy and to which most of the world today aspires. These are *European* ideas, not Asian, nor African, nor Middle Eastern ideas'. This kind of pathological arrogance raises an important question: if Europe is the only source of all that is good, valuable and necessary, then what need is there for multiculturalism? Other cultures should either commit suicide or abandon themselves to total assimilation in the West.

If no good can be seen in other cultures and their enduring values, multiculturalism is as impossible as it is futile. A civilisation with the arrogance to exonerate itself from any need for guilt, that cannot even acknowledge that slavery and colonialism are crimes against humanity, is intent only on retaining the hierarchies of history and the power structures of dominance by permanent denial of the history and philosophic and moral complexity of the rest of the world.

Second, multiculturalism is all about transformation. Here we are not just talking about transforming the poor inner-city blacks and Asians by providing them with economic and educational opportunities but also of transforming Western society itself, so we move from the irrational premise that 'they' – all the ethnic others – see the errors of their ways and become more like 'us', to the humane idea that Western culture is as deeply flawed as all other human cultures. Multiculturalism does not require more commitment to liberal values in Western societies, as Bhiku Parekh argues in *Rethinking Multiculturalism*. Rather, it requires a transformation of liberal values to more inclusive forms.

What we assume to be naturally good and wholesome in liberalism often turns out to be rather limited. For example, the classical, liberal notions of 'freedom', all the way from Mill to Rawls, do not have a place for the marginalised and the poor. In his essay *On Liberty*, Mill excluded 'the backward nations', women and children from the rights to liberty; and John Rawls, in his celebrated *Theory of Justice*, acknowledges that societies where the basic needs of the individuals are not fulfilled do not fit into his framework of liberty. There is no way you can build multiculturalism on such exclusivist ideas.

Transformation requires that we move from the simplistic notion of multiculturalism as a tolerated extension of Western liberalism to a sophisticated process that aims to transform and transcend liberalism itself. This process has to begin with the realisation that liberalism is neither a Western invention nor a Western concern; it is, and has always been, part of all traditions. We need to transcend the hegemony of such ideas as liberal individualism to realise that groups and communities too have rights. And we have to realise that multiculturalism is a partner project – it requires full and equal partnership with other cultures in shaping modernity, postmodernity and the human future.

The failure of multiculturalism suggests that our cherished notions of cultural diversity and equality are still in their infancy. It should lead us not to abandon multiculturalism but to question the limited nature of our supposedly perfect liberal ideals. Multiculturalism is not something that we offer to 'minorities' and 'ethnic communities'. It is something that the majority white communities need to preserve their humanity. After multiculturalism comes even more multiculturalism.

Noise

I hate to say this, but you are going deaf. In fact, we are all going deaf. If you ever get a chance to listen, and opportunities are increasingly rare, you will realise that we are drowning in noise – inescapable, unnecessary, insidious noise.

A great deal of this noise is merely our machines doing their own thing in their own distinctive fashion. Aircrafts taking off, cars starting and stopping, trains speeding in and out of stations. Televisions, radios, CD players and hi-fis at maximum volume. Traffic, burglar alarms, police and ambulance sirens. Jackhammers, steamrollers, trucks pouring cement on motorways that are perpetually being repaired. Cranes, bulldozers, drills and God knows what else on building sites. Washing machines, dishwashers, vacuum cleaners, central heating pumps in the home. Lawnmowers, hedge-trimmers and shredders in the garden. Phones and faxes ringing everywhere. Whirrs, throbs, hums, hisses, clunks, clanks and thunks of all regular, calibrated and cyclical variety. This is the ever-present, Dolby surround noise of the city, any city, that is always there to irritate all and sundry.

The city, I am inclined to think, was created specifically to abolish quiet. Quiet is a vacuum abhorred by planners, devisers, builders and purveyors of all stripe and hue. The city is the abode of the human creative impulse gone rabid, or more poetically, turned Faustian. The bargain with the devil is noise, the very intimation of hell. The city is the antithesis of silence, an impossible reality that purposefully sets out to deny the existence of an impossible ideal. The essence of the city is the real ghetto blaster. Wherever there is a space, wherever people come together, there must be noise.

If all this noise was not enough, the city is always alive with other people's noise. Think, if you can bear it, of the noise leakage of other people's Walkmans on the tube, as if the underground were not noise polluted enough without their lack of consideration. Or the constant ringing of mobile phones on the road, in trains, buses, shops and restaurants. But the city is also full of purposefully deployed noise that has no other function than to distract us from the noise of the city. There is indeed a highly trained pestiferous breed of professionals whose training consists of thinking up new vacuums to fill with new kinds of noise. So, someone somewhere, and may they be abominated beyond the end of time itself, invented background music. It's not enough that a city makes noise just to exist, you have to layer the effect like icing on an American dessert, inches thick. Is there anyone alive who can remember when music was something you sat and listened to? When music was a harmonic experience that by means of sound transported you to quiet? Of course, the only way to let harmonic sound work its trick is to listen intently. Background music, by design and definition, is merely a space filler, a vacuum denier. Musick, the acronym for what makes you sick, is noise that no one imagines anyone will ever listen to. And they have found whole new vacuums to stuff it into. No longer merely the infestation of plastic hotel lobbies and lifts, it is now, just to edge your hellish experience up a notch or two, poured directly down your earlobes while you are hanging, almost at your wit's ends, on telephones. The Internet is full of it, as are computers, which bleep, bloop and jingle at any and every opportunity, and video games flood their blasting, banging, shooting and walloping with mundane, high-decibel musick.

We are getting used to this kind of noise layering. Think of moronic radio disc jockeys who keep you company with extraneous noise in the midst of honking cars in traffic jams. Or the fact that nowadays, no office is complete without a television set replete with 24-hour broadcasting where you can hear endless background drivel from twittering certifiable idiots while you wait to watch a live non-event. There is CNN, Sky News and BBC News 24. Worse still, Bloomberg, where imbeciles of even greater magnitude talk themselves into paroxysms about the second by second movement of blips that are displayed as the visual pollution accompaniment to all this noise pollution. We city types have been brainwashed to think of all this noise pollution as progress. But, contemplate for a moment the terminology we apply to go-getting in the city – the rat race. The essence of a rat in a maze is the absence of escape – there is no way out. The Faustian bargain writ large. For all those nice nibbly bits at the end of the maze, new and innovative ways to generate noise, you get caught beyond escape in a web of someone else's making, muttering fruitlessly, 'Will it ever end?', knowing full well that it never will.

Postmodernists (these are the witless who have spent their whole lives within the increasingly noise-polluted environment of cities and who therefore make virtues out of inescapable evils) are fond of telling us that words are all we have. Or put another way, noise is it. But if all we have is communication by sound transmuted into noise why is there no place left except, at certain hours on certain days, the reading room of the British Library where you can have quiet? A quiet conversation is as extinct as a T Rex.

Recently a friend and I, bent on earnest discussion, tramped the streets like lepers in search of a haven, trying to find a place where we could have the quiet in which to hear ourselves think what we were saying. Wherever we went, noise, musick, hubbub followed. In restaurants, pubs, coffee houses and hotel lobbies, the hubbub of conversations and dishes bounced from glass, oak and chrome – materials so beloved of nineties designers – amplifying the noise as people shouted to be heard over others who were also shouting to be heard. It has not occurred to anyone that smooth surfaces and hard wooden floors bounce sound waves back and forth, thus amplifying the noise of conversation and cutlery. When you add musick, the effect is thunderous.

Why do we accept this level of noise? Largely because we are afraid of what we think is the opposite of noise – silence. Conventionally, we associate silence with suffering, oppression, isolation and death. Think of Keats' poem 'This Living Hand' where quiet is buried in 'the icy silence of the tomb'. Or Thomas Mann's equation where 'speech is civilisation itself' but the other side, silence, is death and isolation. Similarly, Bernard Shaw saw silence as 'the most perfect expression of scorn', R. L. Stevenson announced that 'cruellest lies are often told in silence' and Friedrich von Schiller declared that 'great souls suffer in silence'. More recently, Harold Pinter's 'comedies of menace' have invested silence with nameless intimidation and suffering. Historically, silence has been associated with denial, particularly denial of the voice of the oppressed – silence denied women and other minorities their right to be heard. In prisons, the worst possible punishment is 'solitary confinement' where the prisoner exists in total silence and solitude.

We thus live in utter terror of silence. Viewed from this negative perspective, silence becomes an enemy that has constantly to be banished. Indeed, we have exiled silence to the realm of an abstract idea, an unattainable philosophical goal. So, what do those who seek silence and solitude do? They leave the city, the civilised society, and go off into the wilderness. Wrong move!

I have spent quite some time living in the wilderness in South-east Asia. My experience has honed my ears to realise that what we city-bred types think of as silence is a mere absence of manmade noise. The actual entity, silence, absence of sound, however, when contemplated in a tropical clime, reveals itself to be a philosopher's fancy. The world without human intrusion is never silent.

My idyllic retreat was an apartment that nestled up close to a dense secondary forest, a long way from city noise, on the outskirts of Kuala Lumpur. When I moved to my hut in the wilderness, I was adopted by a cricket I lovingly called Jiminy. Every night, he would launch into a violent chorus of chirrup, chirrup, chirrup. So Jiminy taught me what nature lovers never tell us. An unrepentant, unrelenting, unsilent insect can drive you to the kind of distraction normally associated with a jack-hammer rearranging the roadways on a Bank Holiday. What is more, while one can rely on union regulations to eventually terminate the intrusions of the jackhammer, nothing known to man can cease the chirrup of a Jiminy.

It was persistence that caused the cricket to acquire its name. I thought if I talked to it nicely it might, just might, leave me in peace. All to no avail. It took weeks that seemed like years to devise a means to bring a tolerable semblance of silence to my bedroom in the clouds with the spectacular view of the rainforest. By the time I had managed to nuke Jiminy into the pesticidal silence of total extinction, and waited for the toxic waste to evaporate, I was a chastened and changed man. No more Mr Nice Guy, no more ecological sensitivities, no more nonsense about primeval quiet and contemplating natural beauty. An entire civilisational tradition of venerating the peace, the silent beauties of nature, had been revealed as a cruel joke.

In the long watches of the Jiminy-ridden nights my fevered brain, sleep deprived, was working overtime. At first it was all paranoid delusions – I went through the lists of all those criminals who might have decided to subject me to unspeakable torture. But, as many a mystic tradition teaches, beyond the paranoia and delusions there is a state of calm where many things are revealed to the adept willing to subject themselves to the discipline of insight through silence. Thanks to Jiminy, I have been to that place.

There are much simpler ways, of course, to arrive at a new relationship with a sound-filled world. I always thought mystics made a mountain out of some fairly simple molehills, and have you ever listened for the sound it takes to make a molehill? From the very outset I should have realised that my own tradition actually makes explicit what all those mystic traditions have been trying to make us see, but then fail to make apparent because they are off on another kind of trip. In its undiluted, unmystified version, Islamic teaching holds that the natural world is full of signs, signs of God and His creative power. Well, what else does an effective sign do but jump up and down and say, 'Hey, look at me'? All noise, natural or manmade, is a form of advertising.

There you have it: the natural world is just as noisy as the city. It is a sound-filled arena of flashing neon signs with an intermittent oscillating current. Left to its own devices, it is a ghetto blaster-infested domain where every living thing is sounding off to show they exist. They cheep, chirp, chirrup, rasp, grate, rustle, clack (ever heard a stand of bamboo in a breeze?), thunk, occasionally thud and they all have their own distinctive sounds of display, despair and daily routine. The sea is never silent; it's a kind of perpetual generator. The forest or woods, tropical or temperate, are never silent. There's always some activity going on among the foliage, if only the effect of a breath of air – even growing roots signal their displacement of soil if you listen long enough. Then there is the activity of innumerable inhabitants of the natural world out on a spree of showing off their signs. The more you listen, the more you clear away extraneous noise, the more sounds you hear. So where in all this world of hyperactive signalling is silence?

Back to the Jiminy-induced mystic musings. Silence is a transport of elation. The day Jiminy ceased I had one of those mystic highs yogis experience transcendentally. It was not a case of the absence of sound. No, the silence I experienced as seraphic splendour was the removal of irritant sound that had become noise pollution. So silence, by a little reasoning, turns out to be a state of mind. It is a means of slowing down, of becoming aware and opening one's self to a reality greater than the one we live in in our so-called civilised world. I venture to suggest it is a condition of being in harmony with the background and foreground. Silence is an acceptance of sound where no irritant intrudes to disturb the balance, and that means you too Jiminy, oh long departed mystic cricket.

Now that we've hit the mother lode of philosophic insight I can go even further. All this noise pollution is not only taking us to an early grave, it is also making us unbalanced and unhappy people. Noise increases stress hormones, which, as we all know, leads to heart disease. But noise also disturbs us internally. We are constantly chatting to ourselves – the natural quietness of our minds is consistently disturbed by an endless stream of worries, irritations, memories, deliberations, plans. This inner noise, over which we have little control, is aggravated by external noise. Now, we have more of this inner noise inside us than ever before. Our minds are perpetually restless, our attention is always distracted, so wherever we are, whatever we are doing, we are never completely *there*. In short, we are not truly conscious of anything, including our own self. This is a recipe for everlasting unhappiness.

Under such circumstances, silence becomes an act of will. When my children were small they each in turn were what is politely termed in medical handbooks 'hyperactive'. You want signs and extraneous noise, they knew every device to create same in abundance. I, a writer seeking silent contemplative peace to effect my bread-winning livelihood, developed a great ability to filter out all but the life-threatening effusions of my brood. No special talent, it's part of the life support system we parents all develop. Or, thinking more precisely, it's an innate gift of self-absorption we are all equipped with. Ever tried to make a child listen to you when they have something more interesting to think about, listen to or override with their own noise? An act of will, the self-absorption that renders everything else silent. We all have it, and we all learn how to apply it to envelop ourselves in our own silence. Mystics call it meditation; most of us just call it switching off for self-preservation, tuning out the overburdening sounds and noise to catch a quiet breather.

But self-preservation is becoming a dangerously difficult activity. The ridiculously frantic pace of postmodern life, the massive amount of external stimuli and noise we are bombarded with, the barrage of useless information that we have to constantly assimilate mean that our minds are now more restless and active than ever before. We must juggle dozens of different problems to get through a single day, and every sound, every piece of information, starts a whole new train of thought to occupy our overactive minds. Both inflated inner chattering and exponentially increasing decibels of manmade noise make it more and more difficult to 'turn off'. Indeed, the threshold of will required to 'switch off' into sanity and silence has almost become insurmountable.

What happens to a society that has to seek silence as a conscious act of will against insurmountable obstacles? Well, it goes deaf. It cannot hear anything, including the dissatisfaction of its own Self or the ripples of its own thought. Indeed, it is so exhausted, so desperate, so out of sync with itself that it cannot really think. It worries me that the generation now being born will never experience true silence. We are producing an entire civilisation of tired and emotional beings deprived of quiet. They will undoubtedly find Shakespeare incomprehensible: 'Please Sir, what does "The rest is silence" mean?' They will certainly find it difficult to think, for genuine thought requires total presence, a conscious awareness and contemplation of the world. What for them will knit up the revelled sleeve of care? Can harmonic sound transport to silence from a base of hard techno? What will conversation mean to young people weaned on clubs where it is impossible to hear anything?

A civilisation that knows no silence is the logical end of the contemporary practice, the practices we are busily making ourselves familiar with. It is the postmodern dispensation where everything is on offer instantaneously and simultaneously and they all therefore, ipso facto, make noise concurrently. This is life as we have made it. No wonder New Age rebels dream of becoming anchorites and stylites in imitation of Old Age mystics – the only problem is, you try and think of somewhere to set up your pole that is not surrounded by the extraneous noise of the rest of the world. Yes, Old Age mystics had it easy. That's how they could come up with the idea of silence. They could contemplate a world of sound and concentrate on its harmonies until they invented the idea of silence, a quiet in which they could think improving thoughts and have the calm quiet in which to communicate them. Today we have talking books – need I say more?

Odour

Something really strange is happening to our sense of smell. More and more people are finding it difficult to cope with ordinary odours. Come summer, we all start to suffer from hay fever and a host of other allergies. One in five babies is now born with asthma and immune systems so weak that almost any kind of smell can trigger an allergic response. Anosmia, the medical term for the loss or impairment of the sense of smell, has now become worryingly common. We seem to be in danger of evolving our sense of smell out of existence.

Indeed, in certain parts of North America smell has become so problematic that it has been outlawed from work and public places. In Halifax, Nova Scotia, a 'no-scent encouragement programme' is strictly implemented and people wearing perfume, deodorants or any other kind of fragrance that can cause allergic reactions in passers-by are dealt with speedily. Many US firms now have a smell policy that declares 'employees will wear no perfume or cologne during business hours'. The movement for 'fragrance-free zones' is gaining ground in California, Texas and other states. Environmentalists are threatening to file personal injury class action suits against perfume, deodorant and other industries specialising in the production of pong.

There is a sensible reason for this apparently insensible action. A growing number of people (in the US, between 15 and 30 per cent of the population) are suffering from the new disorder of multiple chemical sensitivity (MCS). That is, they have severe reactions to scented products. These reactions can be limited to headaches, nausea, dizziness, memory loss and breathing difficulties or they can be, particularly if airways swell shut, fatal. Where America leads, we follow. It is only a matter of a few years until MCS, and smell policies, become a major issue in Britain.

So, why are our noses getting so sensitive? The answer lies in the fact that we have banished natural odours from our daily lives and spend most of our time smelling artificially created, chemically enhanced, poisonous stench. The postmodern smells that surround us affect our well-being throughout our lives. And what aromas have we surrounded ourselves with? There is the stench of traffic fumes, the whiff of tarmac, the stink of industrial effluents and numerous other unpleasant aromas of urban odour formations. But that's only part of the problem. Inside our homes, in enclosed environments like the car, we use a plethora of artificial air fresheners whose fragrance makes ordinary breathing hazardous to health. Indeed, I cannot remember when I last entered a taxi or a mini-cab that was not a positive cornucopia of chemically simulated smells.

Our houses have become a veritable paradise of artificial reek. Just look around you. Air fresheners, plug-in air purifiers, electrical ionisers, chemically enhanced pot pourri, pongy soaps, smelly shampoos – the list of household items with artificially enhanced smells is endless. When did we discover the need for coathangers filled with lavender? Some time after the arrival of the roll-on underarm deodorant and all the other noxious personal hygiene paraphernalia on which we spend so much of our disposable income before the application of aftershave, cologne and perfume. We have developed a fetish for the hint of 'fresh pine', included in any number of household cleaning products. Having arranged for the rapid disappearance of actual pine forests, we can imagine ourselves strolling through forest glades as we visit our loos in the heart of a sprawling conurbation. Or maybe your chosen household cleaning fragrance is lemon, and off you waft to a distant Mediterranean hillside as you mop cat pee from your non-slip terracotta kitchen tiles. It is hardly surprising that our nasal odorant receptors cannot cope with this ridiculous chemically enhanced overload.

Smell is inherently evocative, which is undoubtedly why manufacturers spend millions including them in their products. Further millions are consumed by the advertising industry making maximum use of olfactory evocation to get us to buy the smells the manufacturers have inveigled into their wares. Soon, artificial smells of camphor, musk, peppermint and exotic spices will be streaming from our computer terminals. Smells will have been digitised and can be attached to your e-mail, Word document, interactive game or the music you download from the Internet. There will be no escape from the world of the artificial odour.

Have you by now sniffed out an emerging pattern? We have rigorously filtered acceptable fragrances, waft and odour, the things we are prepared to ingest through our nostrils. And the rule is that they should be artificially simulated natural fragrances of a certain ilk. The path of evolution is rigorous avoidance of such natural fragrances as might, in the normal course of our lives, mingle with our activities.

Indeed, Western culture has developed a deep aversion to natural smells, including the odours of real human beings. There is something shameful, we teach our children, about the smell of human sweat or our normal bodily discharges. Only cats and dogs use smell to locate their food, recognise each other and perform other social functions. Civilised behaviour means one must be totally free of natural smell.

I am reminded of my experience in a small European hotel. The modest pension had a toilet that resembled a throne room. One entered the loo and approached the throne itself up an impressive flight of steps. Every vantage point in this small airless chamber was occupied by some form of artificial device spewing forth powerful, chemically enhanced smells. So overpowering was the effect that one emerged doubly relieved – not merely of bodily waste but also of the inner lining of one's lungs, which had been seared by the corrosive array of chemical smells. As I lingered in the vicinity, gasping for breath, I overheard the response of a group of nice British ladies who were next in line to use the facilities. One by one they diced with suffocation, warning the next in line to hold her breath and be quick. The last in line, obviously 'a character', finally emerged and announced without hesitation to all and sundry: 'Give me the good honest smell of shit any day!'

Ah, the candid smell of shit! It is, of course, the worst of all possible smells. Not for nothing is 'shit' considered to be a taboo word; and 'bull-shit' has become one of the most derogatory words in our language. Our entire history, indeed the course of human evolution, has been marked by efforts to escape the smell of shit. Or at least this is what we are told by the emerging, hip and cutting-edge discipline of Evolutionary Psychology.

In Leda Cosmides and John Tooby's college textbook, *Evolutionary Psychology: A Primer*, we learn that our neural circuits, our brains as modular computers, were designed by natural selection to solve problems our ancestors faced during our species' evolutionary history. And what was the most important problem confronting our Stone Age ancestors? It seems that out on the African savannah our evolving species had to acquire 'appropriate' behaviour – they had to learn how to get away from the smell of faeces. 'Appropriate', we are told, means different things to different organisms. For example, the dung fly is hugely attracted, not to say aroused, by smelling faeces and will make a beeline, or dung fly dive, to the steaming pile to mate and lay her eggs. 'But for you', write Cosmides and Tooby, without a hint of humour, irony or indeed much intelligence, bullshit is 'not food', or 'a good place to raise children' or arrange a date. 'Because a pile of dung is a source of contagious diseases for a human being, appropriate behaviour for you is to move away from the source of the smell.'

So there you have it. Latest research into the origin and development of humanity confirms that the good honest smell of shit was as inappropriate to our ancestors as it is to their latter-day descendants running a European pension. It is not only in our genes, it is imprinted in our neural circuitry. The meaning of being human is avoiding the unavoidable smells of human bodily functions – thus we become aware we are not dung flies but sentient life forms.

This argument is, as indeed is much of Evolutionary Psychology, nothing more than bovine excreta. If we take human history to actually include non-Western cultures we find the totally opposite to be true. Far from wrinkling their noses with universal disgust, a large part of the human race regards dung as a vital economic resource to be gathered and utilised with care, if not reverence. The villages of India are fuelled by cattle dung; the family meal is as likely as not cooked on fires fed by this gift of mother cow. The earliest recorded annals of ancient China show that the regular collection of nightsoil has been a source of civic organi- sation and pride, the collection of noxious ordure being a basic form of recycling for fertiliser that grew the food that fed and bred the most pop- ulous nation on earth. The villages of Africa are composed of mud huts plastered with a fine coating of animal dung, which, being naturally fibrous, makes an excellent form of cement – you remember the old adage about no bricks without straw? It wasn't too long ago when in Britain entire urban populations hot-footed it with bucket and shovel to collect horse manure to nurture city gardens and allotments.

I remember in my days as a development journalist the serious concern with which biomass converters were devised and tested. I trav- elled extensively throughout India and China looking at biomass converters, which generated electricity from cattle dung and human bodily waste. Indeed, they were supposed to solve the energy problem of developing countries – and would have done if someone had bothered to get the technology right.

History without the honest smell of shit is an impossible concept. As Patrick Suskind showed so brilliantly in his 1989 novel *Perfume*, before the invention of squeamishness, the cities of Europe were alive with all variety of natural smells. Streets ran with human waste, rivers were civic cess pools, and piss pots, according to the finest literature, were regularly emptied out of upstairs windows, causing a minor hazard to passers-by on the pavements. Indeed, even the best French perfume needed traces of faeces to make it distinctive. It was the rich pattern of urban living, rich in smell.

Lest you think I am advocating mucky living, let me make it clear that cleanliness and natural odours are not mutually exclusive. It is hardly more than a hundred years since Europe discovered the benefits of personal hygiene. In contrast, public baths were common in Baghdad and Damascus over a thousand years ago. Indeed, daily washing and bathing were made a prerequisite of faith in both Islam and Hinduism millennia ago. The most sophisticated sewage system in the world, built by the Ottomans in the 14th century, can still be found under the hills of Istanbul. I have walked through this network, which cleverly uses the differential currents of the waters of the Bosporus to take effluent out to the deep sea.

So cleanliness is not a Western discovery, even though it was the Victorian passion of the water closet and laying municipal sewage systems that did more to enhance survival rates of the industrial working class than anything else. The water closet and the sewage drains ended the scourges of cholera, typhoid and dysentery that made a misery of the lives of and often carried off the urban poor. But the Western world, cultural neophyte to cleanliness, has become paranoid and totally unbalanced on the subject. It now wants to banish natural odours from the planet altogether and replace them with simulated, artificial varieties.

The consequences of continuous avoidance of natural smells are quite devastating. An average human being has the capability to recognise over 10,000 separate odours. But over-exposure to manufactured pongs means most of us are incapable of recognising more than a dozen smells. Something smells like roses, like pine, like lemon, like burnt wood, like sweat, like bad eggs, like ammonia, like shit. That's about it. Even our vocabulary for describing smells is rather limited.

Quite apart from losing our sense of smell, we are doing irreparable damage to our children. Our over-hygienic homes and sterile lives free of natural odours fail to expose children to certain bacteria that kick-start the immune system and enhance its protective abilities. This is why our children are increasingly unable to fight off allergens, and why asthma has become a curse of modern times. Most of these bacteria flourish in the bowl – so we return to shit again. Indeed, the latest cure for preventing asthma and other allergies involves feeding, or injecting, bacteria from the bowl to babies a few weeks old.

Avoidance of natural smell is also undermining our humanity. Before artificially induced hygiene became a fetish, the aristocracy and nobility might have wandered around with their nosegays near their nostrils and used high-priced spices to make pomanders – but they stank like everyone else. Stink was a shared, universal inheritance. But now only the poor stink. This point was impressed on my sizeable nasal cavity only the other day as I travelled on the London Underground. I was sharing a carriage with sundry aromatically arrayed Londoners when a homeless dosser walked in. He stank, he reeked, he was fetid and ripe – and we all turned away and tried to envelop ourselves in our costly, shop-bought personal odours as we tried not to look at him. A few people even got up to change carriage. The odour of poverty is indeed the most noxious – it even prevents us from looking the poor straight in the eye. If you smell like shit, you shouldn't be surprised at being treated as such, as a contemptible, worthless person, outside the pale of humanity.

So now only the poor know what our noses were really made for. In the housing estates of Britain, in the black ghettos of America, in the shanty towns of Asia, in the villages of Africa, the scent of poverty is the most evocative odour of them all. Smell is a class issue. It reminds us of the existence of a premodern, unreconstructed waft of humanity in our middle-class, hygienically wrapped, postmodern world of artificial odours. Only the poor know the truth – that our olfactory abilities are a ladder of atrophying human compassion and concern. Smell is the sinbin of society where we consign and leave to fester all those we are not prepared to include in the fragrant primrose path of consumer abundance.

So, if you want to save your humanity, save your children, save the world, then save your sense of smell. Go out and smell some real bullshit. It would do you a world of good.

Pain

The arse is connected to the brain in more direct ways than we imagine. The significance of the connection has only just become evident to me. Recent events have made me realise that this intimate connection is the fundament on which rests the edifice of civilisation as we know it.

For almost two decades I suffered from what the 11th-century Muslim philosopher and medic, ibn Sina, called 'the disease of scholars'. This disease, he suggested, arose because scholars spend a lot of time sitting in contemplation – both in the study and in the lavatory. Consequently they are perennially constipated. Furthermore, the constipatory process receives added pressure because scholars – the good ones at any rate – carry the burdens of society on their shoulders.

In today's parlance, this condition goes by the unromantic name of 'haemorrhoids' – and it is largely associated with long-distance lorry drivers. A clear indication that scholars and writers are not what they used to be.

On the whole, my piles served me very well. Ever present, often swollen and painful, they kept me on edge. More particularly, they made me think and write faster – when you can't sit in one place for too long, you have no other choice but to get the job done as fast as possible. But then, my condition reached a critical point. I started bleeding profusely. None of the palliative treatments worked. Blood kept pouring out of me as if I were a fountain. There was no option but to submit to the surgical knife. I was told the operation would take less than an hour and I would be back on my feet within 10 days.

Now, I always try to do everything to the best of my ability; and my haemorrhoids were no exception. I had three – each, according to the surgeon, 'the size of an apple'. Therefore, the operation was anything but short and simple. It took four hours – the last two of which were spent in a frantic attempt to stop me bleeding to death. I survived, as I usually do; but only after I had eight pints of alien blood pumped into my system.

So while the rest of the world was watching the World Cup, another form of sophisticated agony, I was ruminating on the nature of pain. I was being transposed between two extreme positions: excruciating, unbearable pain and no pain at all, thanks to the appliance of science known as painkillers. Painkilling was a new experience for me. It made me realise where my convictions came from! In the euphoria of my induced transitions I came to realise that the wrong organ has shaped much of my life and thought.

Along with the rest of Western civilisation, I had assumed that pain was a necessity, essential for creativity and a vital component of any worthwhile experience. What was it Keats said? 'The world is full of Misery and Heartbreak, Pain, Sickness and oppression.' After all, the central image of Western culture is the crucifix – the epitome of suffering and pain. In the crucifix is the idea of the perfect, innocent and blameless, the peaceful made to undergo all the agonies human imagination can devise. In emulation of its central image, Western world has vaunted pain as a path to virtue, pain as the means to improvement. In truth, we have been conditioned to see the rise of civilisation itself as the product of pain.

Fallen 'man' is sent to earth to suffer out 'his' life. This Judeo-Christian idea was inextricably fused with Greek thinking. The Greeks, as we all know, were into pain in quite a fundamental way. The apex of creative imagination for the Greeks was tragedy, and so it has remained. Only pain it seems can raise our thoughts to sublime heights. In Greek tragedy nothing can exonerate or break the cycle of tragic consequences that is the human lot; it all ends in blood and tears.

Quite what the ancient Greeks made of all this I am never sure. But ibn Sina, surely the greatest non-Western philosopher of all time, was much troubled by all this. He mastered Plato and Aristotle by the age of 16 but totally failed to fathom the mysteries of Greek tragedy. Why is it inevitable?, he kept murmuring on his deathbed! I suspect he had a point.

The Greek mythos makes pain the master narrative of existence – the good man, morally inspired by the tales of gods and heroes, must just soldier on regardless of the pain, which is inescapable. Join that happy prospect to a religious worldview whose central image is agony and it's no wonder that ease, content and happiness, not to mention 'niceness', get something of a bad reputation. To get better, as T. S. Eliot phrased it, the patient must get worse. You take your dose of pain and hope for bliss hereafter.

It is not just a Romantic like Keats who capitalised and apostrophised pain and its associates as the cardinal principles of the world – though it is interesting to note that he didn't think oppression made the grade – and the human condition. Western philosophy from the outset has venerated the Greeks and secularised Christian notions make our whole way of thinking and working with ideas pain dependent. Hobbes translated the Christian idea of fallen man into the developmental origin of human society. Life began as nasty, brutish and short, in other words drenched in pain. Locke tried to circumvent the notion of original sin and take a more optimistic line, but his individual blank slate of a human person had to struggle and strive, inch painfully forward. The blood, sweat and tears brigade have always had the upper hand, the point being blood, sweat and tears are the conventional triumvirate of the Good Friday ethos centred on pain, even when pain is not mentioned. If it is not inherent in the nature of man, it's inherent in the nature of the world that conditions human existence.

Even dear old Captain Kirk, the pan-galactic embodiment of so much

Western philosophy, wallows in pain. He could never leave a stable, happy, content, pacific society to its own devices. Non-interference directives notwithstanding, he invariably argued that what made humans great was struggle, pain, blood, sweat and tears – the only ingredients that enable the achievements of civilisation to be incrementally accumulated. Or as Orson Welles put it in the film *The Third Man*, making his own memorable and appropriate addition to Graham Greene's script: in 500 years of brotherly love, democracy and peace Switzerland produced the cuckoo clock, while in just 30 years Italy under the Borgias had warfare, terror, murder, bloodshed and they produced Michelangelo, Leonardo da Vinci and the Renaissance. Pain is not merely unavoidable, it is the essential spur that makes us great. Perhaps that's why Oliver Cromwell's favourite oath was 'in the bowels of Christ', the complete union of the point I have been trying to make – the motif of bum pain, constipation and worse has shaped our thought and history.

Of course, the secular epitome of all this is Darwin. Natural selection and survival of the fittest have a great deal to do with nature red in tooth and claw, or as one might otherwise state it, soaked in pain. The upward escalator of human progress puts priority on the pain and a good deal of the progress made has been demonstrated in increasing sophistication in the arts of inflicting pain.

The more the West has become addicted to the pleasure principle of consumerism, the more its artistic vision has come to glory in pain – an exact reversal of the genesis of Romanticism. Whichever way round you work it, art is to be found only through misery, the latest manifestations being the host of 'look at me, I am suffering/dying' accounts that have received so much praise in the review pages recently. I find this to be perverse; even though it is central to Western thought and philosophy.

My experience leads me to the opposite conclusion. Pain is not what existence is about. It is certainly not the route to beauty as the designer violence gang who have Hollywood by the throat assert, a perverted set of latter-day Romantics all. Existence is about the joy and liberation that comes from relief of pain – that's what art, literature and philosophy should be all about. More of this alternative outlook might redress a balance that went horribly out of alignment in the 20th century. That century, which saw 'the triumph of the West', was the most blood-soaked, pain-drenched century in human history. It has taken the abominations of creating pain to new, total and apocalyptic proportions, unimaginable at any previous stage of human existence.

When pain is considered virtuous, while ease and comfort are roads to perdition, it is no wonder that the eradication of pain as an existential force does not take centre stage. When suffering and all the pain-related conditions – including a capitalised and apostrophised 'Oppression' – are seen as somehow ennobling, we can never summon up the will and commitment to work steadfastly within the conditions of the world for their abolition, their total eradication.

The Romantics are the prime example of where the pain-to-brain connection has led us astray. The Romantics vaunted beauty and sought it through pleasure principles because they could not envisage a victory over the awfulness of the pain-drenched world in which they lived. The more pain and suffering this brought down on their heads, the more perfect the beauty and bliss they could imagine in their art, with death as the ultimate symbol of perfect liberation – or victory by a technical knockout for the pain brigade.

The truth is otherwise. Pain is not ennobling; bearing pain does not make us better people; there is nothing courageous about putting up with excruciating pain when you have no alternative. And when you do, you waste no time in swallowing painkillers. The rise of a civilisation that cannot contain its will to create and inflict pain is not worthy of the name of civilisation. Pain gives rise to bitterness, pain dehumanises, pain justifies the unjustifiable and rationalises the intolerable. To convert to the party of the abolition of pain, however, presents a mega problem. The entire weight of the ages of thought and action is ranged against us. Where can we find the positive endorsements of both ends and means for a pain-free world?

I have surgically ejected my principal pain centre. Gradually I attempt to walk, painkiller-assisted, my talk. But there is so much pain in our world for which we have to take responsibility, the responsibility of engaging practically with and thinking through to its eradication by painless means. We can only make pain a scourge ripe for abolition and cutting off from human consciousness when we deny it any form of glorification and see it as the horror it is. When pain is no longer the essential spur to beauty as truth we can take a sensible inventory of our responsibility for the manufacture of pain by dint of human error that is our history.

Therefore, I refuse to celebrate my haemorrhoids, the unbearable pain they have caused me, the near-death experience they inflicted on me – even though they have led me to a new perspective. I will not be writing a literary book about them – that is exactly the primrose path to ruin we have all been seduced along from the outset. I celebrate the painless state, I dub it normal and basic and from now on I will investigate, analyse and conceptualise through the medium of pain reduction to the point of eradication as the purpose and meaning of existence, and only such things that have nothing of pain about them at all shall I deem beautiful. I offer this insight as an essential counterblast to all the apocalyptic, pain-drenched millenarian visions that swept us, like a tidal wave, into the 21st century under the weight of newsprint, books, articles, films and critical endorsement from the old dispensation.

Predictions

The world is awash with predictions. Images of the future are being hurled at us from every direction. We are constantly being asked to imagine the wonders of the future, dream about the things tomorrow will bring. But the images and dreams we are being fed have a rather unsavoury, undemocratic underbelly. We are being force-fed into thinking that there is only one way life in the future can be lived; and only technology can determine what the future will bring. As such, forecasts have colonised the future.

Even though thinking about the future is a tricky and hazardous business, it has become big business. Tricky because our conventional way of thinking does not normally incorporate the future. We need to make a considerable and conscious effort to imagine what the future may unfold, what anticipated and unexpected possibilities lurk on distant horizons. Hazardous because the future is always unpredictable and any prediction runs the risk of being way off the mark. But this has not stopped the business of forecasting from spreading like a global fire.

But predicting and forecasting are only one way of exploring the future. There are numerous other ways, such as building scenarios, modelling future societies and developing visions of alternative futures. Forecasts have acquired dominance because they are the easiest and most undemocratic way of dealing with the future. No matter how sophisticated the techniques on which they are based – and they are becoming more and more refined and complex – forecasts are little more than the extrapolation of the present into the future. In most cases, forecasts project a selected past and an often privileged present on to a linear future. Thus the future based on forecasts is nothing more than the continuation of the present – with all its inequalities and injustices, but with faster, more sophisticated, more awesome technologies. The ideal dispensation for postmodern times.

In general, forecasts about the future come in two categories. The future will either be a technological utopia or a nightmare. Utopian forecasters tend to be academics, management gurus, corporate types and advertising people; dystopians are often science fiction writers or filmmakers.

Business and corporate books, with titles like *Megatrends* and *Managing for the Future*, available at any airport anywhere around the globe, tell us we will all be Internetted, tuned in to hundreds of channels, working from home, and generally living in technological bliss in the decades to come. For example, in *Rethinking the Future* a collection of leading management experts inform us that advances in science and technology will enable us to manage uncertainty and generate new methods for creating tomorrow's advantages, strategies for growth and reinventing the basis for competition. The future, therefore, will not be much different in at least one respect: corporations will continue to dominate and they will have new theories and tools to maintain their domination.

In the future, the folks at the Open University 'Futures Observatory' tell us, people will routinely have microchips inserted into their brains to store data and communicate directly with computers. According to *The Sunday Times'* 'Chronicle of the Future', within the next two decades we will be able to cure evil by electronically controlled implants into the 'left orbito-frontal cortex', superbugs will be trained to mine precious metals, and little girls will be able to play with 'living Barbies'. We will be living on the Moon, colonising Mars, and will be forever young thanks to anti-ageing drugs. In her book *Next*, Marian Salzman, a director of brand futures at global advertising agency Young & Rubicam, predicts the imminent arrival of a sleeping machine for insomniacs, robotic lawn mowers for obsessive gardeners, intelligent kitchens for food nuts and mail order children for childless couples. Writers such as Michio Kaku and Nicholas Negroponte envisage a future where the Net (and not some foolish notion of Truth) will set us Free and Technology will Liberate us from our own Biology. We are, if we believe these and other technophiles, already on our way to a new digital Jerusalem.

This message is translated into visual metaphors by television programmes like the BBC's *Tomorrow's World* and advertisements for cars, mobile phones, digital and satellite consumer goods – all asking us to reflect on how new technologies will transform not just our social and cultural environments but the very idea of what it is to be human. We have all seen the advertisement for a car that shows a futuristic landscape, with spherical steel balls floating in space, a sort of post-Concorde plane with a novel-looking propulsion unit, a glowing clock-face on very fast forward – all mixed up as a drug-crazed dream sequence. The message is simple: in the future we will all live in a fast-moving, high-tech world of pure luxury. A sonorous voice says: 'Designed for the next millennium – the Vectra from Vauxhall.' According to one mobile phone company 'the future is Orange'. And British Telecom would have us believe that 'in the future' we will all communicate instantaneously, be permanently logged on and constantly in touch, so why not, concludes the advertisement, 'change the way we work'.

In sharp contrast to images of the triumph of technology, we have extreme dystopian projections of the future. There has been a plethora of books predicting the collapse of the nation state and an ensuing economic chaos that will have us all fighting for survival. Then, television series such as *The X-Files* and *Millennium* and films like *Armageddon* and *Comet* constantly hammer the message that there is something happening 'out there' that is forcing our world to resemble more and more an image out of a science fiction novel. In Andrew Niccol's literary film *Gattaca*, the future is divided between 'invalids', a new sub-class of genetically inferior beings, and the genetically perfect who have higher privileges. Technology thus becomes an instrument for perpetuating racism and injustice. But the classic nightmarish image of the future is of course the *Terminator*: futuristic cyborg gone irredeemably mad.

An advertisement for the city of Ontario sums up the point of all this. 'In the future', it begins, 'we will have intelligent buildings', and it continues to make other, similar technologically oriented predictions. The catch-line: all of these predictions have already come true – 'Ontario. The Future is right *here*'. Precisely. The future has arrived even before we have had a chance to experience it as the present. As the title of Michael Lewis's book and the BBC television series based on it makes explicit, *The Future Just Happened*. It is all happening very, very fast; and in some cases it has already happened. The future is an autonomous being that will happen whether we like it or not. There is nothing we can do about it. The sheer repetition and the intellectual and visual power with which this message is hammered home has profound consequences for our future consciousness. It is thus not surprising that the vast majority of humanity thinks of the future only in terms of advertisement clichés, corporate strategies and gee-whiz technological gadgets.

Forecasting plays on this notion of an autonomous future where people have no role and technology determines all. The only actors in this game are those who can turn the predictions into profits. Forecasting thus increases the sense of helplessness in ordinary people. By its very nature, it is incapable of incorporating the democratic aspirations of all members of society. It has to concern itself with things that can be easily and safely extrapolated from the present onto a linear future.

Forecasting thus turns the future into a commodity that can be consumed here and now. Forecasts enable us not just to know the future – even if that were possible – but also to hold it, touch it, feel it, examine it as a gadget in the comfort of our living rooms. The future comes ready-made, packaged, gift-wrapped. As the ad for 'Futuroscope' tells us, it is a theme park that you can visit 'as a part of your holiday in France'. Hell, you can even wash your dirty linen in a washing powder called 'Ariel Future'.

While the future has been turned into a commodity, forecasting itself has become an ideology. Technological predictions have become so important because all ideologies have lost their impact – particularly Marxism, which has a strong predictive element. Even liberal secularism is losing its appeal and has probably passed its 'sell by' date. Forecasts and predictions are filling the ideological gap because they offer a modicum of certainty and control in rapidly changing times. Forecasts imagine the future as a mighty river with comfortably fixed boundaries and contours, moving in an established direction. All we have to do to 'manage' the future is to navigate the rapids; and the functions of forecasts is to point out what rapids lie ahead.

The ideology of forecasting is based on two basic assumptions. First, things change. But it is not just that things change; they are changing at an accelerating rate. Indeed, the rate of change itself is accelerating. This argument, which is a cornerstone of all thinking about the future, has become such a widespread part of our mental furniture that we accept it uncritically. Yet, we can raise a number of fundamental questions regarding 'ever accelerating change'. Why, if change is accelerating, are we actually growing backwards? Economic growth was considerably lower in the period 1973–92 compared to 1950–73. Asian tigers may have been growing at a phenomenal rate at the peak of their economic strength, but after the crash they actually returned to a pre-growth state. The gap between the rich and poor is widening, not just between North and South but within Western societies themselves. The United Nations Annual Human Development Report has pointed out that despite a six-fold increase in global consumption, poverty in Britain and the United States has actually increased. In Africa, absolute poverty has increased almost continuously for the last decade. We thus have a paradox: things may be changing at an accelerating pace, we may be producing more and more wealth, but since the sixties we have experienced an ever decelerating rate of growth and as a human collective we are actually worse off than ever.

Second, as things get faster, smaller and more connected they become better. This too is open to question. Faster and faster cars are actually not taking us anywhere except straight to a gridlock. It has been estimated that traffic in London is slower than in the days of the horse and carriage, and they were certainly more environmentally friendly. Faster, intelligent and 'perfect' computers are creating more problems than they are solving – and I don't just mean viruses, accelerating computer crimes and the increasing ability of hackers and unsavoury characters to bring net-worked society to its knees. The computerisation of the market, with software programmed to automatically buy or sell according to market conditions, has brought us, on a number of occasions, to the brink of economic collapse. The computerisation of ministerial 'red boxes', which used a minister's fingerprints to access government documents, had to be abandoned in Britain because the whole thing was just too complicated, not very reliable and even with all that high technology not very safe! The computerisation of Railtrack's signalling system has been little short of a farce. London Transport's electronic public information system now frequently tells underground users to simply 'check the front of the train'. Moving fast is simply an illusion for not getting anywhere.

Being connected is a substitute for being a real community, which has all but ceased to exist. All technological advances contain nightmarish underbellies and generate ethical paradoxes that are almost impossible to solve. The reality is that we have reached a technological plateau. New technologies may appear to be better, faster and more promising, but in reality they do not improve our lives, or deliver greater material benefits to most of humanity, or make us happier. The dominant trends that are being projected into the future in countless forecasts have, in our own time, not led to a world of peace, prosperity and plenty. They have pro-duced a world that is devastated and diminished in nearly every respect. There is no reason to believe it will be otherwise in the future.

In reality, progress is made not in terms of exponential curves but through peaks and troughs, rather like the booms and busts of economic cycles. We need solace during such bumpy rides to the future; and that's just what forecasts provide. So we constantly extrapolate the good or the bad in the present in the hope of a future paradise or fear of a future nightmare – the hope or fear comes from our faith, or lack of it, in technology. This is why forecasting has made such a fetish of technological development.

But there is another reason for forecasters' obsession with technology. As the distance between the future and the present shrinks rapidly, forecasts limited to a few years into the future become less hazardous. Indeed, some forecasts are realised – particularly those related to information and communication technologies – even before they are made. Mid-term forecasts too are acquiring a habit of coming true because of a self-fulfilling effect.

Predictions and forecasts create representations of the future that are full of meaning. So a description of what we can expect in the near future is a picture with meaning, just as the images of the future we see in advertisements are images with meaning. This meaning is often translated as a prescription. Predictions thus become prescriptions; and images of the future become graphic prescriptions. There is thus a continuum: prediction, prescription, image. The continuum ensures that predictions – particularly of a technological nature – have a higher probability of becoming a reality.

Thus all those predictions about how, for example, we will be cloning ourselves in the future are actually creating a future where human cloning will be the norm. Far and above the ethical and moral problems of cloning, the predictions create the fallacy that cloning is inevitable; the images of technology that will ultimately lead to cloning further entrench this fallacy in the mind of the public. All that is needed now is for this fallacy to be justified in social terms: step forward the infertile heterosexual couple desperate for a child; the child suffering from a genetic disorder; the consumers queuing for designer babies. The moral debate goes out of the window and the future arrives in the very shape that it was predicted to be.

Thus in a very subtle way, predictions and forecasts silence debate and discussion. They present technology as an autonomous and desirable force and project the future as unavoidable. The desirable products of technology generate more desire; its undesirable side effects require more technology to solve them. There is thus a perpetual feedback loop; the future constantly feeds on the technological present. One need not be a technological determinist to appreciate the fact that this self-perpetuating momentum has locked us in a linear, one-dimensional trajectory that has actually foreclosed the future. The future is thus – it cannot be otherwise. As such, forecasts – utopian or otherwise – are inherently undemocratic. Indeed, the very idea of prediction works against plurality and for a single, linear future.

The future need not be a continuation of the present. There is no logic that says we have to see the future only in terms of technology and then only in utopian or dystopian perspectives. To break the stranglehold of binary, technologically dominant but myopic projections, we need to think of the future in pluralistic terms. The future need not be like a mighty river; it can just as easily be like an ocean. In this ocean, we can sail almost anywhere, in any direction. There is thus no such thing as the future; there are many, many futures. Moreover, we should be concerned less with what the future could or would be and more with what it ought to be, what we want the future to be. There is nothing inevitable or determined about the future. It can be made and shaped by all of us according to our desires.

Opening up the future to democratic and pluralistic possibilities requires us to make people, and not technology, the focus of the future. The future, any future, will affect us all; so we all have a right to participate in shaping it. Thinking about the future then becomes an enterprise of social involvement – in debating and discussing policy and participating in policy making, in raising future consciousness of communities, in articulating the future hopes and desires of communities, and in involving citizens in efforts to shape their own futures.

Shaping desirable futures has little to do with forecasting and a great deal to do with scenarios and visions. Both scenarios and visions are about rejecting the passivity involved in the notion that 'things change'.

Instead, they concern themselves with actively changing things in a desired way. Rejecting the 'inevitable' future predicted in forecasts, they provide invaluable help in choosing and creating a desirable future.

Scenarios represent alternative possibilities. Unlike forecasts, which impose patterns extrapolated from the past onto the future, scenarios are plausible, pertinent, alternative stories that can be used to shape policy. Scenarios have been used by local people to develop and work towards alternative futures for their area. By asking what else is possible – apart from the obvious stated in forecasts – and linking current decisions with alternative future outcomes, scenarios can often generate opportunities where only problems are visible. In many American cities, inner-city communities faced with chronic employment, homelessness and forecasts of doom have used scenarios to dig themselves out of the quagmire. One of the most successful is the Time Dollars initiative, which generates social capital by using a system of bartering time. People earn Time Dollars by helping others and then use them to buy essential goods and services. In Suffolk County, New York, unskilled mothers on public assistance bought computers, mastered advanced computing skills and became employable. They paid for their computers in monthly instalments, providing services to neighbours by responding to 'classified ads' accessed through a computerised Time Dollar bulletin board. One outcome of the Time Dollars scenario is an organisation called Habitat for Humanity, which sells houses to the homeless that are paid for by doing fixed community work over a (long) period of time. In Britain, the action-orientated think tank New Economic Foundation has developed a similar scheme. It started in a doctor's surgery in south-east London, then took root in a computer recycling facility in Brixton, before spreading all over Britain. Together with 'Skill Swap', where people can use know-how instead of money, 'time banks' are firmly established in over 40 cities across the UK.

In Hawaii, scenarios have been used to 're-invent' the judicial system. The old courts in Hawaii were concerned less with 'justice' or speedy trials and more with parking fines. Frustrated citizens got together and developed alternative scenarios based on the question: what functions can courts perform in shaping a viable future for Hawaii? The resulting scenarios were used to shape policy and force the governor to reorganise the judiciary as a 'public agency' accountable to the public and, more important, as an institution for changing and improving the lot of citizens. Similarly, in Denver, Colorado, an alliance of communities used scenarios to transform the local health system; and the public transport system in Washington, D.C. owes a great deal to imaginative scenario work by a coalition of communities.

Visions focus on desirables, and like forecasts they too can be self-fulfilling. Visions are the shared commitment by a community to the future it will create. And community visions of possible and desirable futures can usher in genuine, pluralistic change by nurturing the real seeds of change. Radical change seldom emerges from the mainstream; it almost always comes from the periphery. Conventionally, visions have been the province of the Prophets, the wise and unconventional men who came from the periphery and transformed the centre. Today's equivalent of the Prophets are the communities whose voices have been silenced – the non-Western societies and cultures, inner-city poor, women and children, and the 'outsiders' such as immigrants, poets, artists and philosophers – people unimpressed by the Great White Technological Future but concerned more with preserving our humanity and such mundane things as social justice and equity.

Visions are usually based on long-term perspectives. They are used to imagine the potential and possibilities that may be realised 20, 30 years from now. How do we realise our visions? By making sure that planning, policy-making and governance processes incorporate the basic elements of our visions. Visions are therefore not abstract things; they are concrete and have policy and planning implications. A number of cities around the world, such as Toronto, Istanbul and Madrid, have developed visions of their future with the help of the World Health Organisation's 'Healthy Cities' initiative. These visions are then used as the basis for shaping environmental, transport, public health and other urban policies. Citizens are involved both in developing the visions and fighting for plans and policies that would lead to their realisation.

Of course, visions and scenarios are not an end in themselves. But they do emphasise the fact that we need not accept the future passively as a given. They stress that ordinary citizens have a major role to play in shaping the future and thus transform the future into a site of both real and symbolic struggles. The future, or rather futures, become an arena of action — a place where we can create new alternatives and options; attempt to truly widen human choices; rethink political, social and cultural ends; and contain and transcend the social pathologies that have divided humanity.

I believe it is the responsibility of all those who still believe in humanity to subvert the inevitable in the future, which is, after all, only another name for tomorrow that dares not be anything other than a linear projection of yesterday. Next time you see a forecast or prediction, ignore it. Instead, go out and change the future.

Qawwali

This world, the old Sufi mystics used to teach, is a mirage. There is a higher Reality that exists by its own essence. The purpose of existence is to love the higher Reality more than this mundane world of illusions. Like the (oblivious?) selfless moth immolating itself in the candle flame, Sufis direct their passion towards 'fana', or the annihilation of self in the higher Reality of the One. In the particular form of Sufi devotional music practised in the Indian subcontinent, Qawwali, the function of the performance is to enable the self-annihilation of the listener.

In recent times Western audiences have been alerted to Qawwali through the work of one of its great exponents: Nusrat Fatah Ali Khan. How Nusrat became a chic cult in the West is, however, only part of my tale. Appropriately, since our subject is Qawwali, mine is a story of annihilation, involving considerable self-immolation. It is the amazing adventure of the one Qawwali most people in the Western world are likely to have heard: Nusrat's 'Dum mustt qualander', or *'Mustt Mustt'* for short. The story of *'Mustt Mustt'*, how it came about, how it evolved, changed and transmogrified, is a revealing narrative of our postmodern times.

To set the scene, I must begin at the beginning, with the origins of Qawwali, a compendium of the Indian subcontinent's musical traditions, itself. Its invention is attributed to Amir Khusrau, an immensely colourful and influential character in Indian music and literature. A court poet of Ala-ad-Din Muhammad Khilji, Sultan of Delhi (1296–1316), Khusrau is credited as the first Urdu poet in history. Sufi tradition also credits him with introducing such musical instruments as the sitar and tabla to the subcontinent. There is an apocryphal account of how in a spate of invention he cut the *pakhavaja* (a drum with twin striking surfaces) in half, thus creating the two small drums of the tabla, one to be played with the right hand, the other with the left of the drummer. Khusrau also innovated new vocal forms, as well as *rags* and *tals*.

Rags are central to Indian music, but they have no counterpart in Western musical theory. Loosely, *rag* is equivalent to melody, which in Indian classical music exists in free rhythmic form. The concept of *rag* is that certain characteristic patterns of notes evoke heightened states of emotion. Each *rag* can be described according to its ascending and descending lines (which may involve turns), as well as its characteristic melodic figures.

Indian melody can also be presented in its metric form, its tempo governed by the *tal*, a particular time measure. *Tal* is a cycle with both quantitative and qualitative aspects: the quantitative concern the duration of a cycle measured in terms of time units or beats, which can be slow, medium or fast; the qualitative concern the distribution of stresses or accents within the cycle at different levels of intensity. In a *raga*, a composed piece, the character is derived from the specific deployment of the *rag* and *tal*. There are over 200 extant *rags*, each a melodic basis for composition and improvisation, each performed at a different time of day or season to enhance particular emotions.

Qawwali is a fusion of the emotive power of Indian music with the emotional content of Sufi mystical poetry. The work of poets such as the Arab Sufi ibn Arabi or Turkish mystic Jalaluddin Rumi is difficult to fathom for rationalist minds. In a society where one has to 'freak out' or 'drop out' to pursue mystical leanings, the idea of infinite emotion that is both unbridled passion and controlled, purposeful, spiritual endeavour is difficult to grasp. For Sufis, poetry is not just a vehicle, it is a transport of direct mystical experience. It represents and perpetuates the legacy of Sufi saints and teachers. This is why Sufi poetry provides such a vast range of aesthetic expression for mystical love, often utilising stylised imagery of human love as a metaphor for the manifestation of spiritual passion:

> *O wondrous amorous teasing, O wondrous beguiling*
> *O wondrous tilted cap, O wondrous tormentor*
> *In the spasm of being killed my eyes beheld your face:*
> *O wondrous benevolence, O wondrous guidance and protection.*

Amir Khusrau wanted to combine the passion of Sufi poetry with the heightened emotions of a *rag*. However, since Sufi poetry often incorporated a verse from the Qur'an or a saying of the Prophet Muhammad, it was important that the texts remained intact and their meaning was not distorted, a tricky situation to which Khusrau provided an ingenious solution. He was also the originator of the *tarana* style of vocal music, a type of singing in fast tempo using syllables. To an ordinary listener, the syllables appear meaningless but when they are pieced together they form recognisable Persian words with mystical symbolism. Khusrau introduced a few syllables of *tarana* to add balance to the *rag* in which the piece was composed (called *shudh kalyan*) and Qawwali was born.

The word Qawwali itself is derived from the Arabic word *Qaulah*, meaning to speak or give an opinion. As an artistic form, it is strong on opinion: the Urdu or Persian couplets that form the invocation and mystical text of the Qawwali are all-important. This distinguishes Qawwali from a classical *raga* where music has primacy over text. The *tals* used in Qawwali are also distinct, being of a type seldom used in classical music. But the real difference between Qawwali and all other musical idioms of the Indian subcontinent is its specific mystical function and context of use. Qawwali is designed to perform three specific functions: generate spiritual arousal, convey the mystical message of the poetry and react to the listeners' diverse and changing spiritual requirements.

Sufis consider a rhythmic framework and an emphatic stress pattern or pulse, reflecting the heartbeat, to be essential for stirring the soul. The reoccurring beat suggests the continuous repetition of God's name and guides the Sufi towards ecstasy. The rhythmic framework itself is characterised by two techniques. The first is handclapping; the second is a particular drumming technique that uses mainly open-hand or flat-hand strokes. With the downbeat of the drum, the listener's head moves in silent repetition of God's name; indeed, the drumbeat alone may cause ecstasy. By the time the Sufi utters the word *Allahu* (God Is), he is already on the way to another realm. It is said that the 13th-century mystic Sheikh Qutbudding Bakhtiar Kaki was so overwhelmed by ecstasy that he died while listening to Qawwali. Many Sufi saints, like the Indian mystic Sheikh Nizamuddin Chishti, have been known to go into a deep trance during Qawwali and remain oblivious to the world for days on end.

So, Qawwali is basically a form of mystical worship. Subcontinental Sufis often describe it as *zikr*, remembrance of Allah, which is the basic pillar of Sufism. Therefore, the music must serve to clarify the text, both acoustically, by making it clearly audible, and structurally, by placing emphasis on the salient formal features of the poem. Acoustic clarification of the text is sought by volume, singing at a high dynamic level, often with strong and exaggerated enunciation of consonants. Group singing reinforces the solo voice; the solo performer picks out the pertinent units of text, which are repeated by the group.

As a form of spiritual communication, Qawwali is not a one-way exercise; singer(s) and musicians must themselves react to the listeners, respond to their changing requirements, adjust their performance to their audience's state of being and ecstasy. The interaction requires the Qawwali to isolate both musical and textual units and repeat them as necessary, amplifying or cutting short any unit of the text, rearranging or even omitting an element, going forward, backwards or proceeding in an infinite loop. Or, it may require the creation of additional musical units as a setting for portions of text that may need to be inserted out of the blue! I have heard the same poem presented in two minutes and performed for over two hours. The audience and musicians are mutual participants locked in a mystical encounter. The listeners' ecstasy can impose a particular structure upon the music and take the musicians for an unplanned ride.

This incredibly versatile and rich musical tradition has been sustained since the time of Amir Khusrau by the Sufi communities of the Indian subcontinent in the *mahfil-e-sama*, or the Assembly for Listening. Through the act of listening – *sama* – the Sufi seeks to activate his personal link with his living spiritual guide, with saints departed, with Ali, fourth Caliph of Islam who was the cousin and son-in-law of the Prophet Muhammad, with the Prophet Muhammad himself and ultimately with God. By opening himself to the Qawwali, the listener means to transcend his mundane, materialist and conscious existence by kindling the spiritual flame of mystical love. Once ecstasy has been reached, the goal of both Qawwali and the listener is to sustain the intensity of the experience and, well, go *Mustt, Mustt,* or totally lose oneself in the love of God.

One cannot have a more profound or vivid Qawwali experience than at an *urs* – the commemoration of a noted saint's own final union with God, held at the saint's shrine on the anniversary of his death. Throughout the Indian subcontinent, shrines continue to be the centres for mystical teaching and tradition, and therefore prime foci for Qawwalis. At any time of the year one can find an *urs* in progress somewhere on the subcontinent. I have attended Qawwali *mahfils* in Lahore and Pakpattan, two important centres of *urs* in Pakistan. But the *urs* to beat all urs, where the Qawwali reaches unparalleled heights, is the *urs* of the great saint Nizamuddin Auliya and of his favourite disciple, Amir Khusrau himself, which takes place in Delhi.

The Qawwals, the performers of Qawwalis, not surprisingly, tend to be both followers of the Sufi path and highly versatile musicians. The ideal voice for a Qawwal is considered to be loud and full, a voice with life and strength, rather than one that is melodious or modulated. As Qawwals have to project their voices in huge assemblies that gather at shrines, they tend, like operatic tenors, to be rather large. Enter the subject of our story: the late Nusrat Fatah Ali Khan.

Nusrat was not just a big man with a big voice; he was big in every way. And as befits big men, he is shrouded in myths and legends, much like Amir Khusrau and Sufi saints of yesteryear. The popular story of Nusrat's life that circulates in the towns and villages of Pakistan is an enchanting narrative of dreams, remote viewing and mystical encounters. These begin at the beginning: with his name itself. Apparently, his original name was Parvez, meaning 'conqueror', 'lucky', 'happy', a common enough and perfectly acceptable designation amongst Muslims of the subcontinent. Yet, one day a mystic by the name of Pir Ghulam Ghaus Samadani came to see Nusrat's father, Ustad Fateh Ali Khan, himself a noted Qawwal. Our hero entered the room and when his father introduced him as 'Parvez' Samadani was startled and enraged. 'Change his name at once,' he thundered. 'Do you know who Parvez was? He was the king of Persia who tore up the letter sent to him by the Prophet Muhammad. This name does not augur well for a boy destined to be a global Qawwal. It should not be the name of someone who will sing the rosary of Allah.' There and then, the fat boy's name was changed to Nusrat.

The word 'Nusrat' means 'God's grace' and 'success with His help'. So the young Qawwal was only too conscious of his prospects. On the way to his global triumph he is said to have performed several musical miracles. Take, for instance, the occasion when he was called upon to accompany the Indian classical singer Pandit Dina Nath on the tabla. The good Pandit had declared himself disappointed by all the tabla players in Pakistan – none of them could keep sufficient tempo to enable him to express himself fully. But the youthful Nusrat and his nimble fingers did such a brilliant job that Pandit had to declare, 'I am defeated. Nusrat is highly talented.'

It was at the Amir Khusrau Festival in Islamabad in 1975, marking the poet's 700th anniversary, that Nusrat performed his breakthrough musical miracle. All the great Qawwali singers of Pakistan were invited to the festival, which was broadcast live on radio. However, Nusrat, as yet an unrecognised Qawwal, was the last to be invited. So, by the time he and his party arrived the other Qawwals had already picked all the more popular poems and songs of Amir Khusrau for their own performances. It seemed there was nothing left from the Khusrau heritage for Nusrat. But the up-and-coming artist astonished them all by singing a rare and hardly ever performed poem:

Mein to pia sey nainan mila aayi rey
Par nari ganwari kahey so kahey
Mien to pia sey nainan mila aayi rey.

I am not thirsty, I have met my beloved
Whatever the ignorant girls of my village might say
I am not thirsty, I have met my beloved.

After that, Nusrat went on to perform one of Amir Khusrau's most difficult compositions in a particular style of Qawwali known as the Qaul Qalbana. Divided into five *tals*, Qaul Qalbana is only attempted by the most accomplished artists, those confident in their total mastery of their art. This was Nusrat's way of telling the other Qawwals and everyone listening not only that he had arrived but also that he was on his way to higher places.

So far our tale has been of the world of tradition, Sufi tradition that continues to circulate and whirl around its own concerns. Clearly, Nusrat was established, so much within his proper ambit that his own life took on the form and character of popular Sufi narratives, replete as they are with the little miracles of daily life. But we live in one world, and eventually even the unworldly are tracked to their assemblies and whirled by centripetal forces onto the global stage. And so it was that Nusrat was propelled on a trajectory no other Qawwal had ever taken, or even dreamed might exist – to the recording studio of Peter Gabriel.

Gabriel is the unquestioned doyen of world music, the eclectic genre of chic that merchandises the illusion that we are real aesthetes, full members of a pluralist global culture. The great achievement of World of Music, Arts and Dance (WOMAD) and 'RealWorld', the organisation and record label founded by Gabriel, has been to purloin, appropriate and commodify traditional genres of music from distant corners of the world and thereby make fortunes for recording companies, but few, if any, of the traditional musicians involved. The world, as the Sufis say, is a mirage, a distorted flickering image of reality. Or as a Western poet once noted: the world is too much with us, late and soon, getting and spending. I merely note that what world music commodifies is the lure of other worldliness, in easy, though contextually incomprehensible form. For the West, spirituality, mystical power is the continuing domain of non-Western, natural man. The three-fifths of the world who remain bereft of the worldly goods of modernity have only ethereal consolation in other worldliness to warm their hands and stir their mess of porridge by. It has become a natural order in quite a different sense of the word, one where the combination of poverty and mysticism is taken as natural.

World music summons an assembly of listening for the global mirage based on the assumption that by being fascinated by what we do not understand we actually belong to one world. It is a delusion because it lacks exactly those defining criteria that make Qawwali: mutual endeavour for a common higher purpose. Yet, if world music fails to transport us beyond the dynamics of the mundane natural order, at least it sounds nice.

And so it was that Nusrat was drawn to participate in that most bizarrely eclectic and truly postmodern exercise of adding a Qawwali to the soundtrack of Martin Scorsese's *The Last Temptation of Christ*. What better accompaniment to the deconstruction of Christology could there be than decontexualising another spiritual tradition? Postmodernism is nothing if not the vehicle to transport us all beyond the meaningful content of grand narratives of belief. In the studio, goes the story, Nusrat performed a number of *ragas* and Gabriel kept on recording the recital. Then Nusrat did something unusual. He sang the tunes of Darbari *ragas* in higher tones, rather than his characteristic falsetto. Gabriel liked it and it ended up on the soundtrack of the film.

When the recording was complete Gabriel said, 'I wish you could do something with Western musical instruments.' Again the postmodern refrain, the quest for fulfilment by losing all meaning in hybrid fusion form. Decontextualised, uprooted and free-floating postmodernism would have us absorbed in genuine meaningless pastiche. Nusrat started to hum and play on his harmonium in an absent-minded way. After a little while, he rendered the scale:

sa re sa: ni sa pa ni ma pama ni ga re ga.

Nusrat immediately realised the significance of what he had done. Peter Gabriel so liked what he heard he proceeded immediately to record it. Thus was born Nusrat Fatah Ali Khan's masterpiece, '*Mustt Mustt*'. When cinema audiences heard the intriguing sounds of Qawwali they asked for more. They too wanted to go '*Mustt Mustt*', and lose themselves in dreams of postmodern inclusiveness. Nusrat became a must on radio and in record shops far and wide.

Irony is a special delight of postmodernism. The first incarnation of '*Mustt Mustt*' was released on the RealWorld label. Although guitar and other Western instruments are there, the Qawwali is sung in the traditional way largely to the accompaniment of tabla. The text is a mixture of Urdu and Punjabi and its *subject* is Caliph Ali:

Dum Mustt Qualander, Mustt Mustt.
My remembrance moment by moment
Ali in my every breath.

The text is not all together original. Rather, it's a variation on the old Punjabi Qawwali '*Dama dum mustt Qualadar*', which I have heard many a fakir sing in the streets of the Pakistani province of Sindh. As Qawwali, '*Mustt, Mustt*' exists within the traditional orbit of improvisation, with a new element added out of the blue. It includes some enchanting *tarana*, and Nusrat presents the whole performance as a showcase of virtuosity and talent. A passive assembly for listening among the uninitiated can be transported by fascination without commitment, yet it also works within the terms of a committed assembly for listening.

The opening words of the Qawwali are very significant. The word 'Dum' has the double meaning of 'life' and 'breath'. 'Mustt' is the state of being lost to this world, or being located in another realm, or intoxicated in the love of God. Qualander is a mystic. So, collectively 'Dum Mustt Qualander, Mustt Mustt' signifies a mystic lost to this life and breathing the very love of God. The Qawwali is both an expression of mystical experience and an invitation to abandon worldly life and adopt the mystical way, the way of the Qualander. The nod towards Western music and tastes is quite marginal; as a global recording phenomenon this Qawwali speaks its own language, as it ever has.

And now our story takes another turn, ascending cadence becomes descending. The infinite loop of improvisation cuts short, backtracks, goes forward, amplifies and lays its stress on something quite unexpected. It is the responsibility of the Qawwal to react to the listeners. Nusrat himself now proceeds to produce two further versions of Mustt, Mustt. In its second incarnation, the Massive Attack Remix, Nusrat seeks to engage with that assembly for listening that is his new Western audience. As all Qawwals must he searches for a means to keep in step with the spiritual capacity of his audience. So at the second turning of this story he brings instrumental music to the fore and renders the text, the words that are anyway incomprehensible to his listeners, secondary. Some of the conventional Qawwali vocal features disappear altogether. But, for all that, the subject of the Qawwali is still Ali, a refrain simple enough to be repeated emphatically and picked out by the most untrained ear.

The third turning of our tale describes a loop back to the ground on which Qawwali was first born. '*Mustt, Mustt*' returns home, this time to know its birthplace as it has become. In its third incarnation it is released largely for audiences in the Indian subcontinent. It is the function of the

Qawwal to attend to the changed spiritual requirements of the assembly for listening, a subcontinental audience that can both understand and know the tradition and engage with the path presented. So what is one to make of '*Mustt Mustt*' mark three, released in the subcontinent under the title '*Mustt Qalander*'? To what realm does it transport one? It is a fast-paced affair with Nusrat joined by female vocalists. The synthesised music drowns everything and all is lost in funky *tal*. Although Ali is still there, he is no longer the subject of the song. What was meant to be listened to in devotion and ecstatic contemplation now becomes disco dancing music – ecstasy of quite another kind.

It was at this point, with just three versions in hand, that I determined to make '*Mustt Mustt*' a subject of a diatribe on the awful assaults of global postmodern popular culture on my heritage. My assembly for listening was to be, appropriately enough, in Delhi. Listen to this anti-progression, this heedless descent into meaninglessness, I began. I played the three incarnations only to become aware of a certain lack of reaction in my audience. Were they not concerned at how our tradition was being debased by the pernicious influences from the West? They had news for me. Never mind three versions, now there are four: 'But you chaps living in the West would have no idea about that', they noted. Feeling like some innocent abroad I listened as they brought me up to date.

The fourth incarnation of '*Mustt Mustt*' appears in the Indian film *Mohra*. Here the original subject disappears totally and becomes an object: an object of material and sexual desire. The lyrics are changed slightly so the original idea of losing oneself in the love of God evaporates and objectified sex comes into play:

Tu Cheese Bari Hay, Mustt Mustt.

The word 'cheese' translates as 'things', 'commodities' and 'material'. In the original version the word 'bari' refers to higher saints. Here, wordplay is used to connote the idea that a purely sexual object of love can also be divine and you can get 'high' on material things too! The changed spiritual requirements could not be more explicit. This is a world turned upside down but, as my audience in Delhi clearly pointed out, the turning was a home-grown revolution. There was more to come. You should get yourself a copy of the new compendium edition, I was told with a certain impish glee by my audience that had now become my teachers. They sent me in search of the appropriately named 'The New Massacre' version of '*Mustt Mustt*' by Boota and Master G. Here, a number of different versions of the Qawwali – including the original and the Indian film version – are brought together in a postmodern blend. But instead of *tarana*, we have rap. The entire amalgam is defined by absolute meaninglessness. The *object* now becomes a pure extrava-ganza, a fusion of sounds that is 'with it', a commodity that is only a commodity.

Like a moth irresistibly drawn to the flame, I followed the path of '*Mustt Mustt*' to the final immolation, the *coup de grâce*. It was delivered during the 1996 Cricket World Cup. Where once the subcontinent had spiritual passion it now has unbridled devotion for cricket and, inciden-tally, leads the world in betting syndicates that corrupt that erstwhile gentlemanly path as well. The sponsors of the game broadcast a special advertisement on numerous satellite channels throughout Asia and selected countries in Europe. The advertisement features a group of young children playing cricket in a Pakistani village. On the soundtrack '*Mustt Mustt*' is just about audible. It's a joyous occasion with much colour and excitement around the game. Then a child hits the ball, which flies towards the sky, spins as if catching fire and revolves into the symbol for Coke. The soundtrack swells with the unmistakable sound of '*Mustt Mustt*' at full volume. What became a commodity now promotes another commodity, one with rather imperialist tendencies. Nusrat Fatah Ali Khan's crowning achievement, the Qawwali that brought him the acco-lade of 'Shahen-Shah-e-Qawwali', the King of Kings of Qawwali, is finally drained of all its original meaning. Its real essence, intoxication in the love of God, is reduced to the desire for Coke: 'the *real* thing'.

I remember asking Nusrat, shortly after '*Mustt Mustt*' took off, whether it was a good idea to Westernise the Qawwali. 'I cherish the tradition of classical music more than my life,' he said. 'I consider its protection and preservation as my spiritual duty. As an experiment I do not mind the use of Western musical instruments. But it will be great injustice to introduce any change in classical music. I use Western musical instruments because I believe that you can dress up a pretty child in any clothes and it will stay pretty. But the more important thing is that the child should not get injured while putting on those clothes.'

In the case of '*Mustt Mustt*', the clothes did much more than injure the child. Innocence, as the Sufis are quick to point out, is no barrier to annihilation. But the story of '*Mustt Mustt*' has a strong moral. We live on one planet, in multiple worlds. We are different assemblies of listeners for we have not yet the wit to learn how to communicate across and through our differences. I am that traveller that returns to tell we have more problems than we know. There is not only one postmodernism out there. There is not merely one global popular culture that proliferates the meaningless mundane cause of pure commodity. The world is busy building many and different postmodernisms – we are all rushing headlong to meet each other on the common ground of nothingness. The flames are dying out all over the world.

Rights

Postmodern times have played havoc with our most cherished and sacred ideals. Most notions of truth and sacredness have been dethroned; all have been shaken and seriously damaged. But the ideal of human rights has remained unaffected. Nothing, it seems, will shake our confidence in human rights, the sacred canon of liberal humanism.

Based on the older idea of natural rights first formulated in the 17th century by Locke, human rights are rights 'men' are conceived to have by virtue of their humanity. These rights do not need a decree, law or convention; they are innate to all human beings. Nevertheless, there are conventions, from the Universal Declaration of Human Rights to the European Convention on Human Rights, which give these rights a quasi-official status. Considering that they are concerned with the right to life and liberty, freedom of expression, protection of the law, and freedom from torture, inhuman or degrading treatment, and other wholesome and praiseworthy things, no one in their right mind would be against human rights. Right?

Wrong! Most of the world – that is, all of the non-Western world – regards human rights as a highly evolved form of Western imperialism. And I am not referring to nasty dictators and despotic types but legions of concerned scholars, thinkers, activists and communities. As the theory of human rights is a cardinal belief for liberal humanists, it is almost inevitable that its critics are viewed as morally questionable, folks who are in favour of promoting sin. But to have misgivings about human rights does not amount to rejecting that we have innate rights by virtue of our humanity. Neither does it indicate that one is in favour of autocratic and despotic regimes nor that one is indifferent to the protection of those persecuted, tortured or imprisoned for their beliefs or politics. What it does suggest, however, is that we ought to think more deeply about what it means to be human.

It does not take much to establish that our current notion of universal human rights is problematic. To begin with there is the question of the self-righteous irrationality that denies the right to food and shelter but insists on the right to self-expression.

Then, there is the practice of using human rights as a form of instrumental rationality: it is the long and powerful stick with which the West constantly beats the Third World. It often provides a rational justification for 'structural adjustment', 'liberalising' or opening the economy to 'free markets', for withholding aid, and expressing the fear of difference. In other words, the whole idea of human rights has become a political device used for defending the status quo and maintaining the dominance of the West.

What really concerns critics of human rights is the fact that it is grounded in an idealised abstraction called the individual. The whole concept of human rights assumes a social order based on liberal democracy where society is simply a collection of 'free' individuals. But the individual is not the whole person. A person has links with family and community, history and tradition, environment and nature, the cosmos and the universe. The individual is simply a truncated and selected conception of the person constructed for the sake of practical convenience. The individual exists as an atomised unit. A person incorporates his/her parents, children, extended family, ancestors, community, friends, enemies, ideas, emotions, self-image, perceptions, visions, the entire gamut of self-identity. Violence inflicted on a person equally damages the whole community; and violation of the rights of the person affects, and can even destroy, the entire community.

From the perspective of the whole person, rights cannot be individu-alised.

The insistence of many non-Western cultures and religious traditions on consensus instead of majority opinion is based on their belief in the corporate and collective nature of human rights. These traditions see God as the source of all morality and originator and guarantor of all rights and duties. Theological worldviews regard the idea that humankind is the source of morality as misplaced arrogance and the notion of an autonomous individual as naive. They see the view of the human being presented in the Universal Declaration as a defective reading of what constitutes a human being: are humans simply packages of material and psychological needs, wrapped in an atomised micro-cosm? Is this all there is to being human?

Since an autonomous, isolated individual does not exist in non-Western cultures and traditions, it does not make sense to talk of his or her rights; and where there are no rights, it is quite absurd to speak of their denial or annulment. However, this does not mean they renounce the idea of the individual entirely nor that individuality is totally unpro-tected. Indeed, general propositions about individual dignity and the respect due to each individual exist in all non-Western cultures, even though they may not be formulated as 'universal' theories. Since the starting point is the complex web of relationships between an individual and his or her personhood, a balance is sought between rights and duties. In Hinduism, for example, the notion of *dharma*, one of the fundamental concepts of Indian tradition, leads us to a symbolic correspondence with the Western idea of human rights. *Dharma* is a multi-layered concept incorporating the terms elements, data, quality and origination as well as law, norm of conduct, character of things, right, truth, ritual, morality, justice, righteousness, religion and destiny. In Sikhism, the prime duty of a human being is *sewa*: there is no salvation without *sewa*, the disinter-ested service of the community without any expectation of reward. The rights of the individual are thus earned by participating in the commu-nity's endeavour and thereby seeking *sakti*. That's exactly what the Sikh gurus did themselves. Cultures based on such notions as *dharma* and *sewa* are not concerned with the reductive exercise of defining the 'rights' of one individual against another, or of the individual as against society. In such cultures the individual is but a single knot in the whole complex web of material, social, cultural and spiritual relationships. His/her duty is to find a harmonious place in relation to society, the cosmos and the transcendent world.

Indian thought on human rights, therefore, contrasts sharply with the Western model. It does not see the *humanum* as constituted in the individual *only*. Nor does it see human rights as human only. They concern equally the entire cosmic play of the universe, from which even the gods are not absent. All sentient beings and animate creatures are also involved in the interaction concerning 'human' rights. The human is a particular being, to be sure, but neither alone nor essentially distinct. Moreover, human rights are not solely rights. They are also duties and both are interdependent. Humankind has the 'right' to survive only insofar as it performs the duty of maintaining and looking after the world (*lokasamgraha*). Human rights are not mutually isolable. They are interrelated to the whole cosmos and all their corresponding duties; they form, among themselves as well, a harmonious whole. And finally, human rights are not absolute. They are intrinsically relative. They are relationships among entities — entities determined by the relationships themselves.

We find similar ideas in Islam. In contrast to the liberal tradition of personal freedom, which signifies the *ability to act*, Islam emphasises the *ability to be*, to exist. The principal concern and emphasis is on creating a material, social and spiritual environment in which the individual can realise his or her full potential to be. Thus, the idea of human rights (*haqq al-insan*) in Islam is not limited to individual and personal freedom but includes economic, social, cultural, civil and political rights as well. The poor in Muslim societies, for example, have a right to the wealth of the community: *zakat* (the 'poor tax' or obligatory welfare contribution) is one of the five pillars of Islam and is on a par not just with prayer and fasting but with the very declaration of belief in the unity of God. Moreover, Islam makes numerous other provisions for individuals to be: for example, all persons, in a Muslim society, have a right to meet their basic necessities of food, shelter, clothing, education and healthcare irrespective of age, sex, colour or religion. But, like Hinduism, Islam also combines rights with responsibilities. Indeed, there can be no rights without responsibilities. For example, freedom of expression is a fundamental right but it is also a responsibility that has to be met with a sense of justice and commitment to truth. Similarly, the individual has a number of obligations towards the community: to promote communal values, to safeguard the lives and property of others and to seek socially relevant knowledge.

Other cultures too emphasise the whole person. Native American cultures, for example, stress the importance of the collective, which is more than the aggregate of individuals in a tribe. It includes the history of the tribe, its sacred grounds, animals, trees, rocks – all subsist in a dynamic mutual relationship. Thus for Native Americans the individual exists in a matrix of relationships and only makes sense in a communal framework. The Buddhist notion is similar. For the Buddhist, the self is always changing, evolving and devolving. Defining humans as the sole inheritors of the planet at the expense of other animate beings leads to hubris and evil. In Chinese thought, which emphasises harmony more than anything else, the relationship between the person and nature is the supreme positive value. It is not just the person who has rights; nature has rights too.

Indeed, Western culture is unique amongst all human cultures in reducing the person to an individual and then placing the individual at the pinnacle of humanity. Almost all non-Western cultures have more elaborate notions of human rights than the ones we find in the Universal Declaration.

Even in the West, there have been critics and detractors since the idea of human rights was first proposed. For Jeremy Bentham, the 18th-century English philosopher and champion of utilitarianism, the very idea of such rights was 'nonsense on stilts'. For Edmund Burke, the 18th-century statesman and political philosopher, their 'abstract perfection' was also their 'practical defect'. And for moral philosopher, Alasdair Mac-Intyre, human rights are fictions, like 'witches and unicorns'. In his classic *After Virtue*, MacIntyre argued for a recovery of virtue in the classical sense as an antidote to a paranoid preoccupation with individual rights.

Why are we so attached to a specific version of human rights that is so out of sync with the notions of the rest of humanity? All non-Western cultures, without exception, frame human rights within human needs. And Western capitalist societies, as Indian scholar Upendra Baxi suggests, find the problem of needs rather annoying. It is frequently transformed into a contest between 'bread' and 'freedom' and freedom always wins in the Western perspective, despite the fact that without 'bread', 'freedom' of speech and assembly, of association, of conscience and religion, of political participation, are all existentially, and often practically, meaningless for its 'victims'. Indeed, it is characteristic of classical and contemporary Western liberal thought to ignore the entire problematic of basic human needs. Yet, history clearly shows that agitation and activism to secure what we now term human rights occurred predominantly in periods of improved economic conditions rather than periods of depression, recession or any other formulation of hard times, times when bread was scarce. Furthermore, the leaders and participants in such activism were not those worst afflicted by the scourge of poverty and need.

Liberalism also has a serious problem with the notion of community. The liberal perspective sees the egalitarian approach of non-Western cultures as denying the basic characteristics of personal freedom. Belonging to a community consciously demands both discipline, which may include pressure to conform, and self-sacrifice, personal willingness to forgo certain choices, opportunities, indulgences or gratifications in favour of fulfilling one's allegiance, loyalty and responsibilities to others. That it does – no community can exist if every individual goes his or her own way and defines his or her own morality. Indeed, we in the West are unable to deal easily with any kind of collective identity except one defined by geography.

However, despite our myopia, the narrowly conceived definition of human rights cannot be sustained for long. The concerns of the majority of humanity, doubts amongst Western thinkers and statesmen, as well as practical experience gained from fighting for human rights on the ground will ensure an eventual shift towards an all-embracing notion of human dignity.

In the minds of most people, the admirable Amnesty International is equated with the struggle for human rights. As such, what Amnesty fights for, or fights against, is taken to be the sum total of the human rights agenda: detention without trial, disappearance, torture, extra-judicial executions and capital punishment. But the human rights activists in many Third World countries have been forced by experience to go much beyond this agenda. In India, for example, human rights action has taken the form of the organisation and empowerment of the tribal people, the *dalits*, and the marginalised rural poor. Many of these people cannot meet their inherent right to survive without social empowerment. Thus the Indian human rights movement had to move, by necessity, from a narrow focus on civil liberties to wider issues of basic needs and social empowerment.

The rights that are argued for in the idea of 'universal human rights' are rights against the state: the state should ensure freedom of expression and dissent, should not engage in persecution or torture on account of political, religious or ethnic affiliations, should guarantee the civil liberties of citizens and a libertarian attitude towards expressions of individual tastes, feelings and desires. But the state, argue the more open-minded human rights groups, is not the sole adversary: there are the local power structures, the structures of global dominance and the multinationals – all of whom are collaborating with the state to deny basic rights to the marginalised. This collaboration, they argue, has led to particularly inhuman models of development that reduce vast segments of the rural population to abject poverty, rendering them helpless and incapable of survival. These models have an in-built bias against the citizens in unorganised and informal sectors; citizens who have to be kept in their place as a perpetual source of cheap and trouble-free labour, a predicament that has generated untold indignity and eventual loss of the ability of these citizens to survive. So the battle for 'human rights' is also a battle for appropriate models of sustainable growth. It is a redundant theoretical abstraction whether *dalits* and other marginalised communities in India have any rights if they cannot actually survive.

As a Western construct, the whole idea of human rights has developed in ethnocentric and rather egocentric ways. The 'human' recipient of these rights is perceived as of a piece with and in the manner of Newton's clockwork universe and Descartes' dualistic rationality. It is time we saw the human as a complete person and human rights moved into the age of quantum physics.

Human rights, as Declared Universally, are a sophisticated system that answers the historic conundrums of Western society. Sophistication is not the same as subtlety. There is a chronic lack of subtlety as well as sophistication in purblind determination to save people from problems that have no meaning in the conditions of their existence for the sake of corralling them into the confines of a way of life that will either condemn them to the perpetual human indignity of poverty and disadvantage or inevitably lead to their slow, painful and uncomforted extinction. Theoretically, the doctrine of human rights is about compassion, the activation of our highest sensibilities, the application of our most civilised and intelligent attributes in care for the well-being of our fellow human beings. Compassion is only both sophisticated and subtle when it meets the needs of the needy in pragmatic terms and by practical means commensurate with their needs and in conformity with their aspirations as they define and understand them. In human rights, as in so much else, one size does not fit all. Nor should we persist in insisting it should.

Only one common human intent fits all: a collective commitment to be humane. Beyond that consensus, we need to explore and mutually support the great diversity of efforts to ensure the common intent is delivered in real, usable, life- and person-enhancing forms as and how it meets actual needs of actual people and communities. That should become the Declared Intent, the objective towards which we should all devoutly work.

Sex

Sex has become impossible. It has turned into an essential, mindless, egoistic, explicit, league championship event. It has become a public performance art in which instant gratification must lead to total satisfaction. But the equation that sex equals satisfaction just does not compute. On the contrary: sex is increasingly becoming synonymous with misery and unhappiness.

It is, of course, the pre-eminent spectacle of our time. Sex is everywhere, and impossible to escape. Sexual voyeurism is the fastest growing genre on television. Late-night output of Channel 4, Channel 5 and satellite channels like Sky 1, Living and Bravo is largely devoted to programmes ranging from smutty (*Greece Uncovered*, *Prickly Heat*) to soft porn (*Sex and Shopping*, *Red Shoe Dairies*) to more explicit stuff.

Elsewhere, explicit and extensive discussion about dysfunctional sexual performance is a chat show, a game show, any kind of show as long as it is on television. The airwaves are full of graphic pop songs and talk-ins where people phone in to talk about their sex lives. The mechanics of sex — sweaty rutting, attentive pawing and scraping, and athletic not to say ergonomically challenging engagements — are essential elements of virtually every Hollywood production. Newspapers, magazines, advertisements and billboards constantly flash sex all around us.

The sheer quantity of sex around us is quite unprecedented in history. We are the first generation ever to be constantly watching, listening to, thinking about, preparing for, engaging in and recovering from sex.

Yet, all this sex, instead of producing any joy, is simply leading to more and more angst. The more we flaunt our sexuality the more therapists, counsellors, pop psychologists, agony aunts and uncles we spawn to minister to our deep unhappiness and misery. It's rather like the *Rhyme of the Ancient Mariner*: 'water, water everywhere, nor any drop to drink'. The Ancient Mariner was doomed to survey the abundance of salt water that could neither satisfy nor sustain life because he killed the albatross. We too have killed the albatross of sexual happiness; and appear to be dying of thirst among the murky bitter waters we have made.

The evidence of our sexual misery is everywhere. It is best captured in films like *Happiness* and *Romance* that try to represent the sexual spirit of our time. The three sisters of *Happiness* are doomed to grotesque fates in their perennial quest for sexual fulfilment. One of them has a disastrous date with a man who, after being rejected, kills himself. The second seeks an encounter with a habitual maker of abusive calls but finds him too tame. The third, an apparently happy housewife and mother, discovers that her husband is a paedophile. *Happiness* explores almost every kind of sex – including necrophilia. Yet, nothing satisfies its characters – they remain pathetic, lonely individuals doomed to misery.

Like *Happiness*, the plot of *Romance*, one of the most explicit films to go on public release, revolves around a succession of humiliating and degrading encounters. But no matter how far-out the sex, there is just no fulfilment to be had.

The world at large reflects the sexual misery we find in such films. A recent survey by the University of Chicago, published in the *Journal of American Medical Association*, and billed as the most comprehensive investigation into adult sex habits since the famous Kinsey report of 1948, paints a very bleak picture of sexual satisfaction. One in four American women do not enjoy sex and one in three men in all age groups think they are sexually inadequate. Some 27 per cent of women in the 18 to 29 group get no pleasure from sex and consider it a necessary ordeal. The rest are unhappy and dissatisfied because they think they are not doing it right, or not doing it enough, or not doing it the way their partners want them to do it!

So, why all this sexual dissatisfaction, misery and unhappiness – in an age of total saturation, without inhibition, without limits?

I got my sexual grounding through *The Perfumed Garden*. One day, just after I turned 18, a well-thumbed copy mysteriously appeared in my room. The book was written in 14th-century Tunis, famed for its learning and splendour. In sharp contrast to contemporary Muslim societies, it was an open, sensual society where a healthy sex life was seen as essential for a well-balanced personality, good health, happiness, spiritual fulfilment and many other noble virtues. Not surprisingly, Sheikh Nefzawi, the author, reflects the candour of his times.

Nefzawi is often seen in the West as a dirty old man. But he was a poet and a philosopher with a truly wicked sense of humour. He wrote the book with an eye on the market so there is a strong accent on technique – the widely available translation by Richard Burton is only a fraction of this section. But for Nefzawi sex had another, altogether different dimension – a dimension that comes out through the aphorisms, epigrams and sayings of 'wise men and sages' that are scattered liberally throughout the text. It is this dimension beyond the physical act that we have totally lost. Indeed, it seems to me that we have turned the ancient wisdom and metaphors of people like Sheikh Nefzawi on their head – that's why sex has become such an unattainable goal.

Nefzawi taught me three basic lessons. First, sex is a product of deep passion. Satisfying sex has to be based on something much greater than the base desire of the groin. Good sex cannot be had from a cold, clinical relationship – the kind personified by characters in *Happiness* and *Romance*. It requires all the passion in our soul.

In place of passion, we now have obsession. So obsessed have we become with sex that many of us are happy to mutilate our bodies in the pursuit of it. In an age of aerobic exercises, hard bulging bodies, oversize silicone breasts, bleached hair, nose jobs, the absolute necessity to look good at all times under the most minute scrutiny, and the need to deliver hydraulic-quality performance, and – well, is it any wonder sex is angst? Passion in contrast requires romance, commitment, pain, inconvenience – all those things we shun.

I am reminded of an episode of the cult teenage zeitgeist programme of our time, *Buffy the Vampire Slayer*. In one episode our heroine, the slayer, reaches her 17th birthday and celebrates by exercising her newly acquired legal right of being a fully sentient, rightfully liberated woman – by having sex with her boyfriend, who just happens to be a morally confused vampire! Whatever turns you on. The moral, forgive what seems like a prostitution of the language, of the tale is clear. Sex is every new adult's legal entitlement; not just a right, it is a necessity. The conscientious citizen, therefore, had better waste no time in exercising their right before liberty vanishes from the land.

What struck me so forcefully was the sheer cold-blooded deliberation, the calm calculation of Buffy, the model teenager for millions. There was romance, however bizarre, but it was decidedly subordinate to self-possession, total lack of passion, and strategic logic of what it is to be a person in postmodern times. I have no doubt the programme-makers regarded their storyline as educational and responsible. But these mores are not conducive to a fulfilling sexual life.

Second, sex is about relinquishing power. It is essentially about giving and giving everything. And the most important thing to give up is your own ego, the barrier between yourself and sexual happiness. In Nefzawi's terminology, sublime sex emerges after the total annihilation of the ego. Selflessness gives you self-control and self-control is the key to that illusive, long-lasting organism, the recipe for happiness.

But if sex is a power trip, an uncontrolled expression of ego, then you are cooking with the wrong ingredients. It is quite impossible to have satisfying sex with power-mad, self-centred, selfish imbeciles such as those represented in *Sex and the City* or *Ally McBeal*. The high-powered, thirtysomething singleton women of *Sex and the City* treat men as sexual playthings and reap the consequences: when they do have sex it is never satisfying. Ditto for men who treat women as sexual objects. The characters populating *Ally McBeal* are just too obsessed, too self-centred for anything as elevated as satisfying sex – they have to settle for plumbing jobs.

We have reduced sex to an arena of personal self-disposal, an exercise of personal power for as much individual gain as possible. Sex is selfishness writ large. It is a transaction judged by personal, individual benefits. It is about taking everything for yourself; not sharing or giving. If you make sex into an end in itself for the purpose of personal gratification you should not be surprised to end up as a lonely individual. A full sexual encounter still takes two, and making both parties lonely individualists out of their own ends results in double the amount of dissatisfaction. It geometrically expands the possibilities and potential for unhappiness.

Third, sex requires sincerity and time. Good sex is not possible without tenderness, and tenderness requires sincerity. But sincerity cannot be expressed instantly; it has to be demonstrated. That means you need bucketloads of time. You are not going to be sincere with someone you have just picked up in a bar! Or someone you are having a passing relationship with. Sincerity is totally at odds with our ironic postmodern society. In a society where everything is accelerating time is rather rare. Sex is thus little more than an insincere, breathless activity. It is, as promoted by so many chat shows, lad's magazines and women's glossies, a lifestyle. Something you slot in between the office, picking up the kids, checking your e-mail and the shopping trip. Or it is a leisure activity – the outcome of a good night out. It is hardly surprising then that it has become so oppressive and unsatisfying.

Ideas of sex expressed in Eastern classics like *The Perfumed Garden* horrified and attracted Europe in equal measure. When Europe expanded its bounds and launched its colonial career it did so denouncing the East for libertine licentiousness, fornication and generalised sexual perversions. And countless Europeans headed East in search of liberated sex they could only dream of in Europe.

But if the East was a continent content with sex it was because it circumscribed sex within a philosophy. Sex, as we are told in the *Kama*

Sutra, another classic that everyone has heard of but no one has actually read let alone understood, begins and ends in the mind. And an empty mind, a hedonistic mind, a mind devoid of imagination and conviction, is incapable of satisfying sex.

Indeed, sex is like the *Kama Sutra* itself: difficult, intricate and mysterious. The West has made sex easy and explicit. It has therefore drained it of its nourishing and spiritual content. Sex has become so easy that it is brandished as a metaphor for everything, everywhere in our postmodern culture. Sex sells. Not just cars and holidays but even instant coffee, toothpaste and insurance. It is so explicit that nothing is left to the imagination. The mind, the heart, the soul, have no part to play in its execution: everything is reduced to simple mechanics.

This is why the debate about sex education focuses on operation and orientation. Sex education has all the sophistication of a computer user's manual for proficient performance and proper maintenance. But we teach a lie. We teach that sex is easy, an effortless, uncomplicated part of everyday life – an activity divorced from philosophy and outlook on life. By leaving out the most important parts of sex – passion, sincerity, selflessness, time, imagination and mystery – we make sex so impossible for our children. An education based on sex for sex's sake is no education at all. That's why all the sex education in the world has no impact on teenage pregnancies or shattered family lives.

It is time we understood that sex is not an infantile pursuit. The more we pursue sexual happiness for selfish ends, the more it will recede from us. Satisfying sex is an adult endeavour. Sexual ecstasy requires the agony of mature sentiments, hard work and integrity. The only way to make satisfying sex possible is to place it within a philosophy where it is neither the sole purpose nor an end in and of itself.

At the very least we need to relearn and appreciate that satisfying sex is a shared experience. Anything that is shared requires mutual give and take. Mutuality is central to sexual happiness. Mutuality is the idea that we are much more than mere individuals. It is the idea that our greatest personal fulfilment will arise from merging our sense of self in selfless care for the well-being of someone other than ourselves – simultaneously giving and receiving. It is the concept that strict personal accounting fails to calculate the more infinite possibilities and potential of looking at things from other than the perspective of one.

Of course, mutuality has a great deal to do with love. We do pretty well with sex as metaphor for self-love. But we have lost entirely the sense of sex as a passport to the love of anything beyond self. And that used to be the sublime mystery, so fascinatingly outlined in the *Kama Sutra*, that sex implied and expressed.

Classical Persian and Urdu poetry is awash with love, with potent sexual inferences and references; yet, it is actually religious by metaphoric intent and generally understood meaning. Sex is a metaphor for love and love is a metaphor for spirituality. In ancient, Eastern wisdom it is through the mutuality of human relations, fully functional sexual loving of another, and loving and parenting the offspring of a sexual union that we acquire the experience and the concepts to understand the divine. The mutual, mystical union of two people was, and is, the metaphor for creative benevolence, or the principle of God. Mutuality puts sex in its place as part of a more profound conception of what it is to be human in a world where life is us and other people, me and you.

Without some notion of mutuality, sex is well nigh impossible. If we think of sex as easy, casual, fast and uncomplicated, we turn it into an albatross, a dead one, hanging around our necks and leading us into untold misery and personal unhappiness.

But if we return a touch of mystery to sex, temper our egos with some modesty and selflessness, and are willing to devote time, energy and integrity to sex, it would become the true fountain of happiness. When my sons turn 18, and mysteriously find a copy of *The Perfumed Garden*, this is the idea they will grow up to imbibe.

Shopping

Shopping, as we all know, is much more than a mere cultural experience. It is an existential ritual. It confirms we are alive. 'I shop, therefore I am' is the watchword of our time. It is the source of our identity in a society that identifies us by our accumulation, presentation of and indulgence in material goods. In these postmodern times, where we shop and what we buy defines who we are, what we are, where we are coming from and where we are going. Shopping unites the increasingly fragmented bits of ourselves: we shop to complete the Self.

But there is a serious problem with shopping. Most men actually hate it, and with the exception of those with excess cash to burn, most women do not like it much either, as numerous polls and surveys have confirmed. We would rather do the crossword puzzle than hit the shops. Indeed, shopping has become so stressful that most of us prefer to work late at the office than go shopping. But go we must – to lug in the weekly provisions, to find that perfect gift on Mother's Day, Father's Day, Valentine's Day, not forgetting the nightmare of all shopping expeditions, Christmas.

If normal shopping is hateful, then shopping for that special birthday or wedding or congratulatory gift compounds all the inherent tensions and stresses of incipient postmodern existence. It crystallises them into pure existential angst. It confronts us with all our inadequacies – existential and corporeal as well as financial. It is the ultimate ordeal of going

Shopping

from shop to shop trying to find something suitable but never, ever, suc-
ceeding. It is the constant rebuff from harassed, rude attendants uttering
the dreaded words, 'Please pay at the cash desk'. Words that consign us to
demeaning penal colonies of interminable queues.

Even more hateful, Christmas shopping is the acute commodified
quandary writ large. Hours standing bemused and distracted to the point
of dementia: will this one or that one be exactly the thing great uncle
Mordecai will be delighted to return as soon as the shops re-open?
Hours of foot slogging to the point of certainty that bipedalism is a
flawed system of locomotion. Hours of 'oh what the hell, it'll do',
knowing full well it will not. Then, moments of demonic possession, the
kind that impel a theme spree, selecting one trendy novelty idea to serve
all. 'Uzbek goat cheese! Yes! This will be the year of Uzbek goat
cheese!' Succeeded by hours of certainty it was a personal statement too
far.

One is confronted with abundance of everything, defying all rational
and deductive powers of selection, taste and judgement. And you do it
every year, like clockwork, setting new achievement records each and
every time in conspicuously redundant consumer excess.

But now, it seems, we have a comprehensive, not to say simple and
elegant, solution to the central problem of Western existence. Virtually
perfect, e-shopping. Technology has finally been put to the service of
humanity and we can now shop from the comfort of our homes. The
Internet is now the biggest shopping mall in the world. Get on the Web,
and get anything you want. Or, if you prefer, 'push your way to the front
of the queue' with Open, the interactive shopping experience of digital
television.

With e-shopping it can be Christmas every day of the year. You can
shop in delectable peace and security, from your favourite armchair, and
find just what you are looking for. Since e-shopping can be done at any
moment of leisure any time, at any hour of the day or night, from anywhere in the world, there is no need for frantic panic decisions.
Selections can be calm and rational, appropriate and thoughtful. Indeed,

some Internet vendors will thoughtfully help you with even more ideas on what to get for whom. They may even prompt you to treat yourself to a personal reward for all the money you are saving on train, bus and taxi fares, petrol and parking, and those stops for a quick coffee and a reviving bite to eat.

Above all else e-shopping means transcending the existentialist's ultimate conclusion. No need to worry about other people looking over your shoulder, or giving you disapproving glances when you try on that dress. In e-shopping there is only you. Finally, at long last, the destination, the evolutionary pinnacle has been attained: individual freedom and total personification, unrestrained, untrammelled aloneness, with everything at your disposal. All you have to do is click on the appropriate buttons and then wait for your goods to be delivered to your front door.

But while e-shopping solves certain problems, it creates certain others.

E-shopping denies us sublimation. What e-shopping gives as comfort it takes away as time. There is the endless frustration of logging on, clicking your way through useless Web pages only to realise you forgot to bookmark the one site you really need to use. And, once you have ordered your goods, you have to wait for them to be delivered. Pizzas and burgers may take an hour, but everything else takes ages. One can wait up to a month for a book to be delivered or six weeks for a pair of shoes to materialise. This languorous yet fretful interlude extends without resolving the uncertainty principles of shopping.

We are denied the instant gratification of staggering home, fingers bisected by laden plastic bags. These characteristic stigmata console, they are proof of the 'no pain, no gain' thesis of shopping as purgatory. E-shopping provides no tangible confirmation you have fulfilled the primal urge. It gives you even less idea of the effect the whole procedure has had on your bank balance. Is it real money when you click goods into virtual shopping baskets?

We have so much experience of the problems of catalogue shopping that e-shopping should give us pause. Who does not know that things never materialise through the letterbox resembling the pictures in shape, size or qualitative expectation? No matter how carefully you choose your size, it never fits on arrival. Indestructible items always arrive in several small pieces. Bargains often turn out to be junk.

E-shopping performs all the mechanics of the process without any of the elation or spiritual highs of the conventional variety. For all its click-ing of buttons it lacks the old tactile satisfaction of touching and feeling the goods. It denies the spiritual effect of sitting in a crumpled heap in a bus or the Underground surrounded by the visible evidence of one's share of abundance, or painfully, spinally challenged, loading one's loot into the boot of the car by the bag full.

And there is absolutely no substitute for endlessly trying on different clothes and smugly walking out of the shop without buying anything! With e-shopping only a machine knows you are there and cares not when you huff offline underwhelmed.

Nor is there much joy in haggling with a machine. Nor is there much chance of a chance encounter, of discovering something unusual and joyful, something you know you've got to have because the first time you held it in your hand you knew you were meant to have it. E-shop-ping takes the cognisance that shopping is hateful only to make it an even more alienating experience.

Shopping is such a bore, such an empty experience, because it is no longer shopping. It is merchandising. It demeans our humanity by reducing us to rampant materialism. It reshapes our physical environ-ment and human consciousness into arid landscapes. The out of town, purpose-built, one-stop malls that are palaces of merchandising are also ugly temples to materialism. Merchandising has remodelled our high streets into barricaded enclaves that are difficult to access and are of no use for anything except merchandising.

Merchandising is a transaction, an impersonal be and do what you want to, to which everyone else is indifferent. Merchandising can only show indifference to our existence and essential humanity. Merchandis-ing takes the human contact out of humanity and replaces it with jostling through faceless crowds. It tells you to invent who you would like to be, rather than rooting you in recognition of who you really are. It is a game, a role playing where material things masquerade as your humanity. And that's why we hate it. E-shopping takes merchandising to a higher personal level. Now it's just you, in your isolated loneliness, the computer, and all the faceless shops of the world!

Shopping used to be something different. It used to be a social relationship. Remember corner shops, remember family stores, remember local arts and crafts shops? In such places one interacted with vendors who spoke to you civilly, who knew who you were and cared that your requirements were met to your satisfaction. Shops were places for interaction and reaction, conversation and human contact, places people stopped and talked to each other, chewed over the gossip. Shopping was not one-dimensional, self-transactional wish fulfilment (with all the unwelcome psychological overtones verging on narcissism and self-abuse). It was closer involvement in community while acquiring the necessities of material existence. It was not performance art of the person, it was up close and personal face-to-face encounters where human contact, not dead objects, told us who we were, and made sense of other people.

That is why I love shopping at my local, mostly Asian, stores. The families of shopkeepers and assistants are always inveterate chatters. Here, you will find gossip without parallel, inordinate interest in who and what you are. They will quiz you, in depth, in pertinent detail as they manoeuvre you among the available goods. As they learn of your circumstances and problems they negotiate you to sensible choices as well as delightful indulgences. By the end of the process, if you have properly entered into the relationship, they will offer to give you a discount. This is not the merchandiser's prominent ploy to make you part with more money. It is the individual shopper's earned reward for polite and entertaining social engagement, a gift from the vendor. It is shopping as vindication of humanity and interconnectedness, a relationship that makes you appreciate other people, who appreciate you right back.

Shopping

So shop till you drop in malls of your choice or e-shop in your aloneness if you must and secure the end of civilisation as human community.
But give me human scale and human contact every time.

Terrorism

Terrorism has gone postmodern. Not only has it acquired a global reach, it now follows the logic of consumerism. It is 'manufactured' and 'delivered' like other global consumer goods. A computer, for example, may be manufactured in several different places, assembled in another, and sold anywhere on the face of the earth. Similarly, terrorism can fester in several places, terrorists recruited from many countries come together in one place to hatch their plans and then deliver their deadly payload wherever opportunity presents itself. In a world devoid of meaning and fuelled by perpetual doubt, we have an added uncertainty: meaningless terror, the lurking fear that anyone can be the next target, the next innocent victim – the constant anxiety whose only function is to feed insecurity and breed more uncertainties. Welcome to the 21st century.

In its postmodern mould, terrorism has a deep and intrinsic relationship with the media. Terrorists live for the media: they plan and strategise in virtual reality. They die on air: recall how the execution of Timothy McVeigh, the Oklahoma bomber, was delayed for several minutes to ensure that the video link was up and running. The actual acts of terrorism, from hijackings to bombings, are often played out in the full glare of global television as though they were some sort of reality show. This is why the distinction between fictional and real terrorists is often blurred. Think of all those Hollywood movies depicting Islam and terrorism as synonymous – such as *Rules of Engagement*, *True Lies*, *Executive Decision* and *The Siege*. The message of these films finds a ready echo not just in tabloid journalism, but in respectable broadsheets and political rhetoric of all shades. In their turn, terrorists themselves have begun to resemble the mindless killers of the films, hell-bent on destroying, as *Rules of Engagement* tells us, 'the infidel Americans, their allies, including civilians, and plunder their possessions'.

But while terrorism has embraced the virtual reality of film and television, its final outcome is old-fashioned realism. Terrorists have surveyed the postmodern world and in answer to its layer upon layer of simulation, its pastiche of flirting with disaster, they make film maker's conventions into flesh, broken and burnt flesh. When *Independence Day* blew apart New York skyscrapers and the White House, audiences cheered and were amused. It was ironic, a puckish conceit within its genre, in its own way a homage to the power it appeared to deride. Now, if one could look, those cinematic conceits would be revealed as mere shoddy imagery, ersatz, cardboard cut-outs, virtual unreality, the conceit of these simulacra the worst kind of hubris: the pride that came before the fall.

The essence of terror in postmodern times is its capacity to take us beyond imagination. It has the capability to make real the unimaginable in actual, atrocious horror. The postmodern terrorist simultaneously manipulates image and reality in callous calculation. The callous calculation, for example, that made us watch, during the week of September 11, again and again not a simulation, not an artist's impression, not an imaginative leap, but the unimagined reality of devastation and appalling human loss, the fragility of the structures of triumphant worldly success. The callous calculation that tapped into our unfathomable fears of biological terror as 'anthrax letters' arrived at CBS and the Capitol in Washington. The callous calculation of the Real IRA when it placed a car bomb in a busy shopping street in Omagh, Northern Ireland.

Standing at ground zero of a new century, what can we say about the nature of postmodern terror? It is worth noting that we desperately want to misinterpret its nature, its being and its genesis. We seek to make it

Other, the dark alternate of Western civilisation. Osama bin Laden, with his ridiculous beard and gaudy turban, is the perfect idealised Other, drawing into one infernal being all the consistent themes of age-old stereotypes: brutal, barbaric, cruel, the absolute fanatic outside the ambit of Western consciousness, truly the demon Other.

Yet the essence of the Other is to exist within tradition and outside the modern or postmodern. It is in the nature of the Other to be quaint and exotic but also impotent, incapable of challenging the power and supremacy of Western dominance. In which case, the Other simply cannot explain, nor generate a bin Laden. Cave dwellers are not necessarily cave men. The clearest indication of the aberration bin Laden presents within tradition came when the Taliban's own gathering of legal scholars, working on the basis of traditional Islamic law, condemned the attacks of September 11, found them to be culpable, criminal deeds. When the question of terror is put, tradition – no matter how ossified and frozen in history – clearly distinguishes its unconscionable nature; it cannot harbour nor condone the animus of such evident evil.

The 21st-century terrorist is a product of much more than merely demonised tradition. Terrorism is now crafted out of the same materials that made postmodernism, sharing its characteristics and values, its eclectic mix of traditions and modernity, and its concern for collapsing past, present and future. No wonder there is no appetite for fabricating a common definition of terror.

Postmodern terror has four basic features. First, it is about pride. Postmodernism itself has always been a conceit: so secure in its self-confidence it could make a fetish of doubt and insecurity. Postmodern terrorists, in contrast, make fetishes of their particular notions of truth.

They seek the same global space, confidence and pride of place for their own beliefs, outlook and conceits. This is why terrorist goals are often stated in apocalyptic, all-embracing terms. We can see this not just in the pronouncements of al-Qaida, but also read it in the declared aims of American militias and the final testimony of Timothy McVeigh.

Second, postmodern terrorism is about the manufacture of identity. Who were these terrorists? Scions of wealthy, middle-class families, products of acculturated global society, educated in universities and technical institutes in Western cities, at home with all the ephemera of postmodern existence. Indistinguishable in cities, they change identities to move among the ebb and flow of transient populations, taking a course here, renting an apartment there, hip enough to cause hardly a ripple when wanting to try out the ultimate big boy's toy, a flight simulator.

In particular, the postmodern terrorist is adept at assuming the garb of the technology geek. To strike fear in the heart of complacent abundance demands mastery of all that science and technology knows of destructive capacity with coherent, planned precision. To outwit its targets, terror must be more cunningly adept in knowing the technological ability of its opponents. This is why terrorists, the home-grown American variety as well as those with global reach, are always flirting with cutting-edge technology. The mechanics of terror are the routines of sophisticated technology comprehensively understood the better to be inverted and turned against their makers and users.

The ability to change and adopt identities like a chameleon means terrorists are frighteningly familiar with their targets. Consider the September 11th attacks. The targets were carefully chosen for symbolic and real effect: a global centre of the global economy, the World Trade Centre, and the military nexus of the lone superpower, the Pentagon. The weapon of choice one incapable of being detected by any protective laser-guided space umbrella: the normal scheduled transport of an interconnected world made ballistic. In opposition to the high-tech overkill capacity of the greatest military arsenal ever assembled, the simplicity of box cutters. To achieve the end of their well-laid plans the protective invisibility of mingling within a polyglot society.

The terror of terrorism is that it assimilates itself in postmodern society so effortlessly, so unassumingly. The fear it generates is a function of familiarity, not difference. Terrorists wreak havoc because they are at home in the postmodern world. Only the urbane citizens of the border-less, global world of consumer consciousness could pass unseen until the lethal moment when they materialise their abomination.

Third, postmodern terrorism is about total war. It is here that it differs most radically from the terrorism of earlier, conventional varieties. The logic of total war was developed in modern times. Its ultimate symbol is the nuclear weapon that obliterates everything. There have always been wars and wars have always been brutal and brutalising. In the heat of battle inhumanity flourishes; the results are always horrific. Total war, the kind of war devised in the 20th century, is different. The 20th century's wars, particularly the two World Wars, sought to refine the rules of war while simultaneously extending the practice of war to leave civilian populations no hiding place. From the first practice blitz at Guernica in the Spanish Civil War, to the real thing directed at London and other British cities, to the fire-bombing of Dresden and on to the atomic devastation of Hiroshima and Nagasaki, the progress of war in the 20th century was the obliteration of the distinction between combatants and civilians.

The aftermath of the Second World War marked the end of colonial empire and the beginning of the imperialist era of Cold War superpower rivalry. Change seldom comes easily. Colonial powers clung tenaciously to their overseas possessions in the name of the civilising mission – building democracy and bringing the wretched of the earth, the Other, up to the mark of modern democracy. In Indo-China and Algeria, in Kenya and Aden the illogic of colonialism was opposed. It was opposed aggressively by guerrilla war, by striking at the symbols and personnel of the colonial state, it was opposed by terror in the name of freedom. Perhaps the first act in this unfolding new dispensation, the earliest recorded incident of this kind of terror was the bombing of the King David Hotel in Jerusalem, perpetrated by the Stern Gang, the Zionist guerrilla brigade among whose ranks was Menachim Begin.

The tactics were borrowed, adapted and used again and again in country after country seeking self-determination. Guerrilla terror was justified in the name of a higher responsibility to achieve nationhood and release from the injustice of colonial rule.

But this kind of conventional terrorism, with its relatively attainable goals, hence its capacity to be translated into a political process of negotiated settlement, is not dedicated solely to killing civilians or mass destruction. The Kosovo Liberation Army (KLA) seeking independence for Kosovo or the Albanian National Liberation Army seeking equal rights for Albanians in Macedonia are bent on claiming territory rather than obsessed with civilian targets. The routine of Irish paramilitaries is to issue a bomb warning by telephoning the police so that civilians can be evacuated. This is localised terror, a local cause fought on home soil for immediate and local objectives. It involves the conventional brutalities of any war; the longer it continues the greater the brutalities. An end to such terrible conflict, however, is always conceivable: from bullet to ballot box and from one-time terrorist to head of state.

Postmodern terrorism is a totally different phenomenon. It follows the logic of mutually assured destruction of the Cold War period. Everyone and everything is a legitimate target. This is just as true for bin Laden and his followers as it is for the home-grown American terrorists of the McVeigh and Unabomber variety, as well as the right-wing American militias. This breed of terrorist consciously chooses to make war, to seek the destruction of an ideologically defined enemy, to spread insecurity and fear by returning evil to what is defined as its source. The logic of this terror is absolute. It sees hegemonic power, the control and supremacy of American government for example, as the root of all evil and binds itself to do evil to any and all institutions of that power. The acts of terror are selected and directed to destabilise the order it demonises. In the hegemony it opposes, postmodern terror sees no distinction between innocent and guilty. Indeed, the terrorist does not even need the revolting double talk of 'collateral damage', for all who exist within the dominant order of the postmodern world and do not choose to oppose it are legitimate targets.

Postmodern terror, then, consciously locates itself as the antithesis to the thesis of power, the dominant power of the postmodern world and all its ways. Antithesis defines power as comprehensive violence and responds by all-embracing violence of its own. Terror then begets counter-terror. In hunting down the terrorists the normal standards that are supposedly the benchmarks of the dominant civilisation can be suspended because terror exists. So, the rule of law, judicial review and access to legal representation no longer apply, and recourse can be made to torture, in violation of the very principles of human rights and due process by which the individual should be protected from the overbearing tyranny of state power. The state becomes what the terrorists claim is its real nature. Terror justifies the failure to comply with and fulfil the difficult demands of justice in a complex world and this itself justifies the resort to more acts of terror. We have a self-sustaining, mutually reinforcing cycle of absolute opposition. So mutually self-justifying that even CNN's senior political interviewer, Wolf Blitzer, notes his surprise at the number of viewers who want to know why America is not using tactical nuclear weapons against Osama bin Laden! Or as one American expert noted: the war on terror must be fought in absolutes, so thesis and antithesis meet on common ground. In a war of absolutes there are no restraints; ultimate destruction is the only shared logic, the logic that sustains the will to fight.

Ultimately, postmodern terrorism enfolds the State within its own ambit. Terror is the creature of power, the anti-power opposed to dominance, the implacable antithesis created by a shared structure, means and logic of power. It renders the State just as passionless, cold and unyielding as itself. Both exist within a logic that makes no concessions and allows no exceptions. It is an opposition without possibility of negotiation – there is no conceivable political settlement that can accommodate the objective of the terrorist and the existence of the State.

Finally, postmodern terrorism is about release from history. This is best demonstrated in the personality of bin Laden himself. He is being constructed as the Che Guevara of the Muslim world, an icon on T-shirts, posters and postcards. He has been lifted out of history – not just his personal history with regard to what he has actually done, but the history of Islam itself, where heroes follow a well-established code of conduct. As a figurehead, what bin Laden symbolises is a new construction of Islam totally devoid of history. His one-dimensional interpretation of Islam is truly postmodern: it is an eclectic concoction of arid tradition infused with ultra-modern technology. It is infused with romanticised practices located in a virtual past, a fatalistic notion of the future that collapses on the present and moves backwards to the birth of Islam, and a plethora of pieties devoid of all ethical and moral content. It takes what it needs to justify itself out of the moral and ethical context of Islam and recasts these principles as instruments of war in its power struggle with the demonised enemy. All that exists for these rent-a-beard terrorists are two warring blocks of Islam and non-Islam. As a leaflet from Haiz ut-Tahrir, the lunatic British fringe of the Taliban, put it: 'everything other than Islam is falsehood'. As such, the Islam of the terrorists is in a state of total war with everything, everywhere, all the time!

Postmodern terrorism is a new kind of evil. But it is only one amongst many kinds of evil in the postmodern world. The inability to distinguish between reality and virtual reality, the inability to see all victims as equal, the inability to feel the pain of victims you cannot see, these are evils as great as terrorism. There can be no coexistence with the postmodern terrorists, yet merely combating them in the unending cycle of mutually reinforcing absolutes – terror and counter-terror – sustains the insecurities and fears that fuel the deluded pride and misbegotten cult of terrorism. No political accommodation is possible with terror, but there are endless evils that politics can and must address. When we make all human life equally valuable, when we make compassion, tolerance, genuine participation and distributive justice realities for everyone, we strike fear and insecurity among those bent on terror, we disorder the essentials on which it depends, we destabilise and remove its reason to exist. Not by counter-terror but by the intelligent building of peaceful coexistence is terror terrified. It is a lot easier to simply demonise, condemn and combat the terrorist. But the challenge of the 21st century is whether the courage and conviction can be found to end the causes on which terror feeds like a parasite until its manifest evil withers into madness no one can contemplate.

Toys

Christmas, the season of goodwill, is also the season of tyranny. It is the season when little children blackmail their parents to buy the toy that is all the rage this season. Toys are like drugs. Like drugs, they function as artificial stimulants of children's consciousness. They are addictive. Children just can't have enough toys. And like drugs they turn our children into zombies, insatiable consumers who hunger forever for the latest craze, and thereby destroy their imagination and well-being.

So don't buy any toys for the little blighters. Instead, wrap up a huge empty cardboard box and watch how much fun they have with it. When I did that last year, it became a ship that went 'Poop, poop' and sailed across the ocean of our living-room carpet. Unfortunately, this would probably make you the most unpopular parent of the century. Children have been hypnotised by television advertisements and made into little demons whose desires must be fulfilled. When this is translated into peer group pressure it makes children hypersensitive to the number, sophistication and therefore the cost of the toys they receive. How could they tell their friends, hold up their heads in the school playground, if they got an empty cardboard box for Christmas – even if it did provide them with hours and hours of fun? Children and parents who cannot afford the latest craze feel inadequate and alienated. So parents are caught as much in the tyranny of toys as children are.

One of the most evocative places I know is the Bethnal Green

Museum of Childhood in London, an interesting title since it is a museum of toys. What is so evocative about this museum is the ease with which you can tell the social, military and economic history of Britain by looking at the toys. This phenomenon is not a function of childhood, it is a function of adults wanting to imprint their ideas, aspirations and ideals on children. In one sense passing on our culture to children is the job of every generation, the task of continuity. But there is something limited and limiting when toys are our agency of transmission.

Of course, 'children' are not just persons below some critical age. 'Childhood' is a social construction with its own history. To understand how the toy game is played nowadays, it is worth seeing it in the context of how it developed as a part of childhood.

For a glimpse of the Good Old Days, we needn't go further than to the traditional Dutch winter solstice celebrations. There we find the original Santa Claus, who comes every year early in December, with his big bag of toys. Santa first interrogates children about their behaviour: 'Have you been good this year?' Santa's assistant, Black (yes!) Peter, whips those who fail; those who have been (Calvinistically elected to be) good, get the goodies. This quaint narrative takes us back to the days when there was little sentimentality about children, when they were simply small, pre-sexual people who had to be trained to do their future job and to be indoctrinated with the ruling virtues. Although the notion of childhood began to change with Enlightenment sentimentality, which came to full commercial flower in Victorian times, the function of toys has remained more or less the same. Now, as then, toys are used to prepare children for the crucial roles of society.

Today, toys are designed to slot children into the dominant role in affluent societies: consumption. The function of modern toys is to turn children into brainless consumers, the impulsive buyers of tomorrow. Toys are little ideological bundles that inculcate a totally materialistic understanding of desire and satisfaction, enjoyment and happiness. It is the task of children to get Mum and Dad to divert an extraordinary amount of their income into buying toys.

Conventionally, toys were a way of marking distance between children and adults. The principle used to be, 'When I was a child I thought as a child… When I became a man I put away childish things.' Now children think through concepts constructed by obnoxious marketing men and grow into childish addictions for adult 'toys' with no transition period or space to think for themselves. There is a continuous and seamless movement from 'baby's first toy' to toys for toddlers, infants, juniors, adolescents and adults. Each toy, and each step, is an elaborate marketing scheme that demands follow-up buying. Once you have bought Barbie you need to buy a couple of wardrobes, not forgetting her boyfriend, Ken. Computer games require a computer, then the software, and then the purchase of several or more games, then add-ons or new versions of the game, which are released with boring regularity, and so on. Both children and adults are locked into a feedback loop of ideas and experiences that lead nowhere but to more and more toys. Hence, the hype, the crazes, the hysteria over the toys that are sold out, with parents and grandparents flying across continents to queue for some ephemeral junk – it is all part of the act. Witness also the craze for 'collectibles', such as Beanie Babies or Cabbage Patch dolls that come complete with 'adoption papers', which made them the most sort-after toy of the 1980s.

So toys have little to do with play, and everything to do with possession. This is my first reason for keeping children away from modern toys. My second reason for rejecting toys is even stronger. They seriously limit the imagination of children. Most modern toys have one assigned function. A Teletubbie, for example, is a Teletubbie: a stupid person that lives in Teletubbyland. Batman lives in Gotham City and all the details of his miserable world are provided – nothing is left to the imagination. Dolls are no longer just dolls – bland, blank, sterile things used by little girls to create countless imaginative characters. Today's dolls lay down the law. They are Sindies, Barbies, Cabbage Patch dolls or Bonnies. They are not toys but concepts; one cannot play with them in the conventional sense of using one's imagination to create a world since their world is created for you, all the details are already filled in. Children have little to do but to follow the conceptual grid laid out for them.

The limitations placed on the imagination of children are not abstract. They always promote certain worldviews, such as that of Hollywood, in the case of movie-based toys, or that of Western middle-class computer culture, in the case of Playstation and other computer toys. Consider, for example, the message projected by Barbie. If only you looked like Barbie, little girl, you could marry Ken and live happily ever after – that is, be loved and protected unconditionally and always (by the ultimate Daddy-person). Or if you look like the princess, 'Someday, my prince will come', and then you will have the guarantee of growing up just like Mummy (the all-powerful), have Daddy (the even more powerful) and make babies (your destiny). This picture not only denies them a more complex view of their potential but also creates serious confusions. When the stakes for becoming just like Mummy get very high, in puberty and adolescence, they end up with distorted body images. It is hardly surprising that so many girls in our society grow up hating their bodies and faces, which are going through all kinds of untoward changes. Some of them settle for self-loathing, the saddest and sickest try to starve themselves to death (eating disorders) or see fat in the mirror where there is none (body dismorphic disorder). Others simply dumb themselves down to make themselves more attractive to boys.

Not surprisingly, boys are growing up expecting Barbie-type bodies and compliance in every girl they meet. And their own toys reflect the most extreme manifestation of their gender – Action Man, He-man, G. I. Joe and other big and powerful, masculine, macho, well-built and violent figurines. Most toys for boys are based on the idea that war, mayhem, destruction and domination is all there is in the world. Control, being the total master of your universe, is the basic ingredient of all electronic games. What matters is winning, 'scoring', how many points you put up on the board – every computer game has that running tally. You are up against every user who has played the game. All life becomes a contest, not just against a combatant you can see, but also against anonymous combatants – real, virtual and enemies from the future. Domination is the name of the game – camaraderie or compassion is outlawed.

There is a direct and unbroken line, I would argue, between spending your childhood shooting, kicking, stabbing, slaying, punching, hitting and playing war games, doom games, kung fu fighting games, dragon slaying games and the ability or lack thereof to manage aggression and testosterone poisoning in adolescence. From there the step to a full adult who is unable to control his rage and manage aggression is a short one. Witness how many young adults drive their cars as though they were playing a racing video game!

This brings me to my third reason for rejecting toys. By turning today's little angels into the social misfits of tomorrow, toys are seriously damaging our future.

Insofar as play is an opportunity to create, toys best serve play when they leave most room for imaginative creation. Creativity in turn fosters broad and multiple ideas about future possibilities. When toys belonged to the realm of crafts, they were shaped with one's hand and were the product of one's labour. Consequently, I would argue, toys took on a human dimension. Made of simple materials such as wood, clay and paper, they allowed for the greatest flexibility and the application of the player's imagination. They were one way of resisting a mechanical view of the world. Craft toys demanded the involvement of children and their very nature promoted socialisation and co-operation. They assisted children not just in becoming members of society in creative and flexible ways but also in thinking about the future in a myriad of imaginative ways. Children saw the future as full of potential: the world need not be the way adults have shaped it. It could be improved, it could become a better place.

Today, toys embody the qualities of the automon, the robot-like machine. They promote a monolithic notion of the future. The future has only one possibility – the continuation of the war-like present. There is no option for children to imagine alternative possibilities in the future. It is thus; and it will always remain so. In other words, modern toys increasingly embody a reductionist, one-dimensional view of the world where exploitation is the norm and there is no place for improvement or socially enlightened developments.

Moreover, exploitation is central to the way toys are actually manufactured – my last argument against toys. An overwhelming proportion of all the world's toys are made in China and South-east Asia. The Latin American Barbie is manufactured in Malaysia; the Native American Barbie with long black braids and a headband is made in Indonesia; and the Japanese Barbie is produced in China. Barbies and other global toys, manufactured by a handful of giant corporations, are made at the expense of children (as young as five and six) and women who work in appalling conditions and are paid a pittance for their labour. I have visited Thai and Indonesian toy factories where teenage girls, working night-shifts, stitch Barbie's frilly dresses in cramped conditions. Their fingers and palms are often cut to shreds and their eyes are always watery due to the strain of the work. There is a prison-like atmosphere inside these factories – workers are denied any sort of breaks, work perilously close to the hot plastic used for making all variety of dolls and breathe its poisonous fumes. They often sleep and eat in overcrowded 'hostels' next to the factories.

Fires and poisonings are a common occurrence in these factories. Since 1993, there have been a string of reports of fires and death by toxic fumes in toy factories in China, Indonesia, Thailand and Hong Kong. In 1993, a fire at the Kader Industrial Toy Company in Bangkok killed 118 workers, all but 14 of them women and children. The following year, 87 workers died in a fire inside the Zhili Handicraft factory in the Shenzhen region of southern China. In 1998, 220 Vietnamese workers, making toys for as little as six cents an hour, were poisoned by acetone, a chemical solvent used to manufacture plastic Disney characters such as the *101 Dalmatians* dogs. The main ingredients of most plastic toys – high and low density polyethylene, polyvinyl chloride, polypropylene and polystyrene – are all highly toxic. Workers constantly exposed to these chemicals experience headaches and skin rashes. Later, they experience disorders of the nervous system. Exposure to spray paints used in the manufacture of plastic toys results in the loss of white blood cells, weakens the immune system within a few months and frequently causes leukaemia. Women and children who work in toy factories often suffer serious health problems and tend to die young. And they are seldom compensated for industrial accidents.

This, then, is the other side of the cuddly toy. The side that is hidden from our gaze: the Victorian nightmare of little children and their mums slaving away in hazardous conditions for measly sums on the other side of the world. Think of that when you see your children playing with their toys.

Of course, it does not have to be that way. But breaking out of the tyranny of modern toys is not easy. A parent is not a 'good' parent if he or she cannot provide the toys demanded by their children. No one wants their children to think of them as miserly, killjoy mummies and daddies. We want them to think of us as friends. Which reminds me, since we all have been indoctrinated with the idea of being a friend to our kids, what happened to all those games you could play with your kids? What about running around the house, screaming in joy, crying with pain, hiding and seeking, building that snowman, climbing a tree, using our innate imagination and creativity to see things, interpret things, make things, designate things? Perhaps I will wrap up that cardboard box after all. I seem to remember I was required to be the engine room providing the motion across the carpet ocean. And we all laughed together.

Tradition

Tradition has almost become a term of abuse. It is most often associated with romantics, Luddites and chauvinists who want to keep us chained to the past. The very mention of tradition sends shivers of terror through all those who carry modernist and postmodernist heads on their shoulders. But much of the bad press that tradition and traditional societies have received is unjustified.

By modernist convention, we see traditional societies as backward, 'living in the past'. The essential principles of tradition are the cause of backwardness, just as it is in their nature to be incapable of change. Therefore the tradition of traditional societies is a major hurdle towards development and 'modernisation'. The classic texts of development all argue that tradition must be abandoned, indeed suppressed where necessary, if 'backward' societies of the 'Third World' are to develop and 'catch up with the West'. And, in the name of development and progress, traditional cultures have been uprooted, displaced, suppressed and obliterated.

In postmodern times, we have come to see tradition simply as dangerous; we often associate it with 'essentialism' – that is, harking back to some puritan notion of good society that may or may not have existed in history. There is some truth in the assertion that traditions can be essentialist. But this traditional essentialism is itself a product of postmodern times where nothing seems to have any meaning and everything changes rapidly and perpetually. In such circumstances, it is natural for people to hold on to those things that give meaning to their lives and provide them with some unchanging sense of identity.

Traditions become essentialist in two ways. The first emerges with a self-awareness of belonging to a tradition and trying to live by it. Here a few features of the tradition are identified and insisted upon. The St Andrew's society of Kuala Lumpur, for example, has identified Scottish country dancing as the essential element of Scottish tradition. To attend the St Andrew's Annual Ball as a true Scot you have to be able to demonstrate your proficiency at the dances and veneration for the mindset of the world according to Andy Stewart. For Muslim minorities in Europe, to give another example, the female headscarf has become the cardinal element of Muslim tradition. So practices that were voluntary and came naturally in the past now become acts of conscious awareness.

This sort of assertion of tradition can, of course, be seen in reverse – as a loss of tradition, a decline of confidence in one's culture and tradition. One becomes conscious of one's breathing only when it becomes difficult. When traditional societies begin to fear the onslaught of modernity and postmodernism, they begin to flaunt their traditions more openly and aggressively. Tradition becomes the marker of one's threatened selfhood in a mass society.

The second way to make tradition essentialist is to transform it into nationalist politics. Here 'the nation' becomes synonymous with 'authentic tradition' and political expediency shapes the contents of both. It is this form of essentialist tradition – often referred to as fundamentalism – that has produced so much violence and conflict in recent times. What is fundamental about Islamic fundamentalism, for example, is that a romantic notion of Islamic tradition is essential to its vision of the state. State and tradition are fused into a single identity. Similarly, Hindu fundamentalists in India equate romanticised Hindu tradition with being an Indian. There is no place for other traditions and cultures, including other traditions within Hinduism, in their 'Hindustan' (the indigenous name for India).

But essentialist tradition is not tradition; it is traditionalism. Traditionalism is an ideology and, like all ideologies, it has fixed contours and functions solely to secure a slice of political power.

Traditions, on the other hand, are dynamic; they are constantly reinventing themselves and adjusting to change. Indeed, a tradition that does not change ceases to be a tradition. But traditions change in a specific way. They change within their own parameters, at their own speed, and towards their chosen direction. There is good reason for this. If traditions were to vacate the space they occupy they would cease to be meaningful. When tradition is cherished and celebrated the entire content of what is lauded can be changed. Such change is then meaningful because it is integrated and enveloped by the continuing sense of identity that tradition provides. Furthermore change can be an evaluated process, a sifting of good, better, best as well as under no circumstances, an adaptation that operates according to the values the veneration of tradition has maintained intact.

In Britain we have a good example of a very strong tradition – a tradition that has reinvented itself a number of times without losing its basic ingredients. A tradition that has playfully used the notion of authenticity to relocate itself and, in the process, has rediscovered its genuine self. I am referring to the tradition of Indian restaurants.

We have a long tradition of 'eating Indian' in Britain. There is at least one Indian restaurant in every high street. The tradition derives from the historic British craving for curries and empire. When, around 1605, Sir Thomas Roe sought permission to trade in India from the Mogul Emperor, Jahangir, he wanted to import a whole range of curries to Britain. Over the years, curry has become something of a fetish on these isles. When Indian restaurants first emerged in significant numbers, during the fifties and sixties, they were firmly set in a colonial tradition. Even their names suggested their colonial status – 'Indian Curry House', 'Cox Bazaar' and 'Maharajah'. These names were designed to rekindle fond memories of the empire that had recently been lost. But they also suggested that the Indian restaurants, and the curries they served, were firmly at the bottom of the league. Moreover, colonial tradition meant that Indian restaurants were a monolithic entity: all restaurants serving food from the subcontinent of India were Indian restaurants. 'Eating Indian' meant eating anything that could lay a loose claim to being from the subcontinent. Indian, Pakistani, Bangladeshi and Sri Lankan; Punjabi, Mogul and South Indian; vegetarian and non-vegetarian – everything was 'Indian', and everything was a 'curry'. And curry is what the lads had when the pubs closed and they were looking for somewhere to vomit their intoxication. For almost half a century, the Indian restaurants put up with the most uncouth, uncivil and ignorant behaviour from their white patrons.

Then the reinvention of tradition began. The tandoor – the clay oven used for making Indian bread (*nan* and *roti*) – was dragged from the sub-continent and proudly displayed in the high streets of Britain. Real Indian restaurants did not serve curry but food cooked in a tandoor. The names changed too. Tandoori restaurants had names like 'Taj Mahal', 'Agra' and 'The Red Fort'. These invoked images of the rich history and tradition of Indian civilisation. The names were a reclamation of history that had been masked by British pretensions to possession of empire.

But rescuing the tradition of Indian restaurants from colonial moor-ings was not enough. They had to be placed within their own diverse traditions of the subcontinent. In the next phase of reinventing tradition, a new dimension was added. Varieties of Indian ethnicities were empha-sised and the *karahi*, the Urdu/Hindi word for wok, became the symbol of authenticity. Authentic Indian restaurants not only cooked their food in a *karahi*, they also served it in a small *karahi* as a demonstration that genuine authenticity was being brought to the table! The names changed once again to reveal not only an infusion of new ethnicities but also a certain self-confidence that invites Indians to eat Indian complete with their families (grandmothers and grandchildren welcome): 'Lahore Karahi', 'Ravi Kebab House' and 'Bombay Brasserie'.

Next, the reinvented tradition had to be relocated on a different plane. To achieve this a totally daring invention had to be made. Today, all authentic Indian restaurants boast *balti* cuisine. Indeed, *balti* cuisine has become so popular that many supermarkets now sell their own brand of ready-made *balti* dishes. But there is no such thing as *balti* cuisine; there never has been. A *balti* is a receptacle, a pitcher, a vessel, a pail of the kind once used by Jack and Jill to fetch water. In India it is put to numerous uses. It can be used to carry water for washing, for taking a bath and may even be used to flush the old-fashioned squatting lavatory. The roles and uses of the *balti* are as numerous and as diverse as Indian civilisation itself. But one thing the *balti* has never been used for is to cook food. Maybe because it is too deep, too wide, too rough and too undisciplined for the preparation of such a varied and sophisticated cuisine.

The selling of *balti* as a renovated traditional and authentic 'Indian' cuisine has been an effective method for the Indian restaurant to relocate itself to a more august station. It has also been a symbol of resistance. When the Indian restaurants were associated with colonial tradition, they resisted by simply exploiting the ignorance of the white patrons. Curry you want; curry you get – the same curry was served with different labels. So someone eating *rogan gosht*, chicken *masala* or prawn curry was eating exactly the same thing with different bits of meat! (Well, if you can't tell the difference between a curry and a *bhindi*, and in any case if you are going to smother the flavour with tons of chillies in the mistaken belief that all Indian food must be very, very hot, and drown it with gallons of beer, you deserve what you get!) By the time the *balti* arrived, Indian restaurants had reinvented themselves as sophisticated purveyors of traditional Indian cuisine. So the humble *balti* was used to give a more elite representation to Indian restaurants, enabling *balti* cuisine to sit among the cordon bleu pots of Western postmodern civilisation.

In reinventing their own tradition, through both conscious and unconscious processes, Indian restaurants have achieved several feats that demonstrate the qualities of life-enhancing tradition. They have demonstrated that traditions change and transform and even adjust to market demands. It is clear that in the transformation of the *balti*'s role, *balti* itself played no active part. In its native land it still does all those many things that it has done for centuries, but in its new incarnation it has become a pot that competes in the market place to satisfy the increasing need for innovative hype and authenticity. They have also, in arriving at their latest culturally legitimate state, performed a genuinely authentic miracle – they have cosmopolitanised and humanised a very parochial and sanitised people, the British. And quite apart from getting rid of the flock wallpaper, they have discovered their true selves. Today, restaurants from the Indian subcontinent have changed their names to indicate a certain authenticity of expression, a certain earthiness, a self-confidence of having arrived. The names now incorporate Urdu/Indian words: 'Jalabi Junction', 'Café Laziz' and 'Karahi Master'. The cooking area in many of these restaurants, whether upmarket or more humble, is part of the dining experience, providing traditional assurance not just of freshly cooked food but also bringing back the direct and tactile relationship between the hand that cooks and the hand that eats.

What is true of Indian restaurants in Britain is true of traditional cultures everywhere. The trouble is that outside observers, those who witness or even participate in the transformation, seldom appreciate the subtlety as change. So far as British society is concerned it has just become more familiar with the lexicon of Indian food as it was and always will be. The trouble with traditions as a force of change, the essential mechanism that permits meaningful change, is that they are invisible to the outsider. Therefore, observers can go on maintaining their modern or postmodern distaste for tradition irrespective of the counterevidence before their very eyes. The contemporary world does provide opportunity for tradition to go on being what tradition has always been, an adaptive force. The problem is that no amount of adaptation, however much it strengthens traditional societies, actually frees them from the yoke of being marginal, misunderstood and misrepresented. It does nothing to dethrone the concept 'Tradition' as an *idée fixe* of Western society.

There is an unholy triple alliance between traditionalism, modernity and postmodernism. They all have a vested interest in laying claim to what actually constitutes tradition and how it should and should not operate. True, each holds a different view of the meaning and content of tradition. But they are unanimous in one single absolute: tradition is fixed, immutable. Their answers are to deprive it of its power; abolish it; or mock, deride and demean it as the implacable enemy. The triple alliance is a potent, collaborative force; each party knows exactly what it wants – control. The control they have and would continue to wield is bad for all concerned, as the record of their activities here, there and everywhere amply demonstrates.

So the time has come to find a new, humane ally, to make common cause with the real face of tradition. The last best hope for a sane future is to lay hold of what traditional societies have – the adaptive ability to change and remain themselves. This includes all the aspects of British traditional society, the things that have been submerged in the drive for modernity and postmodernism. The only effective antidote to ethnic cleansing, for that is exactly what suppression of tradition amounts to (and the triple alliance are all ethnic cleansers in their own way), is to embrace traditional pluralism. Traditional pluralism is the frightening premise that there is more than one sustainable, sensible, humane and decent way to resolve any problem; and that most of these problems can be solved within traditions. Traditional pluralism is a mark of common respect we are called on to pay to each tradition in a world full of diverse traditions; it is the basic idea that we might just know what is best for ourselves. It is the notion that inventiveness, ingenuity, enterprise and common sense are integral to all traditions, and that every tradition, if given the opportunity, resources, tolerance and freedom, can adapt to change and solve its own problems. In other words, all have the ability to solve their own problems themselves within their own traditions in ways that they find satisfactory. So employing the traditional society option is a new way of arriving at participatory democracy in a most liberal fashion.

The option for traditional pluralism is no instant panacea. It is a complex struggle to unpack all we have been force-fed for centuries. It replaces the trek to become an anonymous cog in a reliable system with the need to discover who we are. It means the willingness to select things that are meaningful and be accountable for the meanings they are capable of bearing, warts and all, while we strive to employ what is valuable in our identity as the means to transform ourselves into something better. Traditional pluralism puts us all on the spot, facing the same problems but with different equipment and circumstances in which to find our own solutions.

Universalism

Universalism has ceased to be universal. The assumption that human societies and cultures have some irreducible experiences, elements of life that are common to everyone and link our humanity, has evaporated. For good reasons and not before time, too. For universalism was basically a euphemism for the assumptions underlying Western values that were held to be valid for all cultures and all time. However, what is replacing universalism is turning out to be just as Eurocentric and oppressive.

Universalism offered what in polite 'postcolonial' circles is referred to as 'a hegemonic view of existence' where values and experiences, hopes and expectations of 'a dominant culture are held to be true for all humanity'. Or, to put it another way: Europe always assumed that everything it did was universal. From its history to the main product of its history: modernity. Therefore, it was easy for universalism to be equated with the ascendancy of Europe and become an instrument of imperialism. To become modern was a 'universal aspiration' and the colonial subject had to be dragged into modern times. Everyone in the world had to be force-fed English literature because it had proved its greatness by depicting the 'universal human condition'. It was not just the English novel that was universal, its reader too was a 'universal human subject'; and if the readers did not appreciate the greatness of English literature, then clearly they were not cultured or totally human.

It was the fact that universalism is so deeply and intricately tied to

Eurocentrism that made it contentious. But the exposure of the imperialistic nature of universalism also revealed problems with ideologies and worldviews with universalist tendencies. These tend to be big ideas that provide coherence and give meaning as well as a sense of direction to our lives, what is known in technical parlance as 'grand narratives'. An idea such as Universal History becomes a yardstick by which all history, of all other cultures and civilisation, is measured. 'Universal Religions' like Christianity and Islam provide another face to the problem, for they have contested each other's claims to universalism throughout history. In fact, it is within the nature of all universals to condition their adherents to what is uniquely 'theirs' as the whole truth, the complete answer, unfailingly superior to any other system, outlook or practice. A universal code encodes everything; it is the answer to everything and the only way to see anything. A universal system is the Sun around which all planets float in orbit, the medium that gives substance to all reality and makes it knowable.

So, the quest for a single fundamental universal principle from which all other ethical principles are derived seems doomed to failure. Worse: even what we do accept as universal turns out to be time dependent. Social consensus is a movable feast, highly mutable and tenuous – anything we regard today as universally valid or universally acceptable could tomorrow be considered invalid or abnormal. It seems that the only human universals that transcend culture and time are our physiological characteristics: breathing, eating, drinking, sleeping, pissing, shitting and sex.

The dethroning of universalism has brought obvious benefits, particularly for non-Western cultures and oppressed minorities within cultures. Their values and ideas are supposed to be, theoretically at least, on a par with Western values and norms. But the move away from universalism has also transformed Western society in three significant ways.

First, the exit of universalism has led to the exit of the very idea of restraint. It used to be a universal premise that civilisation existed in restraint. For the sake of bettering our condition, human beings gave up the licence to indulge their baser instincts and concentrated their efforts on refining the more humane attributes of their nature: the meaning of the term civilisation. This view of society was based on the humble premise of all religious philosophies: that we, as human beings, are neither perfect and infallible nor entirely incompetent. It is a curious paradox that the vision of civilisation as a framework of constructive and supportive constraints became a vision of human bondage. In postmodern times, prudent restraint has no value or virtue. Absolute absence of restraint has produced the other paradox of our times: that poverty of aspiration has become a postmodern pandemic.

Second, the departure of universalism has also led to the departure of our will to struggle. In pre-postmodern times, values – the intangible qualitative measures that exist beyond quantity – defined all the things that locate and orientate individuals within not merely a universe of personal desire but a universe of other people and their desires. Values provided a compass bearing on judgements that assessed human performance: good, better, best; bad, worse, worst; least or most; should or should not; beneficial or harmful. To all of these qualitative judgements postmodern times proffer a 'can do' ideology founded on a teleological dream of perfection. What postmodernism actually delivers is humanity becalmed in a universal dispensation of nothingness. So there is nothing to struggle for or against, because nothing is meaningful. There is nothing to struggle for since licence, the absence of any restraint, is now the natural, liberal endowment of all people. In postmodern times we can recognise nothing that is worth anything because good is as good as bad is bad, and both are indistinguishable. We can thus do whatever we choose, and be whatever we decide to be, because the only thing that defines the human condition is eclectic personal choice.

Third, loss of universalism has led to a serious loss of our humanity. Indeed, it has brought us to the incipient moment of rewriting what it is to be human with no idea of how to respond to questions such as human cloning and stem cell research, the creation of embryonic life to rescue extant damaged lives. Are these developments things of wonder, proof of our creative capacity, or are they poisoned chalices? Discuss. But, how can we discuss such topics when all the terms of debate are so mort-gaged, so beholden to things too few believe, or are prepared to acknowledge might be worthy of belief, to sustain any coherent argument or build any rational consensus? Like everything else, the question of the future of our basic humanity becomes a topic for panic politics, gerrymandered constituency balancing and focus grouped, manipulated presentation. This is the poverty of ambition that defines the politicised domain of negotiation that is the last vestige of the thing we once called civilisation.

We ought to remember that nature abhors a vacuum. The absence of something is not the same as the presence of nothing. All the universal systems, the 'grand narratives', have been 'deconstructed'. They have been shown to be constructed out of untenable, inappropriate, self-serving, self-denying, hypocritical constraints that, in the history of human experience, worked for the service of the few instead of the many. Universalism has universally acquired a bad name and been required to vacate centre stage. Does this mean we are rid of such grandiose thinking? In fact, its central position, the rationale for how things are and should be, has been taken by a new variety of universalism more pernicious than all the universalisms of pre-modern and modern times.

In postmodern times, the idea that has acquired universal connotation is individualism. From the notion that European values and experiences were the epitome of human existence, we have moved to the idea that the individual is the starting point and source of all human actions. But this individual is still largely a specific European construction. To begin with, he/she is defined solely in terms of personal choice. And he/she moves in a utopia that says you should have it all. Yours is the universe and all it contains or can be made to contain. Moreover, the 'freedom' of this individual underlies all the operations of the 'free' market economy. He/she is thus in constant competition with all other individuals; and the only meaningful activity for all individuals in this Western universe is commodity exchange. It seems ridiculous and ironic to accuse such individual idylls of being universalist. But then there is nothing beyond being an individual; the individual is the whole universe, the only universe we can know, influence, order and manage. This is individualism manufactured as universal aspiration.

In a universe defined by personal choice anything and everything can at some level be reduced to special pleading deemed good for some individual. Every act of special pleading is an absolute individual justification for utilising the ultimate extreme of human imagination and inventiveness to perfect the imperfect, the unacceptable or the damaged in an individual life. A 60-year-old woman cannot be denied the right and freedom to have fertility treatment. The childless couple must be entitled to their chance of happiness by the creation of a cloned baby. The young accident victim whose only hope is xeno-transplant should have the option of harvesting organs from any convenient animal. The cumulative effect, however, is that individual choices make decisions that have universal implications. Eclectic personal choice as we now see it practised is not choice for or from among what is. It is the choice of what ought, should or can be made to be. It is in its demands that postmodern individualism betrays its universal vision, a vision of individual perfection, available for a price at a consumer outlet near you. The universal entitlement of individualism is the dream of personal ideal utopias, without the need to recognise constraint, boundaries, taboos and social acceptability. But such personal utopias have consequences for us all and for all our futures.

Postmodern individualism not only shapes the world for us all, it also attempts to shape a universal morality to enslave us all. The morality of individualism is based on the idea that every act or behaviour contains its own moral logic outside the domain of prescribed practices. This is not the same thing as immorality; as a binary opposite, immorality posits a morality and is something that society understands and can cope with. It is the notion that every individual authors its own ontological existence. It is the idea that we are so sophisticated we can transcend societal morals and decide our own as we merrily pass through life. In the final analysis this is the morality of 'anything goes', which in the postmodern, globalised world has become a universal imperative.

So, as a vision of the universal freedom to have and consume all and everything, to be free to do and behave as desired, postmodern individualism is the true inheritor of all universalisms that ever existed. It holds the ring, orchestrates the attack on vestigial attachment to the remnants of all earlier universalisms by defining their limitations. It is in fact a belief system to beat all belief systems, an ideology that surpasses all ideologies, and a universalism that presides over all the lesser breeds of universalisms.

The trouble is, this new personalised centre for each and every individual universe will not hold. To have and have more, self-evidently, we need, depend upon and cannot do without other people. Furthermore, everything we have and desire to have is vulnerable to the choices made by other people. But all these exclusive universes lack the principle of inclusiveness. We can only deal with the needs of others in so far as they comply with and do not constrain our personal desires. Far from being liberation from the limitations of all previous universalisms, eventually the postmodern dispensation ends up with exactly the same problem that has bedevilled all previous versions: what to do about other people.

Other people too have their theories and practices of universalism. We need to acknowledge this just as much as we need to accept the basic fact of the human condition: we are not alone. And we ought to be able to distinguish between different conceptions of universalism. Even consumers recognise the concept of quality control and know that good value lies beyond the common denominator of vested self-interest. If we cannot do better than shop around for universal systems, we certainly ought to know what kind of warranty they claim to offer and whether it comes with a money-back guarantee, home trial and returns policy. *Caveat emptor* – shoppers be aware!

Voyeurism

'Hell is other people', said the French writer and philosopher Jean Paul Sartre. He could have added, there is no escape from other people determined to show just how hellish they really are. And they are everywhere – on television, on the Web, in the video store, on every security camera. Everywhere, they are single-mindedly demonstrating how banal and dumbfounding they are, how unthinking and willing to be manipulated for deplorable ends. The hell they are creating is called voyeurism.

There was a time when voyeurism was the province of a select few. The sad men in dirty raincoats visiting strip joints, the village 'Peeping Tom', the perverts gratifying their perversions. But technology has re-defined voyeurism. Give a man a video camera and see his voyeuristic instinct bloom. Your most private moments could this very instant be playing on someone's VCR. If you have a penchant for exposing yourself, you could, without much bother, get on voyeurcam.com or mybedroom.com. That man in the restaurant with a new miniature camcorder could be shooting up the skirts of the waitresses. If you have made a particularly saucy video, or have a freaky tale to tell, you can always get on television. There is a burgeoning market out there. If the medium is the message, then the message is voyeurism. And we have all become voyeurs.

Voyeurism is a close cousin of narcissism. When we turn our lurid gaze towards dysfunctional others, leer into their private moments, or watch them engaging in banal acts, we are actually looking at ourselves. The enjoyment we get is the pleasure of self-love, the love of our own reflection. Voyeurism seduces us by projecting our own inner hell on to other people. We see in others what we dread in ourselves – but secretly we know we are not all that different, just as execrable, and equally venal. The pandemic of voyeurism is telling us something about ourselves. And it is time we asked just what this means and where it is leading us.

Nowhere is our newfound obsession with voyeurism more noticeable than on television. Having been spared the 'Big Brother' experience in Britain by the simple stratagem of spending the summer in the United States, I found myself immersed in 'Survivor'. The CBS show is a cross between 'Big Brother' and 'Castaway 2000' (which followed a group of people living on a remote Scottish island for a year), survival and inter-personal duplicity presented as a game show. The episode I watched had the contestants, chosen largely for the high quotient of their egos and repulsive nature, eating squirming live grubs. I returned to 'Life of Grime' (a series about those who carry out society's most unpleasant tasks), which provided more insight into the repulsive nature of one's fellow citizens than is strictly desirable to maintain a civil society.

All this in addition to the regular, over-generous diet of freaks, deviants and sad losers one meets on imports such as 'Jerry Springer', 'Sally Jesse Raphael' or 'Rikki Lake' as well as home-grown rubbish like 'Esther' and 'Trish'. These shows are sacrificial baying fests. The 'guests' sacrificially present their grotesque character trait – Women Who Marry Transvestites, Men Who Sleep With Their Mothers, this sort of thing. The studio audience ritually respond with gasps, guffaws, hoots and hollers mixed with some chosen questions. What are these people doing to our society? Should they be allowed to get away with it? Do they have a right to exist? It is not a narrative event, it is a stream of consciousness interlude; the angrier it gets, the more inarticulate and confrontational, the nearer to chewing the scenery and throwing things the better the entertainment. After an hour, credits roll.

It is all so distant from the heyday of the seventies when daytime talk became established in the US as the filler par excellence. In the hands of a Phil Donahue and often enough an Oprah, ordinary people discussed issues that affected their daily lives, with genuflection towards educative purpose. The sleaze and voyeurism came stealthily to attract audiences and then became the only reason for the existence of such programmes. Donahue left the industry in publicly expressed disgust. Where previously the occasional discussion brought bizarre, dysfunctional behaviour before the cameras, now only by being bizarre and entirely lacking in functions of any ordinary kind could one get in front of the cameras.

It is the success of sleaze talk that whetted our appetite for a more overt form of voyeurism. It arrived in the form of reality TV. In Britain the documentary tradition has always been strong. It was a structured and controlled way to meet, observe and be engaged by various genres of people. Then, by an amazing trick of dissembling, the fly-on-the-wall style was born. Instead of pre-packaged stories containing messages, coded or explicit, the entire panoply of making programmes was supposedly swept away. We were to take an unvarnished look at people being, well, people. Banality was born with a great deal of high purpose and portentous self-congratulation on behalf of the broadcasters.

When reality steps in, when cameras strain to catch unscripted and unexpected riveting moments in jerky movements, suddenly all of television looks exactly what it is: stage-managed, produced, researched and edited to a polished glossy sheen. The deception, however, is that as much planning and connivance goes into reality TV as any other kind. There is nothing 'ordinary' about these 'ordinary people'; they have been carefully selected, selectively edited and expertly packaged for our consumption. The only really astonishing thing about reality TV is our collective willingness to accept that, in the symbiosis of camera crew and willing people, an unstructured reality in some measure does percolate through unmediated by media professionals. This is precisely the lure of reality TV. That's why it is the greatest artifice of the media.

The late eighties and early nineties saw reality TV, premised on this damned lie, sweep all before it. Americans succumbed to the lure of vicarious experience as shows with titles like 'America's Most Dangerous Rescues', 'America's Most Inept Criminals' and 'America's Funniest Home Videos' proliferated. Britain followed, as she always does, with drivel like 'Airport', 'Ferry', 'Hospital' and 'Pet Doctor'.

The genre came to dominate prime-time television for two reasons: our insatiable appetite for gawking at others and our total mistrust of our fellow human beings. Careful scrutiny reveals that considerable portions of these programmes are a result of the proliferation of CCTV cameras, the ubiquitous need to record everything on video shared by authorities and employers, every bit as much as the general public's love affair with the camcorder. And it was a lot cheaper than conventional programme making, an unbeatable argument for giving the public what they were prepared to lap up. The ultimate example has to be true confessions of murder, an entire archive of which already exist. It is only a matter of time before tried and convicted criminals regale us with their deeds on prime-time TV.

From reality TV we move forward, at the beginning of the 21st century, to peep shows. It is important to note that 'Big Brother' originated in Holland where peep shows are a national institution. It was only natural that it should be put on national television. What is common to both 'Big Brother' and its American derivative, 'Survivor', is that they are an enactment of the *Lord of the Flies*. The participants who display the most beastly character are most loved by the audience. But why limit ourselves to houses and islands? We can have a peep show anywhere – on a train, plane or a bus. This last mode of transport was in fact a runaway success on Spanish pay TV. 'The Bus' put nine strangers on a specially built double-decker bus wired from top to bottom with cameras and microphones. As they travelled through Spain fighting, shitting and otherwise displaying compulsively deranged behaviour, their every move was broadcast 24 hours a day via a digital channel. Viewers exercised their voyeuristic power through their ability to choose different cameras and camera angles. The winner turned out to be the last person left on the bus after 100 days.

The voyeurism of peep shows like 'The Bus', as well as sleazy chat shows and reality TV – collectively dubbed 'water cooler TV' – plays on our suspicions that ordinary people are always up to no good, being naughty and wicked at every opportunity. One of its main selling points is that it inspires people to talk to each other. In other words, it makes us all as sad as the willing subjects who consign themselves to the experiment before the cameras. We are led to believe it is all about bonding, when in truth it's about human bondage.

'Big Brother' is the lineal descendant of 'Candid Camera', 'Beadle's About' and 'Surprise, Surprise!'. A group of clichéd, not very interesting people are put together under the most artificial of circumstances. They are asked to do idiotic things like making sculptures of themselves to fill in the total boredom of their days as the only alternative to sleeping all day, every day. We are asked to believe these meaningless activities have purpose because their rations will be cut if they fail, in instances where there are no criteria for either success or failure. They are encouraged to talk about themselves, their feelings and their bonding experiences, ad nauseam. And increasingly, as in 'Big Brother 2', they are encouraged to have sex. When the inmates are not talking about themselves, or why they are or they are not having sex, psychologists are drafted in to talk about them talking about themselves. It is a game show, but supposedly it is real, and a practical psychology cum sociology course.

What 'Big Brother' demonstrates is just how gullible we have become as a society, how ever ready we are to be duped. Unmediated 'Big Brother' would mean watching 24 hours a day. What we actually watch is heavily censored, cleverly edited, structured, selected, predetermined vignettes of a structured and controlled situation. Or to put it another way: rats trapped in a very public maze.

People have always been interested in people. But what this unholy alliance of voyeurism and narcissism breeds, feeds and spawns is a dehumanising process that actually lessens our regard for other people. Our desire to see duller, sorrier and more dysfunctional people than ourselves on television means we are prepared to demean anyone to make ourselves feel better about our own less than wonderful, isolated lives. It is all so dehumanising because it objectifies individuals, requiring us to marvel at their exhibitionism, mock their stupidity and laugh at their dysfunctions. We are not there to understand them, to feel for them, to care about them. Voyeuristic television makes people the ultimate commodity. We consume them to fill in a boring evening.

I acquired this insight from none other than Jerry Springer, the master of voyeurism. What, in the name of hell, is this thing called 'Jerry Springer', he was asked on 'Larry King Live' (where else?). 'This is a TV show', he replied repeatedly, as if this mantra were total explanation. It 'is not a serious show'; it's only 'chewing gum TV'. Its attraction is 'you can't make up the stuff people do in their lives'.

'This is a TV show' means it has no significance, it cannot be held responsible or accountable for any untoward consequences that result, it exists only to fill a void in the schedules and the sad lives of those who appear and by inference those who watch. It 'is not a serious show' means its reason for existence is neither to counsel or achieve any catharsis for those who appear nor to provide any insight, instruction or edification for those who watch. It is a freak show, unashamed, unabashed and no one should have any qualms about anything on it. Pontius Pilate has washed his hands.

Callous is a mild word for the world according to Springer. That he is a self-serving bastard is no news. What is worthy of note, however, is that his constant refrain implies something much more. His innocence depends on the implicit argument that we have neither right nor reason to be unaware of the conventions by which his success has been achieved. No one is forced to go on his show and make a public, humiliating spectacle of themselves. Violence, murder (which has actually occurred as a result of going on the show) and unforeseen eventualities are the fault of the participants, for whom Springer has little regard, and the audience, to whom he must assert total submission. Unmediated television exonerates at all levels those who continue to mediate and manipulate all concerned. Springer is content with the reflection that only 10 per cent of the American population, people who deem themselves outside the mainstream, would be prepared to go on television and discuss their life, blow by blow. That makes 25 million people. He expects to be in work for a long time.

Clearly, we have returned with a vengeance to Roman circuses. We are no better than those who watched and bayed for blood as the victims were fed to the lions *à la Gladiator*. But this return to ancient amorality has been greased by two very postmodern traits. First, it owes a great deal to a brand new human right: your entitlement to 15 minutes of fame. Everyone wants to be famous, and that means getting on the 'telly' by hook or by crook. The new forms of voyeurism emerged because television, broadcasting our narcissism, has become internalised, part of our psyche. If exercising this right means reducing ourselves to the base levels of beasts, so be it.

Second, the predominance of narcissistic individualism has turned hedonism into a fashion statement. We compete with each other – as demonstrated so well in shows like 'Ibiza Uncovered' – in expressing our belief that the pursuit of undiluted pleasure is the highest, indeed the only goal of humanity. Having exhausted the conventional channels of pleasure, we turn to, and return to, the barbarian forms. What is a holiday in Ibiza but a Bacchanalian orgy? Our ideas of pleasure remain limited. The pursuit of novelty often leads us back to the spectacles of history.

Other people's hell is the hell that we have created for ourselves. Voyeurism, in all its multiple forms, has reduced us all to objects – dehumanised, unreal sources of meaningless entertainment. In the end, it is our own callousness that enables broadcasters to determine, control and produce ever more bizarre formats of unholy alliance between the willing subjects and duped audience. Thus, subject and audience connive in total manipulation. Truth becomes indistinguishable from untruth, illusion from delusion – we simply see everything as actuality. The savvy consumer is consumed, Big Brother is Us, they have locked the gates of the asylum and Elvis is in the building – and so are we all.

So on with the motley and forget any talk of values, good taste, or understanding our fellow human beings. The fruits of voyeurism come in the form of callousness, disinterest, dishonesty, ratings and vast profits. What else is there?

War

I speak of war and the rumours of war. Of course, the whole point is that war itself is unspeakable. Rumours are another matter, the essential matter of human speech, and we are surrounded with them at every turn. Rumoured menace to all we hold dear, our highly expensive and unsustainable lifestyle, abounds in a world driven by material envy. And no household with children, of any age, is without the rumour of war blasting from a games console: Boom! Schpow! Thunk! Aaagh!

War is one thing that defies the inherent logic of postmodernism. What is unspeakable should be unthinkable in an age when words are all we have and all we are. Yet we think a great deal about war. The only way to make amazing advances in technology pay is to make them into entertainment – hence war games on computer consoles reflecting real war games in the real world, which itself is underpinned by an economic system deeply anchored in war.

Just think how much of our everyday conversation, routine business and fantasies are based on war. We are unable to solve any problem without declaring war on it. We talk of 'war on terrorism', 'war on crime', 'war on drugs', 'war on poverty' and 'war on cancer'. War is present not just on our streets and urban conurbations, but in hospitals as well. Walk into a hospital and you are in the middle of a war zone. Doctors are like soldiers machine-gunning diseases. There is talk of killing pain. When patients are sedated or anaesthetics are administered to them, the process is referred to in medical slang as 'slugging'. The cytotoxic chemotherapy that is used on cancer patients is described as poisoning; in cancer treatment there is also the notion of tumour-kill, derived straight from the language of nuclear war.

In the business and corporate worlds, the language of war is used with unabashed pride. Ruthless military leaders are extolled as role models for American and European businesses. Consider the titles of books selling secrets of business success: *Patton on Leadership: Strategic Lessons for Corporate Warfare*, by an author who himself sounds like a barrel of a gun, Alex Axelrod; *Leadership Secrets of Attila the Hun*, by Wess Roberts; and *Leadership Lessons from General Ulysses S. Grant*, by Al Kaltman. Inside these volumes one finds a world of military manoeuvres, last-ditch battles and gleeful massacres presented as management practice. Axelrod's book, for example, looks like it is a Second World War manual. It starts with Patton's famous speech: 'No bastard ever won a war by dying for his country – he won it by making the other dumb bastard die for his country.' From here on, war values are presented as the only way to live and die – for corporations as well as individuals. But one doesn't have to read the book to get its message. The dustcover says it all: 'Distils Patton's brilliance into 158 essential lessons every leader must know to win in today's merciless corporate war.' Roberts is a bit more imaginative – he 'draws from the imaginary thoughts of one of history's most effective and least-loved leaders to discover leadership principles you can apply to your own situation'. When such leaders rule the corporate world, what a diminished world they create.

The philosophy of blood and guts is, of course, an essential part of most of our entertainment. Whether it's video games like *Doom* and *Lara Croft* or cyberwarfare films like *The Matrix* and *War Games*, the entertainment value is directly proportional to the body count. But cyberspace is not confined to the video screen – it has taken over the real world. So, now we have virtual wars: real wars experienced as video games.

The Gulf War was the first virtual war. It led Jean Baudrillard, the mischievous French philosopher, to make his much maligned declaration that 'the Gulf War has not taken place'. 'Desert Storm' was a totally 'virtual' engagement, he said, and so it was 'idiotic' to be for or against it. Indeed, for most of the world, the Gulf War was largely a television spectacle. It was presented almost as a video game that kept much of the brutal side of the war, including human casualties, nicely hidden from the viewers. But the Gulf War had real casualties on both sides.

But in a true virtual war, the body count on our side must remain – well, virtual. Enter, the Kosovo war, a war totally death free for the Allies. It was fought at a distance – for some 11 weeks, American, British, French and German planes, manned and unmanned, attacked targets in Kosovo, Serbia and Montenegro. Remote weapons fired from remote distances destroyed much of Serbia's economy. The absolute technological superiority of the Allied forces not only guaranteed victory, it also removed death from our experience of war.

The Afghanistan war was also brutally one-sided. Those fighting on the side of the Taliban often described it as 'war of the spacemen': continuous bombardment by planes, submarines and ships virtually decimated the opposition before the Western-backed 'Northern Alliance' troops moved in for ground fighting. The ground action was totally subservient to laser-guided missiles, 'pin point' aerial bombing, surveillance via satellites and drone aircrafts, smart bombs, daisycutters, and other paraphernalia of postmodern high-tech warfare. Almost all of the dead were on the Taliban side; most of those who died on the side of the Northern Alliance and single digit Western causalities were actually victims of 'friendly fire'. Despite the rare odd bit of resistance from the Taliban, it was a war won by the push of a button.

All of which makes virtual war an eminently thinkable and enormously profitable enterprise. It is the pattern of all future wars in the postmodern version of the Boy's Own world of derring-do.

The future often tends to be a function of the past. So it is hardly surprising that the origins of virtual war are to be found in the cold war. The glacial second half of the 20th century was defined relative to villains who were our alter egos – the antithesis of our normality. The cold war was a virtual rivalry that could never have been brought to the test, for to make war in cold war days was simply to be MAD, or march towards mutually assured destruction and planetary annihilation. It was this fact that sustained the dynamic of the cold war, fuelled the riches of the West and the gradual impoverishment of the Eastern bloc.

Two worldviews butted rhetoric, the word war of rumours, but neither contemplated or could permit total engagement. It was a close call with the Bay of Pigs and Kennedy but MAD logic prevailed and sanity returned. But war and rumours of war had to go somewhere. So the people of the Third World became the predecessors of the virtual reality of today: the animated Gameboy figures who could be permitted to fight real wars and die unspeakably, equipped with all the military hardware its makers could not think of using themselves or on themselves. Think how much of Africa has been devastated by the glut of American and European weapons or how Afghanistan has been turned into a lunar landscape by American and Soviet military hardware. What was left of Afghanistan was destroyed by the 'war on terrorism'.

One war between the era of the cold war and the virtual postmodern world of war has made a definable difference: Vietnam. It defined the actual nature of contemporary virtual war by showing how far the Americans would go, or rather would not go, for the cause of a 'free world'. To die in a war you need to believe in something. To retain any credibility, the creed of 'them' and 'us', villains and heroes, has to be based on something worth dying for, a struggle for the survival of something so right it could never be sacrificed or compromised. As Vietnam proved America was not at all sure of its convictions. A generation rose up and protested the minute they were in danger of being drafted into the first war to be watched on nightly television. Vietnam brought all that was unspeakable about war into homes around the world in graphic images of human suffering, callousness and the dehumanising instincts bred by the rumours that sustain wars. Vietnam created the essential dynamic of virtual war – no more body bags containing American soldiers.

Vietnam reached its apotheosis with the fall of the Berlin Wall. When the Wall collapsed, it marked more than the end of Communism. It also revealed that the ethos of 'greed is good', 'materialism is all we have', is a highly potent global dispensation. It was not the birth of the end of history but the true beginning of postmodernism, the absolute relativity of nothing worth believing in because all great narratives were mere lies and rumours of lies, political con tricks it was best to doubt absolutely. Why was this not the end of history? Simple: because history was founded and worked out through war. It is far too perilous to the preservation of economic activity to permit this vital principle of productive power to be dismantled.

The end of the cold war created a new problem: how to sustain war in a world without enemies and when no one believed enough in anything to wish to be incinerated, maimed and traumatised in the least.

So, we return to the manufacture of villains. During the pre- and post-cold war period, the construction of the villains, the Crazy Ivans, was a simple question of turning the on/off rumour machine in one or another direction. Russian peasants were noble workers struggling for freedom in the Russian Revolution. Then demonised hordes when they succeeded in establishing an enduring Soviet republic. Then valiant allies when they died and took large parts of the Nazi war machine with them to deliver victory for the Western Allies. Then once again implacable enemies when they wanted to export their revolution to the 'Free World'. Constructing villains is easy and the West is a past master at the game. Indeed, it has always been the Western way, from the demonisation of the Jews as the 'internal enemy' to Crusading propaganda about the fanatic, bloodthirsty Saracens, via the media frenzy of emotive rumour that converted Belgian babies impaled by the Hun and the Nazi into Kuwaiti babies butchered in incubators by the Iraqis during the Gulf War. Villains come in cycles, are endlessly recycled, moving forward in a trajectory that relies on certain enduring features at its core. When a villain is needed, and any villain will do, there is nothing like falling back on the oldest villain of them all: the Muslim threat. Enter, bin Laden.

With his ridiculous beard and turban, he represents both the ideal personification and accumulation of all the previous representations of the Muslim threat: the Ottoman Saracens, the revolutionaries of Algeria fighting French occupation, and the 'Arab terrorists' of many Hollywood films.

Black propaganda, the rumour mill that churns out war, has been with us since the Crusades. It is practised and ever ready to go into action. The postmodern difference is that the villains are groomed in public, nursed and nourished, and slowly inflated until they, by their own free will, acquire the dimensions of true evil. The trick here is to give them just enough support and encouragement to make the right transformation. Consider how Saddam Hussein was built slowly from a tin-pot dictator, supplied with endless weapons of endless variety, encouraged to attack and carry out a decade-long war with Iran, and nudged to invade Kuwait. Or how bin Laden was set up and equipped by the CIA and openly encouraged by Washington throughout the eighties to help the Mujahadeen fight the Soviet Union. Or how the Taliban were created as a new entity by America, with Saudi Arabian and Pakistani backing, to provide a client state in Afghanistan. To become a perfect target, the monster has to be fed, gluttonised, and then led to the slaughter.

But while Saddam proved that we could have virtual wars to devastate manufactured enemies, the Gulf War wasn't entirely successful. Difficult manoeuvres require ceaseless practice, which alone makes perfect. All the techniques of virtual war were tested, their suitability confirmed. All it would take to make it perfect were a few more practice runs. Enter, Slobodan Milosevic. Kosovo provided the means to hone the machine to ultimate refinement. Moreover, we could go to war to protect worthwhile values: the rights of the innocent in the face of true barbarism, those about to be ethnically cleansed. There could be no question the cause was right, humanitarian and against a genuine evil. And now we could fight for what we believe in by effective virtual means safe from the prospect of body bags and feel good about ourselves.

With virtual war perfected on earth, where could we go next? Why, to outer space. America's national missile defence system, otherwise known as 'Star Wars', is the perfect global answer for a war-based global economy. Its sole function is to generate endless business for the war industry. Its propaganda slogan is defence, not offence, giving it a great selling point. It requires endless rumours of war, thus creating endless work for the propaganda industry known otherwise as the independent media. There is a cycle here, too. Politicians complain about media pressure for 'action'; that generates more copy, that feeds back to the politicians, who complain even more about media pressure – so there's enough news to satisfy the insatiable appetite for perpetual and constant news. How else are 24-hour news channels going to function? They keep 'rogue states' and mindless terrorists in business, because it is the news industry's best business – mindless repetition of unanalysed rumour and fearmongering.

'Star Wars' is the ideal virtual weapon. It has truly stunning computer-generated graphics. Everyone can see how they are being defended while being defended, just as if they were playing on a video game in the local arcade. See how the free world will be kept free with the postmodern equivalent of a light sabre – laser beams in space. We can all feel like Luke Skywalker and tell ourselves we really are safe. What is more, this defensive war shield comes with an absolute guarantee: totally free of any American body bags.

But this virtual war of the future will have at least one casualty. There will be no more old comrades and nostalgia for the days when men were men and did what men had to do. We can see how significant this loss is by contrasting it with the Vietnam War. The Americans who avoided the draft and missed that last great soldiers-in-action war are now suffering from serious missing-the-action syndrome. They have to invent a war record for themselves so they can talk about old comradeships and gallantry under fire. Think of Joseph Ellis, Pulitzer Prize-winning historian, who fabricated an imaginary past for himself in Vietnam and then proceeded to make it an integral part of his history books. Or the actor Brian Dennehy, who claimed to have been wounded while serving as a marine in a Vietnam he has never seen. The syndrome even has a medical name: stolen valour. Exploding a hunk of junk in space doesn't quite have the same valorous ring to it as the famous helicopter scene from *Apocalypse Now!* But progress has its costs; and somebody has to shoulder them.

The benefits of virtual war, however, can be shared by all of us. A globalised economy, where export of weapons is the norm, makes it easy for anyone to obtain all that is needed to engage in virtual warfare. Before long, the technical sorcery that enabled the war in Kosovo to be fought at a distance will be acquired by other states. However, it is not just a question of cruise missiles and stealth planes. Virtual war has its roots in cyberspace and cyberspace will make sure that it becomes a democratic enterprise – involving all, whatever their race, creed or age. Just listen to that teenager hacking away at night. He talks of gremlins, worms, Trojan horses, logic bombs, trap doors, chipping, nanomachines, Herf guns and EMP bombs. They are real weapons of virtual war that can, for example, knock out a power station, crash trains and planes, bring down the New York and London Stock Exchanges. So keep an eye open for that disgruntled citizen, conspiracy theory nut, and right-wing extremist – see how they use their joysticks.

I grew up with the lyrics of Buffy Sainte-Marie, the peace protestors, CND marches and their songs and anti-nuclear weapons campaigns. The postmodern, virtual, rumour-infected wars have no place for the rhetoric of making peace not war. Making peace is a messy, often fruitless, difficult, long and intractable problem. Think of Northern Ireland and Palestine. It does not make for easy stories or good pictures on the 24-hour news channels, just incessant frustrated politicians parading in and out of buildings – a real switch off. There is no glory in fulfilling the conditions for peaceful coexistence. It requires an insistence on giving up, giving in and give and take. It requires annihilating the real enemies – poverty, dispossession, disadvantage, those hardy perennial seeds of all wars. It requires sharing wealth and manufacturing a form of global inclusion that would make everyone as loathe to go to war or die for anything as the American population. No, much safer, more profitable, more cost effective to stick to old ways in new virtual mode.

So I speak of war and the rumours of war because it remains as impossible as ever to speak of peace and gossip peacefully.

Xeno-effect

Postmodern man has never had it so good. It's not just material abundance and infinite choice but all those wonderful appliances of science that make grooming such a delight. Just think how many different types of blade are now available for our shaving pleasure – with single edge, double edge, triple edge; with lubricating strip, without lubricating strip; fixed; moving. I can carry on waxing lyrical. Which brings me to the infinite variety of waxes, creams, gels and sprays, without stickiness and with lasting invisible hold, that we use to keep our hair just the (mostly ridiculous) way we want it to be. But I wonder how many men notice, when they have finished grooming in front of the mirror and take a sneaky peak at their manhood, that something profound is happening down there. To put it bluntly: we are shrinking, *seriously*.

Scholars who study the decline of great civilisations sometimes find an environmental factor behind their fall. The river-valley cultures of the Middle East may have destroyed their habitats by over-irrigation, depleting their soil and making them vulnerable to unfavourable climates. There is a theory that the Romans poisoned themselves with pewter. This is the alloy of lead and tin that they used for their drinking vessels, happily unaware that the alcohol in their wine dissolved out the lead and subjected them all to chronic lead poisoning, generation after generation. We, it seems, are grooming ourselves out of existence.

Something of this sort has been suspected ever since the publication of Rachel Carson's *Silent Spring* in 1965. If a pesticide like DDT could eliminate the songbirds, what could it do to us? Fortunately, the songbirds generally returned once pesticide use was regulated. And the long-term effects of DDT on us have, so far, been negligible. Well, as far as we know!

But other toxins are available to do the job – radiation, PCBs, dieldrin, to mention but a few. Up to recently we could take comfort in the evidence that in small doses their effects are not disastrous. Radiation was an early subject of suspicion. But thanks to public debate, first over nuclear weapons and then over nuclear power, we are well aware of the dangers of radiation. The use of 'Agent Orange' by America in its dirty war in Vietnam also generated a highly politicised debate and the long-term dangers of dioxin were seriously studied. The new evidence of third-generation victims of dioxin in Vietnam is truly shocking. But horrific as this may be, it is not yet a bell that tolls for us all, as the initial dosage of dioxin was massive by any standards.

But now a new culprit has come to the fore. We are being constantly exposed to 'feminising' chemicals that have led to a decline in human male sperm count – a 50 per cent drop – over the last half-century. This discovery, or rather realisation, was controversial at first, but now it is as confirmed as any fact. But that is not all. The size of Western male organs is also decreasing; and I mustn't mention the increase in malformed penises, undescended testes and other reproductive disorders. The cause of all this are certain chemicals that mimic female hormones. The finger of accusation points firmly towards a family of chemicals called parabens, which are widely used in such necessities of modern life as deodorants and skin creams.

Parabens have been considered 'safe' largely because their oestrogenic properties are very weak. So they have been approved by regulators for use in a wide variety of consumer goods. The American Food and Drug Administration has registered over 13,000 products that use parabens. When absorbed through the skin of pregnant women, parabens are believed to act as xeno-oestrogens in the wombs, affecting the normal development of male foetuses. Some 99 per cent of skin creams designed to be left on the skin contain parabens. The cosmetic industry has been shoving this stuff at us for several decades – a few more decades and the cumulative effect could be devastating.

The 'feminising' chemicals, the xeno-oestrogens, provide us with a good example of the real price we are paying for an unending stream of new grooming products with the in-built promise to make us look like stars, transform our natural looks and colour and help us cheat age. But nature is not a free lunch, and vanity can exact a high price. The term 'Faustian bargain' was once used in connection with the civil nuclear power industry. It described our willingness to derive the present benefits of nuclear power, while bequeathing the problems of waste to our descendants. In that case the terms of the bargain were clear: we get the goods, and they will get the radioactive bads. It is difficult for most people to think that grooming in front of a misty mirror can also involve a pact with the devil!

But we can extend the idea of a 'Faustian bargain' to the whole of our material and consumer culture based on science and technology. New chemicals are created, produced and eventually released into the environment at the rate of thousands per year. To test these properly, even against known hazards, would absorb a significant fraction of our productive effort, and would also slow down innovation. The United States Environmental Protection Agency tells us that there are some 87,000 chemicals out there in the environment that have the potential ability to mimic the female hormone oestrogen. That's a hell of a lot of xeno-oestrogens to look out for! As new brands and new chemicals come on the market, regulators in Britain, the US and elsewhere do their best and focus on the most obviously risky chemicals. For the others, the ruling principle is that they are deemed safe until proved dangerous. There is a 'precautionary principle' at work here, but with the precaution almost always applied to the benefit of business and profit.

So, in many ways our innovation-obsessed, technologically driven consumer culture is living on its luck. So far we have been lucky. We have even detected the effect of parabens in time to do something about it. Just as we discovered the ozone layer in the nick of time, found the side effects of DDT before they became serious and, and... The laws of statistics say we can't be lucky forever. If xeno-oestrogens don't get us, then another manmade environmental health catastrophe lurking around the corner will.

Meanwhile, we ought to be aware of the possibility that we could end up following the Romans, minus our penises. After postmodernism comes the post-penis era.

Yahoo!

In Jonathan Swift's *Gulliver's Travels*, Yahoo is the name of an imaginary race of brutish creatures. In postmodern times, Yahoo is a race of real, boorish people who live their lives on the Internet. It is also the name of one of the first and the most popular online navigational guides to the Web, and the name of a magazine that is the bible of 'Internet Life'. Yahoo could be said to personify as well as characterise the Net.

One of the main features of the Net is that it tends to do things in exponential terms. Yahoo!, the directory service for Web pages, is a good example of this. It was started, in April 1994, by two Stanford electrical engineering graduates (David Filo and Jerry Yang) to track their favourite sites on the Web. It grew exponentially in its first six months to become the unofficial starting place for exploring the Internet. When they took their service public, the two graduates become instant multi-millionaires. Within a few years, Yahoo! took over the world. And that's the kind of pace the Internet sets.

Another basic feature of the Net is its mythological nature. Yahoo sometimes stands for Yet Another Hierarchical Officious Oracle. In classical antiquity, an oracle is an infallible guide to the future; it is a place where advice or prophecy is sought from the gods. One of the world's leading suppliers of software for information management, with revenues approaching scores of billions, is also called Oracle. A software for building e-business applications, popular with developers, is called

Delphi. As we all know, the classical Greeks believed that Delphi was the centre of the universe. Zeus himself sent two of his angels to the end of the earth – a flat disc – in order to determine its centre. The divine birds met at Delphi. So mythology, and not just Greek mythology, is quite integral to the institutions, software and conceptual makeup of the Net. Indeed, mythology is the material of which the Net is woven.

When two essential features of the Net are combined, we end up with an accelerating mythology. The world of o's and 1's, created in and by cyberspace, is a mythological utopia where communication is immediate and automatic, friendships emerge instantaneously, and all information is available at the touch of a button. In this utopia, muzak comes out of our beds, medicine emerges from our data sockets, we live in intelligent houses, drive around in self-guiding smart cars, and all of us publish our own books.

Cyberspace, like mythologies, is about redemption. It is the new god of secular salvation. Its priests are the managers of Intel, Xerox, Apple, Lotus and Microsoft – the people who dragged the computer out of their technological temples and onto our desks. Its prophets, sometimes described as 'techno-metaphysicians', search for more profound meaning in the information revolution. These yahoos talk reverentially about 'information society', 'third wave technology', the 'fourth discontinuity' and other claptrap. They make constant prophecies about 'The Next Big Thing', and eagerly anticipate the arrival of the machine 'who' really thinks.

I have no problem with the assertion that computers will improve the way we work and play. But yahoos are not content with this. Computers, they tell us, will not only improve the way we think, they will actually turn us into better human beings and communities. The Net is the realisation of the unity towards which the world has been working ever since we tripped over technology, or stripped the leaves off a twig to make our first tool. At last, we can realise our true spiritual potential, combining material quest with ethereal yearning, and evolving into a higher life form.

Like Greek gods, the postmodern yahoos are lusty fellows. They lust for power, control, perpetually desire for more and more, and of the carnal variety. The computer revolution is motivated by little else. Like all lust, and all mythologies, the lust for computers can enslave and then destroy.

Computer enslavement begins with the lure, the promise of increasing and accelerating computer power and connectivity at decreasing costs. Once you are caught and invest heavily in the use of computers to perform crucial tasks, you become irreversibly committed. Systems have to be perpetually upgraded; new software has to be constantly installed. It's not just that you end up spending accelerating sums of hard cash, you also become totally dependent.

One of the great myths about computers is that they are getting cheaper and cheaper. What they are getting is more and more powerful. And the latest model, with the whirls, buzzes and whistles – the one that *you* want – is hardly cheap. And what constitutes cheap anyway? The machine on your desktop is hardly cheap when what it costs can feed a whole family in Bangladesh for a full year. Computerisation creates a whole new set of dependencies on hardware and software manufacturers. One is trapped in a 'pathological scramble' to keep up with the incredible rate of change.

An equally great myth is that computers lead to noticeable increases in productivity. In truth, administration and management systematically absorb all that ever-increasing power, while workers are not much better off in terms of autonomy, flexibility or greater control. Technical efficiency is just another name for increased control by management. Thanks to computers, management now know exactly what the workers are doing, when they are doing it and with whom. Every keystroke they have made has been logged!

But who needs workers anyway? Computers are making sure that they are, on the whole, on their way out. No matter what the yahoos tell us, the dominant cybertrend is towards destroying, and not creating, more jobs. This is nowhere more pronounced than in the sunrise high-tech enterprises. What early computers did to manual workers, the new computerised networks are now doing to white-collar personnel. Crafts and skills are evaporating fast. When intelligent machines arrive, knowledge workers too will receive their exit orders. Thanks to computers, it now takes fewer people to develop, build and sell a product than ever before. So the gap between the rich and poor is set to widen even more, jobs will become very scarce and security will be a rare commodity.

Cyberspace is the space where delinquents and perverts, radical nihilists and terrorists, roam freely and in exponentially large numbers. Some 40 categories of undesirable activity – ranging from pornography, fraud, hacking, 'freaking', virus creation, promoting violence and cyber terrorism – have established themselves firmly on the Net. New Web sites promoting fascist and extremist ideas spring up with mundane regularity, as do manuals for bomb-making and sophisticated lock-picking techniques complete with DIY diagrams. More than 20,000 new hosts of pornographic sites are created daily. Child pornography, much of it from Eastern Europe, is the biggest growth industry. Eastern Europe also produces some of the best and most fanatical hackers who have the ability to bring down airport flight management computers, power systems, hospital equipment and not least, stock markets such as Nasdaq. Information put on a computer is seldom secure – molecular analysis of a hard disc can reveal much of what was 'deleted'. Dubious files and viruses can be traced to their origins by modern techniques within 24 hours. The techniques used by some to trace hackers and virus writers are used by others to trace and trap human rights activists. That innocent-looking e-mail may be concealing text within text – what is known as steganography. So that purchase order may actually be an order to carry out an assassination.

Complex networks like the Internet suffer from a serious weakness. A network is essentially a collection of nodes. The World Wide Web is a network of Web pages joined together by hyperlinks; the Internet is the physical communication network linked together by routers. All a yahoo terrorist has to do to cause untold damage is to target the most connected routers or Web sites. The average performance of the Internet is reduced by a factor of two if just 1 per cent of the most connected nodes are destroyed; and with only 4 per cent of crucial nodes down, the Internet loses its integrity, becoming fragmented into small, disconnected domains. So, like Achilles, cyberspace stands on clay feet.

But we don't need yahoo terrorists to cause chaos. The Internet is taking us towards chaotic times naturally and in more ways than one. The first signs of this come from the financial markets and computerised trading, which seems closer to the promise of virtual reality than any other human activity. Here, the problem is simple. Given the speed with which astronomical sums of capital fly across the globe, there can be no management in any real sense. Electronic trading has increased market instability by providing automatic responses and by removing the physical limits of executing trades on actual exchange floors. As computerised networks and powerful satellite communication links make markets accessible from almost anywhere on the globe, a new breed of 'paper entrepreneurs' increasingly displaces experienced traders. These are computer wizards who depend on their computers rather than experience. They use computer-trading programs with little or no awareness of underlying economic activity. It is therefore hardly surprising that markets have been crashing with depressing regularity since 1987.

Surely, anyone with an intelligent head over their shoulders should be able to detect that there are serious problems with the computerised utopias that we are being hurled towards. The problem with the yahoos is that they are just too spaced out, too drunk on accelerating technology, too out of breath organising life at the speed of light, to be intelligent. William Gibson, who coined the term in his novel *Neuromancer*, described cyberspace as 'a consensual hallucination'. The yahoos are perpetually hallucinating; and their hallucinations have both historic and physical reasons.

The origins of cyberspace are to be found in the American war machine. Like Teflon and the mini hi-fi, it is a partially expected and predicted by-product of research whose sole purpose is to discover better and more efficient ways to kill. In the sixties, a group of technologically twisted hippies slowly subverted the computer from its Armageddon arithmetic, brought the network out into the open and used it to chat and play games. Today, cyberspace bears all the hallmarks of its hippie subverts – from an obsession with pagan, psychedelic and new age spirituality to sexual neurosis and perversion to plainly daft talk about free information, community and love.

Virtually all the myths about cyberspace have their origins in this history. One of cyberspace's frequently repeated aphorisms, attributed to the 'Whole Earth' guru Stuart Brand, declares that information wants to be free. So, like an ageing hippie, information is a libertarian entity. Yet, nothing of value on the Web is free. What appears to be free is only an invitation to entrapment, like the drug peddler's initial fixes.

Similarly, we are constantly being told that cyberspace is linking us all together, bringing communities closer and producing communities where there were none. Wherever we go in our global village, we can tap into a cellular phone, get online with a personal digital assistant with built-in modem and satellite connection, and surf the Web to our heart's content. But connection does not make a community. Nor does it actually lead to meaningful communication. The community that cyberspace generates is purely an illusion.

Computers may draw us together, but they encourage us to divide and fragment even more. The Net facilitates and encourages a separating-out into endlessly sub-dividing groups. It is populated largely by style groups where people define themselves through their fantasies. We thus inhabit not a global village but a fragmented globe. When you look closely at the world of yahoos, you find discrete, isolated, sad, desperate individuals. You can jerk off using a computer, but you can't develop a meaningful relationship with it.

The real appeal of cyberspace is the fact that it offers a society dominated by individualism what it desires most: a world for one. It is the ideal place for those incapable of saying hello to their neighbours, but ever ready to fire bursts of text detailing their fantasies to complete strangers in newsgroups, forums and countless sites (over a third of the Net) devoted to all variety of perversions. Building communities is hard work. It requires you to be out there interacting in the real, messy world, not sitting in front of a terminal talking to someone you have never met, nor are likely to meet. On the other hand, exposure to the wider world via the Net appears to make people less satisfied with their personal lives. So, if you are hooked on surfing, you don't just end up as an isolated, sad individual, but the odds are you are also a highly dissatisfied individual.

If one tries to form a relationship with a computer, one should not be surprised to discover that it is not physically too healthy. Computer-induced hallucinations are now becoming common. The ever-growing cloud of 'data smog' subtracts from our quality of life, leading to stress, confusion and ignorance. Computer addicts everywhere are suffering a whole array of diseases described collectively as 'fragmentia'. These include increased cardiovascular stress, weakened vision, impaired judge-ment, confusion, frustration, decreased benevolence and overconfidence. One direct product of the information revolution is a brain imbalance called Attention Deficit Disorder (ADD). This syndrome causes acute restlessness, boredom and distraction. Sufferers cannot focus on anything for more than a few seconds. We are, it seems, heading straight for an ADD epidemic.

ADD spells death for the book. The yahoos have all but written off the book. Reading books requires effort. Even electronic books have to be read! You can't surf the book and jump perpetually from place to place like on the World Wide Web. Moreover, now that we can all bundle our thoughts using some desktop publishing package, or some idiot-proof software for writing hypertext, and publish it on the Net, the book really is redundant. But the crap that saturates the Net makes the book more, and not less, important. The Net only encourages vanity publishing on a colossal scale. It's the domain of the unread semi-literate, clutching Web pages, screaming about his undiscovered genius, and stalking cyberspace for victims.

In its extreme form, computer-induced hallucination leads to the idea that the Internet represents the next stage of human evolution. Modes of communication have evolved in a linear fashion, from alphabets to monotheism, reaching their natural apex with cyberspace. So the next quantum leap, the next step up the evolutionary ladder, is the merging of cyberspace and physical space and the dissolution of humanity into virtuality. Individual consciousness will be submerged in the Overmind of the Internet. Soon, in the not so distant future, we will be downloading our minds onto the Net and cruising the world as a digital signal. Virtual reality already makes this possible to some extent. So we should not be surprised when newspapers are published directly into our heads – sidestepping the problem of actually reading them – and poetry and literature are experienced by all directly in digitised forms.

Frankly, I would prefer the yahoos to disappear in electronic blips and leave the world for people with real imagination.

Zapping

Twenty centuries of civilisation, and we end up as a function of finger-flicking virtual reality. After travelling through pre-modern and modern centuries, we arrive today at the apex of postmodern life: today, we live to zap. The awful truth is even worse. We are the products of our own zapping. Zapping is the endless employment of that pernicious little enemy of reason – and even the mildest activity – the remote control.

Remember the old days when there were only two channels and someone, if they dared, had to stand up, walk across the room and physically interfere with *Sergeant Bilko*, *Lucille Ball* and *Dixon of Dock Green*? Now, from the comfort of your sofa, the lightest spasm of a single finger creates a collage of news, soap opera, sport, the latest blockbuster, boring documentaries and dear little animals. No more family feuds about what to watch. Everyone watches everything with the touch of the remote. Zapping, the philosophy of the more you have the less there is to watch.

It all began with MTV. The 24-hour music station created a culture of zapping without the bother of actually using a remote control. The music video is all about fast-moving images – nothing stays on the screen for more than five seconds. Everything from far-off history to spaced-out styles are jumbled together in a feast of images, jump cuts and genres to deliberately defy meaning and comprehension. The MTV viewer is the ideal channel-hopper, the Master Zapper, whose closest acquaintance with a story-line is the plot of an average commercial. The goal is simply to enjoy the spectacle, the intensity, the sensations, to glide along the surface of the images.

Satellite, cable and now digital TV have brought zapping into the mainstream. The countless channels cater for all variety of special interests and individual tastes. And what do we find? Programmes no longer assume our interest and attention. Now they are all made zappable, or zap-proof, in small soundbite-size nodules, all grasping for attention but never delivering. You know the kind of programme I mean, it keeps on telling you what it's going to be about without ever actually being about anything, or getting to the story. So, up with the remote control, a-zapping we will go. We soon discover the delights of channel-hopping, making our own jump cuts between reality and nonsense, sense and sensibility. From channel to channel we create a kaleidoscope, our own merry-go-round, a calliopean swirl, befuddled and intoxicated by the sheer variety and incoherence it creates. And now they tell us this is modern art, the auto-creation of your very own constantly changing spectacle. The art of nothing worth watching.

Do not dismiss zapping as the last resort of the couch potato mentality or *fin de* millennia ennui. The word exists because zapping is vaunted as an aesthetic of and for our time. It's the essence and spirit of what we have become.

Zapping makes us believe we are the masters of choice and abundance. But choice and abundance have become ends in themselves. They make slaves of everyone, politicians, businessmen and viewers alike, we all serve the need for choice, for the mere existence of more things without anyone ever having to give up anything. Finger-flicking is an enterprise of living that erodes the ability to reason out the best possible choice. We have an abundance of everything, but no reason to choose anything. We see so much, we have more information than we can absorb, but we have never been so superficial, so afraid of being ignorant.

And that's the condition of being zapped, being deluded by our supposed sophistication. With remote control we get exactly what we ought to expect: distance, disinterest, disregard – total lack of involvement in anything. The consequence? Zapping turns out to be not aesthetic but an anaesthetic. It's a diversion that deadens the nerve endings of our moral sense. The 30-second attention span, the world of soundbites, means we can be angry for 30 seconds, have an instant opinion, but not the least idea what to do about it, so we move on to something else.

Every time we watch real pain and suffering on our television screens we reach for the remote. The women wail, the bombs drop, and instantly it's on to the next image. Zap! We are bored by what we cannot change, so we flick to another channel.

Zap!

Bibliography

Alibhai-Brown, Y (2000) *Who Do We Think We Are?* Penguin, London

Bell, D (1993) *Communitarianism and its Critics*, Oxford University Press, Oxford

Bellah, R et al (1991) *The Good Society*, Alfred A Knopf, New York, NY

Bentham, J (1980) *Fragment on Government*, Greenwood Press, London

Bloom, H (1994) *The Western Canon: The Books and School of the Ages*, Harcourt, Brace, New York, NY

Bloome, I, Martin, P and Proudfoot, W (eds) (1994) *Religion and Human Rights*, Columbia University Press, New York, NY

Burke, E (1999) *Reflections on the Revolution in France*, Oxford University Press, Oxford

Burnett, F H (1990) *A Little Princess*, Signet Classic, New York, NY

Carson, R (2000) *Silent Spring*, Penguin, London

Chomsky, N (1994) *World Orders, Old and New*, Pluto Press, London

Cosmides, L and Tooby, J
www.psych.ucsb.edu/research/cep/primer.html

Davies, H (1980) *Book of British Lists*, Hamlyn, London

Ellison, R (1952) *Invisible Man*, Random House, New York, NY

Etzioni, A (1994) *The Spirit of Community*, Vintage, London

Fanon, F (1965) *The Wretched of the Earth*, Penguin, London

Federici, S (ed) (1995) *Enduring Western Civilisation*, Prager, Westport, CT

Fishkin, J (1991) *Democracy and Deliberation: New Directions for Democratic Reform*, Yale University Press, New Haven, CT

Galbraith, J K (1992) *The Culture of Contentment*, Sinclair–Stevenson, London

Geertz, C (1973) *The Interpretations of Cultures*, Basic Books, New York, NY

Gibson, R (ed) (1998) *Rethinking the Future*, Nicholas Brealey, London

Gibson, W (1994) *Neuromancer*, Ace Books, New York, NY

Golding, W (1955) *Lord of the Flies*, Coward-McCann, New York, NY

Haley, A (1979) *Roots*, G K Hall, Boston, MA

Hamill, P (1994) 'End Game', *Esquire*, 122 (6) pp85–92 December (American edition)

Hart, M (1992) *The 100: A Ranking of the Most Influential Persons in History*, Citadel Press, New York, NY

Heim, M (1993) *The Metaphysics of Virtual Reality*, Oxford University Press, Oxford

Held, D H (ed) (1993) *Prospects for Democracy*, Polity Press, Cambridge

Henry III, W A (1994) *In Defense of Elitism*, Doubleday, New York, NY

Herman, E S and Chomsky, N (1988) *Manufacturing Consent*, Pantheon, New York, NY

Hughes, R (1993) *The Culture of Complaint*, Oxford University Press, Oxford

Ishihara, S (1991) *The Japan That Can Say No*, Simon and Schuster, New York, NY

Johnson, A (2000) *The Concise Kama Sutra: Based on the Original Translation by Sir Richard Burton*, Hamlyn, London

Kothari, S and Sethi, H (eds) (1994) *Rethinking Human Rights*, New Horizon Press, New York, NY

Kukeni, A (1999) *A View From the Year 3000: A Ranking of the 100 Most Influential Persons of All Time*, Poseidon Press, New York, NY

Lewis, M (2001) *The Future Just Happened*, Hodder and Stoughton, London

Maalouf, A (2000) *On Identity*, Harvill Press, London

MacIntyre, A (1981) *After Virtue: A Study in Moral Theory*, University of Notre Dame Press, Notre Dame, IN

MacIntyre, A (1988) *Whose Justice? Which Rationality?*, Duckworth, London

Makdisi, G (1981) *The Rise of Colleges: Institutions of Learning in Islam and the West*, Edinburgh University Press, Edinburgh

Makdisi, G (1990) *The Rise of Humanism in Classical Islam and the Christian West*, Edinburgh University Press, Edinburgh

Mazuri, A (1990) *Cultural Forces in World Politics*, James Currey, London

Mill, J S (1998) *On Liberty and Other Essays*, Oxford Paperbacks, Oxford

Mittar, P (1977) *Much Maligned Monsters*, University of Chicago Press, Chicago

Nandy, A (1997) *Exiled At Home*, Oxford University Press, Delhi

Nandy, A (1998) *Return From Exile*, Oxford University Press, Delhi

Nefzawi, S (1993) *The Perfumed Garden*, translated by Richard Burton, HarperCollins, London

Negroponte, N (1995) *Being Digital*, Hodder and Stoughton, London

Nesbitt, J (1984) *Megatrends*, Warner Books, New York, NY

Packard, V O (1957) *The Hidden Persuaders*, D McKay & Co, New York, NY

Parekh, B (2000) *The Future of Multi-ethnic Britain (Parekh Report)*, Palgrave, London

Rawls, J A (1971) *Theory of Justice*, Harvard University Press, Cambridge, MA

Rouner, L S (ed) (1988) *Human Rights and the World's Religions*, University of Notre Dame Press, Notre Dame, IN

Sainsbury plc (1998) *Makers of the Millennium*, London

Salzman, M (1998) *Next*, HarperCollins, London

Sardar, Z (1998) *Postmodernism and the Other*, Pluto Press, London

Sardar, Z (1999) *Orientalism*, Open University Press, Philadelphia, PA

Sardar, Z (2000) *The Consumption of Kuala Lumpur*, Reaktion Books, London

Sardar, Z and Ravetz, J R (eds) (1996) *Cyberfutures: Politics and Cultures on the Information Superhighway*, Pluto Press, London

Sardar, Z, Davies, M W and Nandy, A (1993) *Barbaric Others: A Manifesto on Western Racism*, Pluto Press, London

Saul, J R (1992) *Voltaire's Bastards: The Dictatorship of Reason in the West*, Vintage Books, New York, NY

Schlesinger, A (1998) *The Disuniting of America: Reflection on a Multicultural Society*, W W Norton & Company, New York, NY

Seabrook, J (1993) *Victims of Development: Resistance and Alternatives*, Verso, London

Slatalla, M and Quitner, J (1995) *Masters of Deception: The Gang That Ruled Cyberspace*, HarperCollins, New York, NY

Slotkin, R (1973) *Regeneration Through Violence: The Mythology of the American Frontier 1600–1860*, Wesleyan University Press, Middletown, CT

Smith, H N (1978) *Virgin Lands: The American West as Symbol and Myth*, Harvard University Press, Harvard, MA

Sobel, D (1995) *Longitude*, Fourth Estate, London

Stiver, R (1994) *The Culture of Cynicism*, Blackwell, Oxford

Sun Tzu (1983) *The Art of War*, edited by James Clavell, Delacorte Press, New York, NY

Suskind, P (1989) *Perfume*, Penguin, London

Swift, J (1993) *Gulliver's Travels*, Cambridge University Press, Cambridge

de Tocqueville, A (1998) *Democracy in America*, Wordsworth Editions Ltd, London

Tucker, R (1991) *Managing the Future*, G P Putnam's Sons, New York, NY

Wark, M (1999) *Celebrities, Culture and Cyberspace*, Pluto Press, Annandale, NSW

Wieners, B and Pescovitz, D (1996) 'Reality Check', *Wired*, San Francisco, CA

Bibliography

Wood, E Meiksins and Foster, J Bellamy (eds) (1997) *In Defence of History*,
    Monthly Press Review, New York, NY

Yalom, M (1997) *A History of Breasts*, Alfred A Knopf, New York, NY